Pascal Programming for the Apple

T. G. Lewis
Oregon State University

Reston Publishing Company, Inc.
A Prentice-Hall Company
Reston, Virginia

Library of Congress Cataloging in Publication Data

Lewis, Theodore Gyle
  Pascal programming for the Apple.

  Includes index.
  1. PASCAL (Computer program language)
2. Microcomputers—Programming. I. Title.
QA76.73.P2L48   001.64'24   80-25382
ISBN 0-8359-5455-2
ISBN 0-8359-5454-4 (pbk.)

© 1981 by Reston Publishing Co., Inc.
A Prentice-Hall Company
Reston, Virginia

10 9 8 7 6 5 4

Printed in the United States of America

Contents

Preface

Pascal is the most influential contribution to programming made in the past 25 years. It is not only a programming language, but is also a statement about programming style. Thus, one major aspect of Pascal is its impact upon the way programs are conceived and then composed.

Second, the VLSI revolution in hardware is made dramatically available through Pascal software; and UCSD Pascal represents the first of a new generation of software systems for microcomputers. When combined with a microcomputer, Pascal is the greatest microcomputer software advance made since BASIC.

The Apple computer has capitalized on these most recent advances in technology in both hardware and software. Its graphics and sound reproduction hardware are intimately tied to the UCSD Pascal software. Their combined utilization is synergistic — greater than their sum. For example, the data-structures capabilities of Pascal naturally provide easy-to-use graphical symbols. The **type** COLOR = (BLACK, WHITE, BLUE, GREEN, VIOLET, ORANGE) fits into the graphics hardware support without language "extensions" usually found as nonstandard features in other languages.

It was because of this emerging synergism between hardware and software that this book was written. The following chapters are devoted to clarifying concepts of computing, programming style, devices, and information storage/retrieval. In particular, sections are devoted to teaching fundamentals of the Pascal System (Chapters 1-3), reviewing the Pascal language (Chapter 4), and applying this fundamental knowledge to many applications (Chapters 5-10).

Chapters 5-10 were designed to sharpen programming skills while simultaneously introducing new programming techniques. Financial applications are introduced in Chapter 5 and text processing using Pascal **strings** in Chapter 6. Chapter 7 explores a very important area of concern in small systems: how to implement large programs on small computers.

Chapter 8 covers the graphics modules provided in TURTLEGRAPHICS, and Chapter 9 is a short introduction to the musical tone generator, NOTE. Finally, in Chapter 10, we unify and bolster the **file** structure operations casually described throughout the book.

Using and learning about the Apple implementation of UCSD Pascal has been a tremendously stimulating experience. I have had great assistance from many people: Dr. John Couch and Susan Wells at Apple Computer, Evan Sakey at UCSD, and the helpful contributions of Dorothy Hyde, Sharon Bassett and the office staff at Oregon State University. Thanks go also to Peg Vorderstrasse and Ann Puig for their typing.

I hope you will enjoy reading the pages to follow. I know you will benefit from the experience if you take time to study each program in detail.

T. G. Lewis

Chapter 1

The French Connection (The System)

"I chose the name because Blaise Pascal was the first (perhaps one of the first) person to build what we may reasonably call a digital calculator. He did so around 1642 to speed up the tedious calculations when helping his father who was a tax collector."

Professor Niklaus Wirth
July 16, 1979

1.1 PASCAL THE MAN (1623-1662)

He was a sickly child, raised by his father who intended to educate him in the classics and literature. But 12-year-old Blaise Pascal surprised his father by secretly teaching himself geometry. One day he showed his father proof of Euclid's thirty-second theorem — that is the sum of the angles of a triangle equals 180 degrees — and that began his scientific training. He wrote a book on geometry (conic sections) before he was 16 and invented the calculator at 19 years of age.

The seventeenth century was a time of great scientific advancement. It might be compared with the post-World-War-II period of expansion in scientific knowledge. Many great inventions and ideas were being thrust onto the English and French societies during Pascal's lifetime.

William Harvey, Galileo, Newton, Descartes, Boyle, Napier, Kepler, Huyghens, and others lived about the same time as Pascal. Thus it is not unusual that Pascal's genius led him to the formulation of Pascal's Law (hydrostatic pressure is proportional to a cross-sectional area of a fluid) and Pascal's Triangle (coefficients of the binomial expansion).

It may be surprising that Pascal invented an early version of mechanical calculators, since this required the design and construction of precision gears; but about 1641, at the age of 19, Pascal developed a working calculator similar

---

Personal correspondence with Niklaus Wirth concerning the name of his new programming language.

to the odometer system of gears used in speedometers today. It had been 1600 years since the previous advance in such machinery was made by Hero of Alexandria. Pascal constructed about 50 models of his calculator, of which 6 or 7 still exist.

Pascal led the way in "reasoning" machines while others of his time were inventing pendulum clocks (Huyghens, 1656), barometers (Torricelli, 1644), and fountain pens (1657). Even though he was awarded a patent for his calculator, the device was too costly and unreliable to become a commercial success; but his work set the stage for modern computer technology. Indeed, Pascal foresaw the modern-day implications of his invention when he remarked, "The arithmetical machine produces effects which approach nearer to thought than all the actions of animals."* This implication drove Pascal to question the power of the human mind. His contemporary, Descartes, asserted that reason alone separated mankind from unthinking machines and animals. Pascal, on the other hand, believed his calculator to be an example of a machine that could "reason" as well as function as an accountant.

Only free will distinguished humanity from the animal world. This notion caused him to ask questions about God and mankind's place in the world. In fact, Pascal was tormented by religious questions. On November 23, 1654, he experienced a two-hour vision during which his "heart felt God." He recorded the details of this experience and sewed a note to himself into the lining of his clothing. Unfortunately for science, this revelation convinced Pascal to abandon the world. He converted to Jensenism and produced his most notable work, Pensés, while contemplating his religious beliefs. In 1662 at the age of 39, Pascal died believing in the importance of both the heart and the mind. The mind is limited in what it can understand, Pascal wrote, while the remaining mysteries of the universe can only be understood through faith in God.

A thread of history connects the primitive calculator invented by Pascal to the sophisticated machines that run Pascal programs described in this book. Charles Babbage (1792-1871) was influenced by Blaise Pascal, Gottfried Leibniz, and Joseph Jacquard. Babbage's calculating engine was a mechanical computer capable of computing while under the control of a program. In 1937, while a graduate student at Harvard University, Howard Aiken became aware of Babbage's work. Aiken, with financial support from IBM, was responsible for constructing MARK I, the first general-purpose electronic computer. The microcomputers of today are descendants of the MARK I.

In some sense we have returned full circle to Blaise Pascal. Pascal, the man, believed in both reason and blind faith; the language Pascal is both a scientific tool based on simple reasoning about computing and a humanly understandable language based on the belief that simple, efficient languages are the most reliable

---

*J. Bonowski, and B. Mazlish, *The Western Intellectual Tradition*, Harper Torchbooks, N.Y., 1975, p. 240.

tools for writing computer programs. In the pages to follow we will be concerned about the programmer as well as the computer when implementation issues arise. For example, simple explanations for straightforward methods will be preferred over technically rigorous explanations. We will use examples that are easy to read rather than examples that demonstrate sophisticated algorithms. Finally, we will employ *short* programs rather than lengthy, complete programs so that the concepts will be illuminated.

1.2 PASCAL THE LANGUAGE (1971-   )

Niklaus Wirth invented Pascal for two reasons:*

". . . to make available a language suitable to teach programming as a systematic discipline based on certain fundamental concepts clearly and naturally reflected by the language."

". . . to develop implementations of this language which are both reliable and efficient on presently available computers. . ."

It was the expressly stated goal of Wirth to develop a tool for ". . . the understanding of programs by human readers and the processing by computers."

This is also the goal of this book. We wanted to develop a document for human understanding of the Pascal language and for understanding the Pascal *environment*, which consists of both the Pascal system and the Apple computer.

It is important to understand not only the language Pascal but also the environment of the Pascal System, because the environment influences how the language is used. Figure 1.1 gives a user's view of the levels to be found within

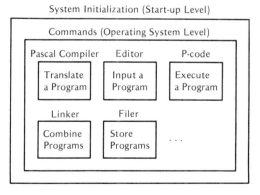

Figure 1.1. The Pascal Environment

---

*N. Wirth, "The Programming Language Pascal," *Acta Informatica*, 1, 35-63 (1971).

the Pascal environment. These levels constitute a kind of Pandora's Box with additional boxes inside.

Each box is at a level within the environment, and each level contains boxes for designing and implementing Pascal programs. We have shown only a few of the innermost boxes in Figure 1.1. For an in-depth description of these boxes, skip to Chapter 2.

The Pascal environment is automatically initialized when the Apple computer is started. The system is loaded from disk into the computer's main memory. When ready, the screen on your computer will announce itself:

Welcome APPLE1: TO
U.C.S.D. Pascal System II.5
Current Date Is 15-DEC-79
Command:E(dit,R(un,F(ile,C(omp,L(ink,X(exute,A(ssemble,D(ebug ?[I.5]

This prompt puts the Pascal System in the Command level where it waits for input of the first letter of the command desired. To open the editor box, type E, and to open the compiler box, type C, etc. Each command is accepted in its abbreviated form (usually first letter).

Figure 1.1 illustrates only the first 3 levels of the Pascal environment. In the next chapter we will examine each box in more detail, but for now we will explain the purpose of the boxes at level 1.

Assembler The Pascal environment includes a generalized machine language symbolic assembler. While we will not be concerned about its use here, it can be used to produce machine code programs. These programs may be tightly coded routines which are used by Pascal programs. In order to combine them with Pascal, we must use the Assembler and then the Linker.

Compiler All Pascal programs must be converted into an intermediate (condensed) form called *P-code*. The Compiler does this by reading a text file created by the user (see Editor), converting it into P-code equivalents and writing the P-code file out onto disk. The converted P-code version is processed further by first Linking its parts together and then interpreting the Linked parts using a P-code simulator (see execute).

Debugger This command is used to set breakpoints in Assembler programs. This is an aid to debugging programs; but since we are not concerned with the use of the Assembler, we will not use the Debugger.

Editor The Pascal environment includes several editor programs. We will describe only one editor — the screen editor. This program is used to prepare Pascal programs. It allows the user to type Pascal statements, edit errors, and save the edited programs on disks.

Filer   The Filer is a program used to save programs on disk files, copy files, delete files, examine files, and set the date (calendar). Each file is named by the user using a dot notation.

VOL:NAME.TYPE

Thus, the disk volume VOL: is given first, followed by the file name NAME and the file extent .TYPE. The most common file extents are program text, .TEXT, program P-code, .CODE, and program data, .DATA.

Linker   The Link command is used whenever separately compiled program units are to be combined into a single P-code module. If a program uses another program unit, then the Linker must combine the two into a single unit before either can be executed.

Run   This command is actually three commands rolled into one. The most frequent commands — Compile, Link, and eXecute — are carried out in sequence whenever R is entered. The Compile step is skipped if the workfile (see Figure 1.2) is already compiled. The Link step is also skipped if not needed. The eXecute step is carried out by running the P-code file.

eXecute   This command causes the P-code simulator to begin interpreting the P-code workfile, or some other .CODE file specified by the user.

?   This command displays additional (less frequently used) commands:

User Restart
Initialize
Halt
? (return to command level)

The H command is particularly useful because it allows graceful termination of a session.

The explanations above discuss a workfile and a P-code simulator. What exactly are they?

The workfile is the single most important object in the Pascal environment (Figure 1.2). The commands available at the Command level access the workfiles as shown in Figure 1.2. To input a Pascal program the Editor builds a SYSTEM. WRK.TEXT file by accepting keyboard input and writing the lines of text to the workfile. The Filer may be used to erase the workfile, transfer it to another file, etc.

The Compiler takes text from the .TEXT workfile and translates it into P-code, which is written to the .CODE workfile. The Linker combines other P-code units with the SYSTEM.WRK.CODE file in preparation for the eXecutor program. (While the Pascal environment defaults to the workfile to process the commands we give it, we can also divert it to other files in the system.)

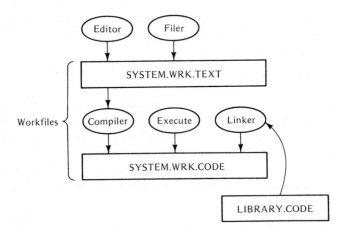

Figure 1.2.   The Workfile: SYSTEM.WRK

The Pascal System is a language and a set of tools for developing programs, debugging them, and running them. The Pascal System is mostly independent of the **machine** environment used to run Pascal programs because of P-code. Therefore, we turn our attention to P-code before exploring the Pascal system in more detail in Chapter 2. Since knowledge of P-code is not essential to understanding Pascal, the reader may choose to skip the next section.

1.3   PASCAL THE MACHINE

One of Wirth's goals was to construct the Pascal System so that it could be easily implemented on a variety of computers. Clearly, the differences among computers are large and, if implemented *directly* on each machine, would consume years of intense labor. Instead, Wirth cleverly implemented the Pascal System on a hypothetical machine called the **P-code machine.**

The P-code machine did not exist when the first Pascal System was developed. Instead the Pascal System needs a P-code simulator before it can work. We must either turn every existing machine into a P-code machine or else build new machines to interpret the P-code produced by the Pascal System. The prospect of selling a P-code machine to everyone who wanted Pascal did not seem like an attractive alternative, so a series of **P-code machine simulators** was developed instead.

At University of California at San Diego, a group headed by Kenneth Bowles initially developed P-code simulators for LSI-11 microcomputers. Later, other simulators (8080, Z80) were developed so that the Pascal System could be run on low-cost microcomputers. These simulators were mainly responsible for the widespread acceptance of Pascal.

The UCSD system developed by Kenneth Bowles is actually a dialect of the original Pascal System. Many features have been changed or eliminated because of the problems unique to such restricted machines. Thus the UCSD Pascal System is only an approximation of the full Pascal System as originally implemented on a large machine. Successive versions of UCSD Pascal are released under different numbers to indicate an increasingly powerful version.

The P-code simulator employed in the Apple computer uses a very different set of P-code "instructions" from the original. It is not necessary to understand P-code in order to use the Pascal System, but it may help to explain the internal behavior of the Pascal System if the general idea of P-code is understood.

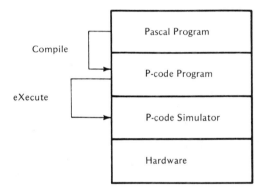

Figure 1.3.   Relationship Between P-code and Pascal.

The P-code "machine" simulates a 16-bit word *stack machine*. A stack is a memory which allows push and pop operations as well as data processing operations like add, subtract, and move. A push loads (copies) a word from one location in the stack onto the top of the stack (tos), as shown in Figure 1.4. A pop copies a value from the tos (top of stack) word and places it in some other word in memory.

Figure 1.4 also shows a HEAP for storing lists (discussed later) and the relative locations in main memory of the P-code simulator and the Pascal system. Note that memory overflow occurs whenever the HEAP grows upward to meet the downward-growing stack.

We can demonstrate how a stack operates by example. Suppose a Pascal program for adding and subtracting is translated into stack operations:

X := (A + B) / (C – D) ;   (* Pascal statement *)

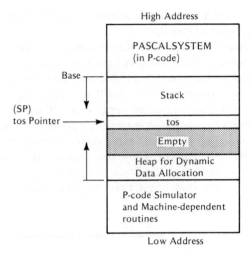

Figure 1.4. The P-code Stack

The corresponding stack operations are:

```
PUSH   A   ;   load (tos) with A
PUSH   B   ;   load (tos+1) with B
ADD        ;   (A+B) is put in (tos)
PUSH   C   ;   load (tos+1) with C
PUSH   D   ;   load (tos+2) with D
SUB        ;   (C–D) is put in (tos+1)
DIV        ;   (A+B)/(C–D) is put in (tos)
POP    X   ;   (tos) is put in X.
```

These operations are managed by a special P-code register called the SP (stack pointer). The SP **points** to the current tos (top of stack) word in the stack. Figure 1.5 shows what happens when the stack operations above are performed.

In the actual P-code machine there are several versions of the PUSH and POP instructions depending on the type of values manipulated and the location of the variables A,B,C,D, and X. We will translate X:=(A+B)/(C–D) into P-code by assuming **global** locations for integers A,B,C,D, and X. This allows us to use LDO to push a word onto the stack, SRO to pop a word, ADI (add integer), DVI (divide integer), and SBI (subtract integers). The Pascal example is then converted into the following P-code.

program when quitting time arrived. If so, SYSTEM.PASCAL would still have the partially completed program in the SYSTEM.WRK.TEXT file. If the program was translated already, it would still have the P-code in the SYSTEM.WRK. CODE file. Fingers couldn't remember what he had done earlier; so from the **Filer:** level he typed,

"W".

"Workfile is APPLE1:JUNK", said SYSTEM.PASCAL. This meant that a *named* workfile was being used during the last session with Fingers. If an Editor command (E) is entered, the text file APPLE1:JUNK is copied into the workfile automatically.

Fingers needed to find out what was going on inside SYSTEM.PASCAL; so he took a walk down the tree of Figure 2.1 to visit *Volumes.*

"V", Fingers typed from /**Filer:**.

"1 Console:
2 Systerm:
4 #Apple1:
Prefix volume is Apple1:"

said SYSTEM.PASCAL in response to Finger's input. This showed that volumes 1, 2, and 4 were assigned to volume names Console:, Systerm:, and Apple1:, respectively, that is, the console and system terminal used by Fingers were connected to hardware ports 1 and 2, while disk volume Apple1: was connected to port 4. Also, all files are (default) prefixed with Apple1: so that if Fingers does not supply a volume name before the file name, then SYSTEM.PASCAL puts APPLE1: in for Fingers. For example, JUNK.TEXT is prefixed by SYSTEM. PASCAL so that it becomes ; "APPLE1:JUNK.TEXT". On the contrary, LEWIS: JUNK.TEXT is not prefixed because it already has a volume name (LEWIS:).

"N",

Fingers impatiently typed to the **Filer:**.

"Throw away current workfile?"

responded SYSTEM.PASCAL. Fingers had better know what he is doing before the workfile is discarded.

"Y",

entered Fingers. He wanted to begin with a clean slate.

"Workfile cleared",

SYSTEM.PASCAL obeyed as always. Of course, the N directive means to erase the workfile and prepare to create a new program. SYSTEM.PASCAL just wanted to make sure Fingers was doing the right thing.

"Q",

Fingers was ready to quit using **Filer:** ; so he terminated it. This session reminded Fingers of the good old days when he automatically started a session in this standard way:

Directive	Comments
F	(*get the **Filer:** *)
D	(* change the date *)
V	(* what volumes are on-line? *)
W	(* what is workfile status? *)
N	(* erase workfile:new *)
L	(* list the volume directory *)
Q	(* quit the Filer *)

Finger's memory was being refreshed by this dialog. For example, the startup volume name can always be abbreviated by the nickname *. So, for example, if Fingers said, *:JUNK.TEXT, the SYSTEM.PASCAL **Filer:** knows that APPLE1: volume is used instead of *. Suppose Fingers wanted to list the file directory of APPLE1:. He would have typed "L" followed by the file name "*".

Let's study some other commonly used directives in the **Filer:**

Filer: "G", typed Fingers in an effort to activate APPLE1: NEWTON. TEXT instead of the SYSTEM.WRK.TEXT file.

SYSTEM: "Throw away current workfile?"

FINGERS: "Y"

SYSTEM: "Get what file?"

FINGERS: "NEWTON.TEXT"

SYSTEM: "Text file loaded"

It could have happened that no such file existed. In this case, SYSTEM would have responded with, "No file loaded". Also, both NEWTON.TEXT and NEWTON.CODE could have existed, in which case both files would be loaded.

Conversely, Fingers would use the S(ave directive to save the workfile in another (named) file.

The R(emove directive is used to remove files from a disk volume once the file is no longer needed. Sometimes is is useful to C(hange a file name, or

T(ransfer the file from one place to another. In each case the **Filer:** would patiently prompt Fingers to make sure the proper action would be taken. Here are some abbreviated conversations between SYSTEM.PASCAL and Fingers.

"R", typed Fingers because he wanted to remove LEWIS: disk volume.

"Remove what file?" asked SYSTEM.PASCAL.

"LEWIS:JUNK.TEST", entered Fingers.

"Update directory?" SYSTEM.PASCAL made sure Fingers wanted to destroy the file.

"Y", insisted Fingers.

"LEWIS:JUNK.TEXT removed".

The **Filer:** is used to perform other important housekeeping chores as the next two examples illustrate.

"M", typed Fingers, meaning "Make a file."

"Make what file?" asked SYSTEM.PASCAL.

"JUNK.TEXT", responded Fingers. But Fingers had forgotten that this response leads to a very large chunk of the disk space being taken by this new file. Instead, he should have entered an estimate of the number of blocks to be allocated to the new file,

"JUNK.TEXT[2]", cautiously entered the wise Fingers.

When disk space becomes difficult to find, Fingers can direct **Filer:** to compress the disk (this squeezes out all vacant blocks in between filled blocks).

"K", typed Fingers.

"Krunch what vol.?" requests SYSTEM.PASCAL.

The system may have to be I(nitialized again if SYSTEM.PASCAL is itself moved by the Krunch function. Another problem may arise when using this directive. The disk may contain bad blocks (worn out or defective sections of the disk). These can be found by typing "B" into **Filer:**. Also, a more detailed volume directory listing can be obtained with the "E" directive.

In summary, the **Filer:** performs the following functions:

G : *get* a named file in place of the workfile

S : *save* the workfile in a named file

W : *what* is the status of the workfile?

N : erase the workfile and create a *new* one

L : *list* the volume's directory

R : *remove* a file

C : *change* a file name or volume name

T : *transfer* a file or volume

D : set the *date*

Q : exit from the filer, *quit*

At the ? extension of the **filer:** we find less frequently used directives.

B : *bad* disk blocks

E : *extended* directory listing

K : *krunch* (compress) disk files

M : *make* room for another named file

P : change the *prefix* volume name

V : display the *volume* names

X : *examine* the disk files (maintenance)

Z : *zero-out* a disk volume

? : *change levels*

2.2 SECOND BLUSH (EDITOR)

The **Editor:** is a program used by the user to compose other programs. It is a sophisticated system in itself because it must be flexible and powerful enough to aid programmers in creating text files, and inserting, deleting, moving, and copying pieces of program text. Margins must be maintained by the **Editor:**, patterns must be searched and matched for replacement, and so forth.

The **Editor:** is screen-oriented; that is, it helps to compose programs by **visually** moving, inserting, deleting, pieces of code on the terminal screen itself. To do this, the user uses a **cursor** which is positioned using the arrow keys on the keyboard.

Once again Fingers took a walk along the **Editor:** tree as shown in Figure 2.2. Here is what he said.

"E stands for edit," mumbled Fingers as he waited for the SYSTEM to answer.

"No workfile is present. File?
:"

checked SYSTEM.PASCAL, because Fingers had previously cleared the SYSTEM.WRK.TEXT file with a **Filer:N** directive. If a workfile had been present, the response would have been different ("reading. . .").

"⟨cr⟩", Fingers immediately typed the carriage return so he could begin building a new SYSTEM.WRK.TEXT file.

"Edit:A,C,D,F,I,J,R,Q,X,Z[E.6f]", snapped SYSTEM. This prompt displayed the very first level of the tree in Figure 2.2. If Fingers already had an active SYSTEM.WRK file he could have performed any of the directives on the existing workfile. However, in this second blush, he had only one choice — to enter a program. To do this, Fingers typed an I for insert.

"I", and Fingers watched as the *Insert:* directive prompted an input. The cursor was waiting at the first character of the second line. So Fingers entered the simplest Pascal program he could think of.

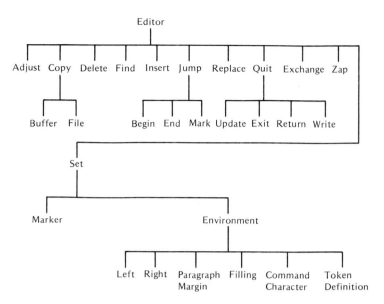

Figure 2.2.   Pascal System Editor Tree

"**program** JUNK;
  begin
  end

and the **Editor:** waited for another line of input. Fingers noticed how the input lines were automatically adjusted to the right whenever he spaced over one column. Whenever the text was updated, the **Editor:** immediately rewrote the program and returned to the **Edit:** level.

"Edit:
PROGRAM JUNK;
  BEGIN
  END.
    ",

said the **Editor:** . Fingers was curious about the other directives; so here is what he did during an adventurous walk along the editor tree. First, the arrows ⟨−, →⟩ on the keyboard (and equivalents of ⟨− and →⟩) caused the cursor to move around on the program text. Fingers made the cursor land on top of any character in the program. This handy tool would be valuable in the directives to follow.

"A", Fingers entered to see what the adjust directive could do. Amazingly, the program statements followed the cursor around on the screen. Wherever Fingers placed the cursor, the statements were sure to follow! After some playful games, the program looked like this:

```
                "PROGRAM JUNK;
BEGIN
                END."
```

"⟨ext⟩", entered Fingers to exit from the Adjust directive.

Next, Fingers entered the Delete directive to see what would happen. Sure enough, everywhere Fingers moved the cursor a character or line of text was sure to be deleted! Since Fingers did not want to delete anything right then, he aborted the deletions (they were ignored) by typing "⟨esc⟩" instead of the "⟨ext⟩" key.

"F", he entered, in order to Find a pattern in the text. This directive automatically searched every line of the text until the pattern was matched.

"Find [i] : L(it ⟨target⟩ =)," responded the **Editor:.**

"/BEGIN/", retorted Fingers, and whammy! the cursor was moved to the end of the first occurrence of the pattern "BEGIN".

```
"Edit:
PROGRAM JUNK;
    BEGIN
END. "
```

responded **Editor:**, with the cursor immediately following the search pattern, /BEGIN/. Notice how the bracketing symbols / and / were used to delimit the first and last characters of the pattern.

Next, Fingers placed the cursor in front of the "END." statement and typed I for Insert. The cursor stayed where it was and the "END." moved over to make room. After entering the writeln statement, Fingers returned to the **Edit:** level with "⟨ext⟩".

```
"Edit:
        PROGRAM JUNK;
            BEGIN
        WRITELN('IT WORKS');
        END."
```

the **Editor:** responded in a flash. Now the program would output a line that says, "IT WORKS".

"R", typed Fingers, to replace "IT WORKS" with "IT SEEMS TO WORK."

"Replace [1] : =⟩", returned **Editor:**, with a prompt. The [1] indicated the number of identical occurrences of the pattern to be replaced. The default to one meant that only the first pattern located would be replaced.

"/IT WORKS//IT SEEMS TO WORK/", Fingers anxiously typed the search pattern followed by *two* **marks** and then the new pattern; but the Editor responded with an ERROR: message!

Fingers should have placed the cursor at the beginning of the program text in order to start the search at the beginning. Thus, the keyboard or arrows must be used to position the cursor to the starting point of the search for "IT WORKS". When Fingers did this, the replacement took place immediately, and the **Editor:** responded with the following:

"Edit:
        PROGRAM JUNK;
            BEGIN
        WRITELN ('IT SEEMS TO WORK   ');
        END."

with the cursor immediately following the new inserted string of characters. Now, Fingers was ready to try the program, so he entered "Q" for Quit, and the **Editor:** responded with a multiple choice.

"Quit:
        U(pdate the workfile and leave
        E(xit without updating
        R(eturn to the editor without updating
        W(rite to a file name and return

"U", entered Fingers. This caused the newly created program to be copied into the SYSTEM.WRK.TEXT file. Fingers could also have saved the program in a new file by typing "W". In either case, Fingers was ready to translate the text into P-code, and then Run the P-code to see what happens. Before we see what happens, suppose we list the directives that are most useful to compose a program.

A: *Adjust* the margins of a program text.

C: *Copy* from either a buffer or file.

D: *Delete* pieces, one character at a time.

F: *Find* a pattern in the text, starting in the position currently indicated by the cursor.

I: *Insert* text in the position indicated by the cursor.

J: *Jump* or move the cursor to either the beginning, end, or to some marker previously placed in the text.

M: *Margin* is adjusted. *Set* sets the left and right margins.

P: Move the cursor one or more pages forward or backward.

Q: Leave the **Editor:** program.

R: *Replace* the pattern found with another pattern. A repeat-factor may be supplied in order to find and replace more than one occurrence of the pattern.

S: *Set* options for the environment, e.g., indentation, margins, etc.

V: Redisplay the screen (*verify*).

X: *Exchange* the character under the cursor with the character typed in.

Z: *Zap* all text between current cursor position and a given position.

2.3 THE MOMENT WE'VE WAITED FOR (COMPILE-RUN)

The easiest way to run a program is to enter "R" at the **Command:** level. This directive will automatically cause the diagram of Figure 2.3 to be followed. At the **Command:** level, Fingers types an "R". If a workfile is present, the workfile is used by the executor. If not, the user is prompted for a file name to be executed.

The executor (see Figure 2.3) must have a linked P-code file to work on. If the .CODE file is missing or not yet linked, the executor passes control on to the linker. We will discuss the Linker in Chapter 7, but for now lets assume the Linker passes control onto the Compiler.

Finally, SYSTEM.COMPILER translates either workfile, SYSTEM.WRK. TEXT, or a named file into a .CODE file. The .CODE file is passed on to the executor.

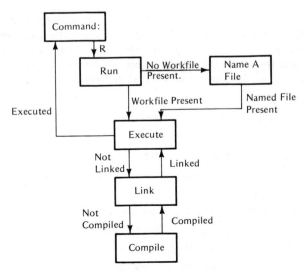

Figure 2.3. Run Command Diagram

The executor *simulates* the .CODE file instructions one at a time. If an error occurs, the simulator stops and reports the segment number, procedure number, and statement number which caused the error.

Here are a few dialogs between Fingers and SYSTEM.PASCAL in the **Command:** level. If the workfile exists, then the results are straightforward.

"Pascal Compiler [1.5] (Unit Compiler)
⟨ 0⟩ . . . . .
JUNK   [1789 words]
⟨ 3 ⟩ . . . .
13 LINES
SMALLEST AVAILABLE SPACE=1789 WORDS",

responded **Compiler** while it was translating program JUNK from 13 Pascal lines into a P-code filename, JUNK.CODE. This particular program used all but 1789 words of symbol table space to store the variables used in the program. Each dot represents a compiled statement.

If no workfile existed, then we would expect something like the following.
FINGERS: "C"
COMPILER: "Compiling . . ."
"Compile what text?"
FINGERS: "JUNK"
COMPILER: "Can't find JUNK.TEXT"
FINGERS: "C" (* FINGERS tries again *)
COMPILER: "Compile what text?"
FINGERS: "LEWIS:JUNK"
COMPILER: "To what codefile?"

"JUNK", Fingers supplied. This will create a file on the * disk. Thus, the output is put into *:JUNK.CODE.

If the program .CODE file had been saved from an earlier translation, we could execute it directly.
FINGERS: "X"
SYSTEM: "Execute what file?"
FINGERS: "JUNK", Fingers slipped up, again.
SYSTEM: "Must link first", reminded the system.
FINGERS: "X", Fingers tried again.
SYSTEM: "Execute what file?"

"LEWIS:JUNK". Fingers gets it correct this time. The .CODE file on disk volume LEWIS: is executed without the translation beforehand.

The **Compiler:** is itself a program and can be controlled by setting *option switches* placed in the program text. The option must be prefixed by a $ and contain no spaces.

(*$option-list*)

Everything between (*$ and *) is treated as an option switch. Multiple switches are separated by commas. Here is a list of options that the reader should experiment with to see how they alter the compiler's behavior. (The default or standard switch setting is indicated with an italicized comment.)

G+, allows GOTO statements in the Pascal text.

G–, *GOTO* not allowed.

I+, Perform I/O checking after every input/output statement.

I–, *No* checking. Errors are ignored by the system.

Ifilename, This is not an I/O switch, but instead interpreted as an include-file mechanism. The file "filename" is inserted into the text at this point. No other switches can appear between (* and *), and no spaces are tolerated!

The include-file option must be used with caution. It must be inserted before all **procedure** and **function** definitions, but after all **var** declarations in order to not conflict with them. Also, the include-file must *not* contain another include-file option.

The include-file option is a very useful feature of the **Compiler:** because it allows large program composition by modules. The include-file name must be of type .TEXT, but the suffix is optional :

```
(*$ILEWIS:JUNK*)
(*$ILEWIS:JUNK.TEXT*)
```

Both of these include-files result in the same action as long as LEWIS:JUNK. TEXT actually exists.

L+ , Save the source program listing under SYSTEM.LST.TEXT.

L– , *No* listing

L , Save under a named file. For example, (*$L LEWIS:LIST.TEXT *) The space following L is necessary.

The listing obtained with the last option switch can be very useful to debugging since each line includes the segment number, procedure number, and number of bytes (code) or words (data) used up to the point in the listing. The executor will report these numbers when an error occurs, so the listing can be consulted to locate the offending instruction.

Q+ , Suppress output to screen.

Q– , *Keep* user informed.

R+ , *Perform* range checking.

R– , No range checking — go for faster programs, but no error checking.

Other (more complicated) option switches are available, but we will not explain them here.

cases the **const, type,** or **var** sub-parts are omitted because they are not needed. Consider the following very simple Pascal program.

```
program PRINTN;
    const
            N = 5;
    begin
            writeln (N);
    end.
```

This simple program defines a constant N as an **integer** with value 5. The program contains only one module: main. The "built-in" procedure writeln is called by merely writing its name followed by a list of variables to be written on the terminal screen. This program produces a single line with the numeral 5 as output.

Beware of the placement of semicolons in Pascal. Almost every construct terminates with a semicolon; however, it is not always simple to identify a construct. We will alert the reader to situations that might otherwise be overlooked.

The simple shell illustrated above is perhaps the most frequently encountered model of Pascal. There is a more sophisticated model of UCSD Pascal, however, which incorporates "non-resident" modules. This is particularly useful when using the graphics capabilities of Pascal. The TURTLEGRAPHICS extension to Pascal may be included in another Pascal program by implicitly defining the TURTLEGRAPHICS procedures and functions through the **uses** construct. The modified shell is shown in Figure 3.1.

program DRAW;

uses TURTLEGRAPHICS; (* fetch graphics routines *)

```
const
type
var                        (* usual declarations *)
procedure
function
```

begin
        INITTURTLE ; (* clear screen, start graphics *)

(* executable statements that draw pictures using TURTLEGRAPHICS
    functions such as VIEWPORT, PENCOLOR, SCREENCOLOR, MOVE,
    MOVETO, TURN, TURNTO, FILLSCREEN, DRAWBLOCK,
    TURTLEX, TURTLEY, TURTLEANG, SCREENBIT, GRAFMODE,
    TEXTMODE, WCHAR, WSTRING, CHARTYPE *)

end.

Figure 3.1. Form Of A Graphics Program

The **uses** statement should immediately follow the **program** declaration. Also, the INITTURTLE procedure should be called from the main body of DRAW before any other graphics procedures are called. Note in Figure 3.1 the long list of graphics procedures and functions available from TURTLEGRAPH-ICS. We will dedicate an entire chapter to exploring these special functions later. (For the eager reader, turn to the chapter now.)

The Pascal System includes a small collection of frequently used procedures that can be called even though they are not defined in the module-definition section of the user's program. The input/output procedures are common examples of these "built-in" procedures which are called *intrinsics* in Pascal terminology. Let us study the behavior of the get, put, read, readln, write, and writeln intrinsics. Edit and compile the following program to observe the different result obtained from each procedure.

```
program ADAM;
  var
    X, Y : integer;
  begin
    get(X);
    get(Y);
    put(X);
    put(Y);
  end.
```

This *incorrect* program defines two integers X and Y. The main module (the *only* module) performs four calls to the input/output intrinsics get and put. When compiled, this program encounters error number 125: ERROR IN TYPE OF STANDARD PROCEDURE PARAMETER. This means that get and put cannot be used to input/output integers, characters, etc., through the user's console; so we should replace them with the text file intrinsics shown below.

```
program BAKER;
  var
    X, Y : integer;
  begin
    read(X);
    read(Y);
    write(X);
    write(Y);
  end.
```

This version of the program appears to perform the same functions as ADAM, that is, a pair of integers is input and then immediately output. But notice the output of BAKER; it is unformatted and difficult to read. We can improve the output format using the following version of this simple program.

The read, readln, write, and writeln intrinsics are best used when doing simple I/O through the user's console. Notice, however, the difference between write and writeln in the next example.

```
program CHARLIE;
  var
    X, Y : integer;
  begin
    readln(X,Y);
    writeln(X,Y);
  end.
```

The readln and writeln intrinsics handle an entire line at a time. Although the readln may not be affected (because of the ⟨return⟩ key⟩ in this example, notice how the two integers were both output on a single line. Note also that the two values for X and Y *could* have been entered on a single line separated by a space, but the output is still crowded together in CHARLIE.

Thus, we must be careful when using the I/O intrinsics of Pascal:

READ and WRITE: Use only with files of characters, e.g., **text, file of char,** or **interactive**—we will discuss these in greater detail later.

INPUT, OUTPUT, and KEYBOARD: These are intrinsic file titles identified with the users console. They are examples of **interactive** files.

GET and PUT: These can be used with any **typed** file. See the chapters discussing file I/O.

Pascal was originally designed to process batch jobs, that is, the user had little interaction with the program while it was running. On a microcomputer, the user will constantly interact with the running program in order to supply data in the form of inputs, and to observe the computed outputs. This form of computing is called *interactive computing.* We will be implementing *interactive* programs in the remainder of this book.

A common method of guiding a user through an interactive program is called *user prompting.* We can use the read and write intrinsics along with quoted *literals* to prompt inputs to interactive Pascal programs. For example, we can prompt the following input using the write and readln intrinsics. On the screen:

```
NAME    :
AGE     :
SALARY  $
```

The program might contain the following:

```
program PROMPT;
   var
      NAMES     :  string;
      AGES      :  integer;
      SALARYS :  real;
   begin
      write('NAME :' ) ; readln (NAMES);
      write('AGE :' ) ; readln (AGES);
      write('SALARY $1) ; readln (SALARYS);
   end.
```

Study the data definition section of program PROMPT. A **string** variable is a variable containing characters as its value. The definition of NAMES defines a class of values (called a **type**) made up of characters from the alphabet. If no limit to the length of the string of characters is given, Pascal assumes 80 characters. If a limit is desired in order to save memory space, the definition should specify an upper limit. To define a shorter string we could have written

NAMES : **string** [18] ;   (* up to 255 allowed *)

and a maximum of 18 characters would be allowed.

AGES is an integer type, that is, we define AGES to be a variable that can only take on values that belong to a class of values defined as "integers". Integers are numbers without a decimal point, while a variable of type **real** is a variable that can hold numbers with a decimal point.

If we wanted to restrict AGES to a smaller class of integers than the class of *all* integers, we could have done so by defining a subclass of values called an integer *subrange*. This is done by explicitly listing the lower and upper bound on the values acceptable to AGES.

AGES : 0 .. 100;

Unfortunately, Pascal does not allow real subranges; therefore it is illegal also to limit the class of values acceptable to SALARYS. The following is *illegal*:

SALARYS : 1.0 .. 1000.0 ;

The next interesting feature of PROMPT is the way we have written the prompts as write statements. The write is used instead of writeln because we wanted the input to be made on the same line as the prompted message. This method will be used throughout the next examples.

Pascal is a *typed* language because every variable name used in every program, procedure, or function *should* be assigned a class of values called a **type**.
We must define every variable along with its type before using it. Therefore, the
study of data typing is of major concern in Pascal. In the next section we illustrate the variety and power of Pascal data typing.

3.2 TYPE CASTING THE DATA

Lets take a closer look at the data definition section of Pascal. We immediately note that Pascal furnishes four basic types:

boolean

integer

real

char

In Pascal terminology these *base types* are called *scalars* because they require
no structuring of their values. A **boolean** is a scalar value of true or false. An
integer is a simple scalar value (usually between –32767 and +32767 on a microcomputer—the last section of this chapter gives a program to discover these
limits). A **real** is also a single value containing a floating decimal point. A **char**
is a single character, whereas a **string** is a sequence of characters.

We can define a datum to be a constant of type **boolean, integer, real,
char,** or **string** by declaring it in a **const** construct. This is the simplest way to
enter values into a Pascal program. Beware, however, the values *cannot* be
changed by the program. They are fixed constants. Here are some examples of
constants. The brackets (* and *) are used to insert comments into Pascal.

```
const
    SIZE    = 10 ;          (* integer valued *)
    FLOAT   = 5.3;          (* real valued *)
    LETTER  = 'A';          (* character valued *)
    GEE     = 'ABACUS';     (* string valued *)
```

Notice that every constant is defined with an equal sign and a value of the
type intended. Every pair is terminated with a semicolon, and only one variable
is defined at a time. Here are some *illegal* definitions:

```
NOWAY   = 10*3 ;                    (* no expressions *)
LIST    = array [1..10] of integer ; (* no structures *)
X, Y    = 5 ;                       (* no multiple variables *)
BAD     = 5..10 ;                   (* no subranges *)
```

The **var** statement within the data definition section of a **program** lists all the *instances* of variables used by all the modules of the program. We say these variables are *global* to the program because they are accessible by any statement in the program (there is a minor exception to this rule discussed later).

The global variables are *declared* (defined and typed) by listing them in the **var** section and assigning a type to each variable. The process of typing in this way is called *instantiation* because it is an example taken from a class of variables, hence an instance of a type. Here are some typical instantiations of data types:

```
var
    FIRST, SECOND :  integer ;        (* multiples ok *)

    CHARACTER     :  char ;           (* single char *)
    STR           :  string ;         (* up to 80 char *)
    SHORT         :  string [10] ;    (* up to 10 char *)
    LIMITS        :  0..50 ;          (* integer between 0 and 50 *)
```

The base types of Pascal provide a collection of minimal data types. Pascal would be an uninteresting language if only these types were allowed. The most significant feature of Pascal, on the other hand, is its powerful type extension capability. Pascal can be extended using two powerful features: (1) structured types, and (2) user defined types.

A **structured type** is either:

string

array

record

file

set

where each one of these refers to structures containing data of one of the basic types. The **array** structure provides familiar indexing structure into a list of identical data types. The **record** structure provides a mixture of data types all within a single "cluster" of data. A **file** is simply a sequential or random access file. A **set** is a collection of scalar values all of the same type but without a prescribed ordering.

The structured types can be used directly in a declaration (**var**), or they can be predefined as a new type to be used over and over again. For example,

LIST : **array** [1..10] **of integer;**

Once these scalar types are defined we can define a subrange type as a partial scalar on the predefined scalar. Thus,

```
WEEKEND = SAT..SUN ;
FALLMO  = SEPT..NOV ;
```

are subrange types defined from DAYS and MONTHS. These types can be instantiated in a variety of ways. Here are some more familiar examples. (Caution: do not use a scalar name in more than one instantiation, i.e., they must be unique).

```
var
    CENTURY :  array [1900..1999] of MONTHS;
    HUES    :  set of COLORS;
    WKND    :  WEEKEND;
    SEASON  :  SEASONS;
```

In the definition of CENTURY each element of the array is allowed to take on the scalar values of MONTH only. The values of HUES include all possible sets of COLORS. For example, HUES can be equal to any of the following $2 \wedge 3 = 8$ sets:

```
              [ ]         ;    (* empty set of COLORS *)
           [RED]          ;
         [WHITE]          ;
           [BLUE]         ;    (* single colors, only*)
    [RED, WHITE]          ;
     [RED, BLUE]          ;
   [WHITE, BLUE]          ;    (* two colors, only *)
[RED, WHITE, BLUE]        ;    (* all 3 colors *)
```

Note that a **set of integers** and a **set of real** would have an infinite possible set of values; therefore, sets are restricted to finite valued scalars or subrange types.

Finally, suppose we examine the usefulness of new types incorporating a mixture of other types. This is done with the **record** structure in Pascal. Here are some examples of new types defined by the programmer using mixed types.

```
type
    CALENDAR = record
                    MONTH  :    MONTHS ;
                    DATE   :    1..31 ;
               end ;
```

```
PERSON      = record
                SEX       :    SEXES ;
                BIRTH     :    YEARS ;
                COLOR     :    COLORS;
             end ;


CARDS       = record
                SUIT      :    SUITS ;
                VALUE     :    (ONE, TWO, THREE, FOUR,
                               FIVE, SIX, SEVEN, EIGHT,
                               NINE, ACE, JACK, QUEEN,
                               KING) ;
             end ;


DECK        = array [1..52] of CARDS ;
```

These mixed-type records are accessed by specifying both the variable name and the corresponding **record** *component*. For example, if we define a deck of cards as above, we can access either the card's value or its suit using the *dot notation* of Pascal.

```
var
    BLACKJACK :  DECK ;
```

To access a BLACKJACK card we must specify its subscript value and its record component name.

```
BLACKJACK [2] . VALUE
BLACKJACK [3] . SUIT
```

Similarly, the **type** PERSON has 3 components:

```
var
    X :  PERSON
```

thus,

```
X.SEX
X.BIRTH
X.COLOR
```

are used to refer to each of the components of X.

Here are some *illegal* instantiations of types to be careful to avoid.

```
var
    ALPHABET    :  [A..Z] ;                (* no sets *)
    LETTERS     :  set of (A..Z) ;         (* not basic scalar *)
    VOWELS      :  ('A','E','I','O','U') ; (* no literals *)
    NUMBS       :  set of integer ;        (* not finite subrange *)
```

The final structured type, file, will be discussed in detail in the chapter dealing with file structures. An example of file declaration is given below:

```
var
    FACTORY :  file of PERSON;
    PAYROLL :  file of WORKERS;
```

We are prepared to study the declaration of modules in Pascal. These modules will access the data we have just studied in order to transform it into output results. When combined with data, the modules complete the necessary parts of programming in Pascal.

Remember,

A. Sets can be of *base type* scalar or subrange only.

B. Unstructured data types **boolean, integer, real, char** are used to construct more sophisticated *structured* types.

C. USCD Pascal provides structured types **string record, array, file, and set.**

3.3 LEARN TO THINK IN PASCAL

Pascal was developed to teach beginning programmers how to write clear, concise, and error-free programs. Fortunately, these goals have been met, in general, and even the most experienced programmer can benefit from the clarity of expression *forced* on the Pascal programmer. Indeed, the simplicity and power of Pascal is the essence of its elegance. Exactly how is this accomplished?

We have already seen examples of the elegance of Pascal data types. Each type is a *cluster* or *data chunk* comprised of scalars or simple structured types. These basic types are combined into more and more sophisticated types using the **type** statement. Thus, every *chunk* of data in Pascal is a well-defined grouping.

The same idea is used to chunk together programs, procedures, and functions. The building blocks of Pascal are (1) program units, (2) procedures, and (3) functions. These three blocks are called program modules, in Pascal terminology, and they may be nested one inside of the other just as we have nested data in order to build more powerful constructs from simpler ones. The "outer-most" modules are declared as follows:

```
program NAME ;
unit     NAME ;     (*program module.*)
```

The module called **unit** will be discussed in a later section. It is used to build a large system of program modules where it is convenient that each module be separately compiled and then linked together in a separate *integration* step.

The ordinary program module defined by the **program** statement may in turn be modularized into *internal* procedures and functions. Suppose, for exam-ple, we cluster together the prompting statements, below, into a reusable proce-dure.

```
procedure PROMPTS ;

    begin
        write ( 'ENTER :' );
        write ( '[1] . NAME :'); readln (NAMES) ;
        write ( '[2] . STATE:' ); readln (STATES);
        write ( '[3] . ZIP :'); readln (ZIPS) ;
        writeln( 'THANKS' ) ;
    end ;
```

This procedure uses global variables which it inherits from the program module, as shown below.

```
program DATABASE;
    var
        NAMES    :  string[18] ;    (* globals.. *)
        STATES   :  string[16] ;
        ZIPS     :  0..99999 ;
    ;
    procedure PROMPTS ;
        begin
            write ( 'ENTER :') ;
            write ( '[1] . NAME :'); readln (NAMES) ;
            write ( '[2] . STATE:'); readln (STATES);
            write ( '[3] . ZIP :'); readln (ZIPS) ;
            writeln( 'THANKS' ) ;
        end;    (* PROMPTS *)
```

```
begin        (* MAIN *)
   PROMPTS ;
   PROMPTS ;
   PROMPTS ;
end.
```

The internal procedure PROMPTS is *called* three times from the main program body. Each time the procedure is executed, it accepts new values of NAMES, STATES, and ZIPS. These values are stored in *global* variables which are accessible to all procedures and functions in the program module. Suppose, however, we include a function SPIT which uses a *local* variable S as illustrated below.

```
function SPIT ( S: char ) : boolean ;
   begin
      writeln (S) ;
      SPIT := FALSE ;
   end ;  (* SPIT *)
```

Notice that function modules accept inputs in the form of a *formal parameter list* and return a value in the form of a typed scalar. Thus, S is the *formal parameter* of SPIT. The value of SPIT is either TRUE or FALSE because it is of type **boolean**. In this trivial example, SPIT returns a value of FALSE.

SPIT could also have used a local variable which was *not* passed to it through the formal parameter list. For example, I is a local variable in the modified function below; but because SPIT is nested within (included inside) the encompassing HAPPY module, the variable I is accessible only to the statements inside SPIT and not accessible by statements in HAPPY.

```
program HAPPY ;
   var
      J : char
   function SPIT ( S ; char ) : integer ;
      var
         I : 0..25 ;   (* local to SPIT *)
      begin
         I := ord (S) - ord ('A') ;
         write (S)
         SPIT := I ;
      end ;     (* SPIT *)
   begin
      readln (J) ;
      writeln (SPIT (J)) ;
   end.
```

Program HAPPY accepts a single character input into variable J: **char** and then passes J as an *actual parameter* to **function** SPIT. Inside SPIT the actual parameter is linked to the formal parameter S: **char** by value, that is, the value stored in J is copied into the value of S. This is called *pass-by-value* and is a safe way to pass data from one module to another.

In pass-by-value communication between modules, the actual parameter cannot be changed by the formal parameter. The function is said to have *side effects* on the actual parameter if the function can modify the value stored in the actual parameter. SPIT has *no* side effect on J because of the pass-by-value linkage.

Inside SPIT we see a local variable I:0..25 defined. SPIT is the *only* module with access to I, therefore we say I is local to SPIT. Next, notice the use of another intrinsic function "ord" within SPIT.

ord (S) − ord ('A') ;

This expression computes the *order* of character S relative to the *order* of letter 'A' in the alphabet. Since the machine-level encoding of the letters of the alphabet may differ from one machine to another, it is wise to compute the relative difference between some character S and the encoded value of the letter 'A'. This number must lie between 0 and 25 as indicated by the subrange type of I.

The value of I is stored as the value of SPIT, and then control is switched back to the main program module.

In the main program module, every function name is treated just like any other variable name. This is why every function module must be typed by its definition. Since SPIT is an instance of an **integer**, the writeln statement outputs the integer result of converting a letter S into a numeral SPIT.

Let's summarize the rules of Pascal modules before going on. These rules are very important to know.

A. Program modules may contain internal modules: either procedures or functions.

B. Procedures are called by writing their names. Functions are called by writing their names in a manner similar to a variable name.

C. Functions return a single value; a procedure returns no values.

D. Both function and procedure produce side effects if they change the value of either an actual parameter or a global variable.

E. A global variable can be changed by a function or procedure that is also defined in the same module as the global data.

F. A local variable can be changed by the function or procedure containing its declaration, or by a call to a module which modifies the local variable through side effects.

G. A parameter is passed by value to a function or procedure unless the parameter is allowed to *vary*. A parameter is allowed to *vary* if the formal parameter list is declared with the **var** statement.

Example: **procedure** SIDE(**var** X: **integer**);

This version of procedure SIDE will allow X to be changed by SIDE. Thus, the **var** allows side effects. This is called *pass-by-reference.*

H. All functions and procedures must be defined before their use (call) unless they are *external* or defined in a forward reference statement.

Example: **procedure** LATE; **forward**;

Example: **procedure** OUTSIDE; **extern**;

Both of these exceptions will be discussed later.

The programmer who thinks in Pascal also thinks in psychological chunks. Each operation to be performed by a program must be broken into pieces or chunks. These chunks are perhaps refined further into smaller and smaller chunks. Finally, the small chunks are encoded as Pascal modules—either programs, functions, or procedures. This is the concept underlying the divide-and-conquer method of programming in levels of abstraction. This is referred to as programming by *stepwise refinement.*

What is the next level of abstraction beyond stepwise refinement of modules? To complete the refinement of a module, we must learn to write individual Pascal statements. This is the next subject.

3.4 THE NITTY GRITTY STUFF

Amazingly, every computer program in the world can be written as combinations of three very simple structures. Every module of Pascal can be constructed from repeated use of the following 3 control structures:

   I.   Sequence

  II.   Choice

 III.   Iteration

These three kinds of module flow are diagrammed in Figure 3.2. A program written as a collection of these 3 constructions is called a *structured* program. In Figure 3.2. (I) the actions of a program are modeled as a *serial* succession of other actions. One activity follows another, and no decisions are needed to decide which path to follow next. In Figure 3.2 (II), the diamond box indicates that a decision is made and the program executes either the upper or lower branch, but not both. Eventually, the two branches join again to provide a single-entry, single-exit structure (SESE).

Every program that is composed of SESE structures is structured. Notice that every structure in Figure 3.2 is a SESE structure. Hence, we can be sure that

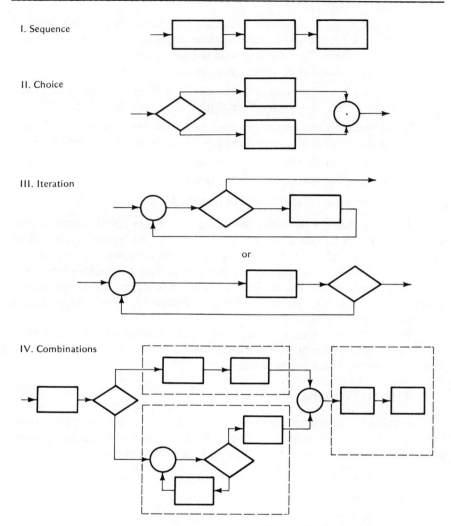

Figure 3.2. Basic Structures of Structured Programming

Pascal programs are structured if we stick to these elementary structures. It has been suggested that structured programs are easier to read and maintain than unstructured programs. Therefore, we will advocate Pascal programs that are restricted to SESE (single-entry, single-exit) control structures.

Both looping (iteration) structures of Figure 3.2 (III) are SESE structures. In the first loop, the choice (decision) is made before entering the loop, while in the second example, the choice is made after the loop body has been executed *at least once.*

Finally, study the combination of all three basic kinds of program structure as illustrated by Figure 3.2 (IV). The dotted-line boxes outline three *nested* SESE structures which are themselves SESE structured. Repeated use of these structures in a nested or serial manner also leads to a structured program.

In Pascal, we can write structured programs by noting the statements that perform the same actions as suggested in Figure 3.2. These are listed briefly below.

I. Sequence.

Assignment:	X := A + B;
Call	PROMPT;
	writeln;
	begin .. end;

II. Choice.

IF-THEN-ELSE:	**if** A⟨B
	then A:=0
	else A:=1;
IF-THEN	: **if** A⟨B
	then A:=∅;
CASE	: **case** SWITCH **of**
	1:
	2:
	3:
	end;

III. Iteration.

Counting loop :	**for** I:=1 **to** N **do**.
While loop :	**while** A=B **do**
repeat loop :	**repeat** ... **until** A=B;

We emphasize that **every** program can be written with these elementary statements. The creativity and imagination needed to write any program may not be easily realized, but it is the goal of this book to supply some insight into how to write programs with these simple statements.

Now, we can turn to several examples to show how to apply sequence, iteration, and choice to solving problems. Remember the approach taken in stepwise refinement. Keep in mind that a program is a collection of data chunks (types), modules, and SESE statements.

Consider the following problem. The Pascal language does not define the size of integer number allowed in a program. On one machine the range of values might be –123500 .. 132500, while on another machine they might be restricted to a smaller subrange, –32000 .. 32000. The size of integer data values depends on the number of bits used to encode each integer. This is called the *word size problem*. In general, the word size of an integer is equal to the number of bits in each word of computer memory.

The largest possible number we can store in a *binary* computer is usually

wordsize
2   –1

where wordsize is equal to the number of bits per word. How can we discover the wordsize and magnitude of the largest integer possible in a microcomputer that runs Pascal?

A high level of abstraction for this problem is given in Pascal *pseudocode:*

WORDSIZE:

1. Start with WIDTH :=0 and WORD :=1.

2. Repeat until overflow occurs:
   2.1.   Add one to WIDTH
   2.2.   Shift and add one bit to WORD

3. Output the WIDTH and largest number found before overflow occurred.

We can implement this pseudocode algorithm once we discover a method of detecting overflow in Pascal programs. This requires some knowledge of machine arithmetic, but in simple terms we must know what happens when one is added to the largest number in the machine. On most microcomputers addition of one beyond the largest integer causes the result to go negative. Let's try this approach and see what happens.

Suppose we define the following data chunk for **program** WORDSIZE.

```
const
     BIT    = 1;
     SHIFT  = 2;

var
     WORD  :  integer;
     SAVED :  integer;
     WIDTH :  0 .. 64;
```

The idea will be to start with a WORD containing one bit and then shift this bit to the left (most significant position) while adding in a new bit. For exampmle,

```
WORD            = 0001
SHIFT AND ADD   = 0011
```

```
SHIFT AND ADD   =  0111
SHIFT AND ADD   =  1111
SHIFT AND OVERFLOW = ?
```

This can be done as follows:

```
begin
   WIDTH := 0 ;
   WORD := BIT ;
      repeat
         WIDTH := WIDTH + 1 ;
         SAVED := WORD ;
         WORD := SHIFT * WORD + BIT ;
      until  WORD < 0 ;
```

The shift operation is done by multiplication since multiplication by two is a tricky way to shift a binary number.

The program of Figure 3.3 resulted from another stepwise refinement of this design. When executed on the author's microcomputer, the result was:

```
WORD SIZE IS 15 BITS
32767 IS THE LARGEST INTEGER
```

Try this program on your own micro and see what the limits are to integer subrange types. What do you suppose is the smallest number possible?

```
program WORDSIZE ;

   const
      BIT     = 1 ;
      SHIFT   = 2 ;

   var
      WORD    : integer ;
      SAVED   : integer ;
      WIDTH   : 0 .. 64 ;

   begin
      (*   FIND THE NUMBER OF BITS IN EACH INTEGER WORD.
           ALSO FIND THE LARGEST INTEGER NUMBER POSSIBLE.   *)
      WIDTH := 0 ;                  (* ASSUME ZERO BITS, INITIALLY *)
      WORD  := BIT ;                (* ASSUME A ONE BIT COMPUTER.. *)

      repeat
         WIDTH := WIDTH + 1 ;       (* COUNT THE BITS, ONE AT A TIME *)
         SAVED := WORD ;            (* SAVE LARGEST WORD FOR LATER.. *)
         WORD  := SHIFT * WORD + BIT ;
      until WORD < 0 ;              (* STOP WHEN WORD OVERFLOWS TO <0*)

      WRITELN( 'WORD SIZE IS ', WIDTH, ' BITS' ) ;
      WRITELN( SAVED, ' IS THE LARGEST INTEGER' ) ;

   end.
```

Figure 3.3. Program WORDSIZE listing

TWENTY QUESTIONS

1. What names in Pascal are reserved for Pascal alone?
2. How many characters are significant in a name?
3. What three statements are used to define a data chunk?
4. What are the three kinds of program modules?
5. What is the difference between get and read?
6. What is a Pascal intrinsic?
7. What does the statement; "writeln;" do?
8. What is the difference between the two data types, **string** and **char**?
9. Is **array** a scalar or structure type?
10. Is this legal in Pascal? **var** SALARYS:1.0..5.5;
11. What are the acceptable values for type **boolean**?
12. What is the difference between these two definitions:

    type
        A = **array** [1..80] **of char**;
        B = **string** ;

13. What are the four basic structured types in Pascal?
14. Is this legal in Pascal?

    type
        COLORS   =   (BROWN, BLUE, GREEN, RED);
        EYES   =   (BROWN, BLUE);

15. How many possible set values can be taken on by the following instantiation of the scalar in problem 14?

    var
        PAINT : **set of** COLORS ;

16. In the following example, which variable is a global, which one is local, and which is formal parameter?

    program RABBIT ;
        var
            X1: char;
        procedure CAT (X2: char);
            var
                X3: **integer**;

17. What is the difference between these two formal parameters?

    Y: **string** versus **var** Y: **string.**

18. What is the value of ord('C') – ord ('A')?
19. What are the three basic building blocks of a structured program?
20. What does SESE mean?

ANSWERS

1. Keywords like **begin, end, for,** etc.
2. Eight. The remaining characters are ignored.
3. A global chunk is defined in terms of **const, type, var.**
4. They are **program** or **unit, procedure**, and **function.**
5. Get is for files and read is for the console.
6. A built-in procedure or function that need not be defined.
7. Skips to next output line.
8. **Char** is a single character scalar, while **string** defines up to 80 characters in value.
9. Structure type.
10. No. Real subranges are prohibited.
11. True and False.
12. They are the same.
13. They are **array, record, file,** and **set.**
14. No. Scalars must be unique, thus BROWN and BLUE can appear only once.
15. Since there are 4 scalars in COLORS, there are $2\wedge4 = 16$ possible sets. PAINT can take on one of 16 values.
16. X1 is global; X3 is local; X2 is a formal parameter.
17. The first is a pass-by-value parameter. The second is a pass-by-reference parameter.
18. Two.
19. Sequence, Choice, Iteration.
20. Single-entry, single-exit control.

Chapter 4

Pascal Spoken Here
(The Novice)

Charles Babbage was rumored to have cursed an error-prone steamship timetable which was so vital to commerce in the mid-1800s by exclaiming "I wish to God these had been calculated by steam!" Of course, calculating by steam meant using some form of mechanical engine that could perform arithmetic without human power or reasoning; so he spend a major portion of his life designing the Difference Engine and the Analytical Engine.

Babbage had some success with the Difference Engine but ran into funding and technical difficulties with his proposal for the Analytical Engine. The Analytical Engine was so similar in concept to modern computers that it inspired the design of some very early electronic computers one-hundred years later.

Babbage's proposal for funding was turned down by the British government. The committee that evaluated his proposal was concerned about a number of obstacles that still face computing today. For example, they suggested, "Care might be required to guard against misuse, especially against the imposition of Sisyphean tasks upon it by influential sciolists." We can only guess at what would have become of modern computing had Babbage's Analytical Engine been funded for construction.

4.1 SIMPLE SEQUENCE (ASSIGNMENT)

The rules of structured programming restrict programming to *repeated* and *nested* use of (1) simple sequence, (2) choice, and (3) iteration as discussed in the previous chapter. In this section, we give more exacting definitions and examples of the *assignment* statement along with operations allowed in expressions.

The assignment statement performs nearly all of the calculations and data movement operations of a program. In most applications, 35-50% of the program consists of assignment statements.

The form of an assignment statement employs := as the "assigned-to" operation.

⟨name of structure⟩ := ⟨expression⟩ ;

The left-hand side must be a single variable, but the right-hand side can be any *well-formed* expression. The statement is terminated by a semicolon in most instances, but there are several exceptions to the semicolon rule that we must beware of.

A well-formed expression is constructed by observing two important features of Pascal: (1) the grammar of the expression and (2) the type of the data. The grammar of Pascal expressions is the familiar *infix* notation. The type of data affects the kinds of operators that are allowed in the expression. For example, **integer** data cannot be modified by **real** operators without first being converted to reals.

Integer Expressions

Study the following examples which use these operators and functions:

*	multiply and produce an integer product
div	divide and produce an integer quotient
mod	divide and produce an integer remainder
+	add two integers
–	subtract two integers
abs(J)	absolute value of J
sqr(J)	produce J*J
trunc(X)	discard the decimal fraction of X
round(X)	if X>=0 produce trunc(X+0.5)
	else produce trunc(X)
succ(J)	same as J:=J +1;
pred(J)	same as J:=J –1;

The integer expression below is converted into a real value by a *mixed mode* assignment:

```
var
    X: real;
    J: integer;

begin
    X:=J;
end.
```

Suppose X:=5.3 and J:=3. The result of the following separately executed assignments is:

Statement	Result
X:=J;	X is 3.0.
J:=X;	J is 5
J:=sqr(J);	J is 9
J:=succ(J);	J is 4
J:=pred(J);	J is 2
J:=round(X);	J is 5
X:=(J+1) div (J–1);	X is 2.0
J:=(J+1) mod (J–1);	J is 0

An interesting exception occurs in Pascal when integers are mixed with real operators in an expression. The integers are *coerced* into real values in *some* cases. For example, it is tempting to forget about **div** and use the real divide operator /. Again, assume initially, J:=3.

Expression	Result
J / 2	Should be J **div** 2
J / (J – 1)	Results in 1.5
(J + 2) / J	Results in 1.6667
2 / J	Should be 2 **div** J

Clearly, integers are also used in integer expressions for subscripting array structures. Thus,

A[J]
A[J+2]

are perfectly acceptable uses of integer expressions.

Real Expressions

The real valued expressions always produce a real valued result. However, real valued data *cannot* always be used in the same expressions as integers. For example, subscripts must be **integer**, not **real**, and reals cannot be incremented or decremented in the same way as integers using succ(X) and pred(X) functions. Assume X: **real**, below {"sqrt" through "exp" are library functions which require **uses** TRANSCEND as part of the program}.

Expression	Result
A[X]	Error, wrong type
pred(X)	Error, wrong type
X:=X+1	Increments X

sqr(X)	Squares X
sqrt(X)	Square root of X
sin(X)	Sine of X
cos(X)	Cosine of X
atan(X)	Arctangent of X
ln(X)	Natural logarithm
exp(X)	e∧X: exponential
pwroften(X)	10∧X: exponential
abs(X)	absolute value of X
X/2.0	division
X * Y	multiplication

Suppose we compute the length of the hypotenuse of a right triangle. The base, BASE and height, HEIGHT are substituted into the Pythagorean Formula:

HYPO := sqrt (sqr (BASE) + sqr (HEIGHT));

As another example, suppose we need to compare two real numbers. Due to round-off or internal conversion from decimal to binary, the comparison may fail when it should succeed. For example, 1.9999... and 2.00... are *equal* when infinite precision is allowed, but they fail a test for equality on most (finite) machines!

Instead of comparing equality, X=Y, it is safer to compare two numbers within some small error bound. Consider the following code as an illustration of a reliable method of comparing two real numbers, X and Y.

```
const
   ERROR = 1E-6;
var
   X, Y : real;
begin
   if ABS (X-Y) < ABS (ERROR * Y)
      then
      else
```

This fragment of code computes the relative error between X and Y.

$$abs \left[\frac{X - Y}{Y} \right] < ERROR$$

If X:=1.0000001 and Y:=1.0000000, then abs(X–Y) is 1E-7 and the two numbers are considered equal. Also, note that the equality holds true for the "large" numbers 10,000,000 and 10,000,001, because ERROR * Y gives approximately 10.

Boolean Expressions

A **boolean** variable takes on true or false values only. A **boolean** is a scalar:

type
    BOOLEAN = (FALSE, TRUE);

We use booleans to set flags, make decisions, and terminate loops. Consider the following examples where P and Q are booleans, J is an integer, and F is a file type.

Expression	Result
P:=TRUE;	Set P to TRUE
P **or** Q	TRUE if either P or Q is true
P **and** Q	TRUE only if P and Q are both true
not P	TRUE if P is FALSE and FALSE if P is TRUE
P:=J>0;	TRUE if J>0 is TRUE
odd(J)	TRUE if J is odd
ord(P)	0 if P is FALSE, 1 if P is TRUE
eof(F)	End-of-file is TRUE if file end has been reached
eoln(F)	TRUE only when an end of line is reached
J **in** []	TRUE if the value of J is in the set

An example of the last expression will help to understand the potential value of the **in** operator. Suppose ALPHABET is a **set** of letters, and S is a character.

type
    LETTERS = 'A' .. 'Z' ;
var
    ALPHABET   :   **set of** LETTERS ;
    S   :   **char**
begin
    .
    .
    .
    if S   **in** ALPHABET
            then
            else

Also, we can abbreviate the flag setting operation,

```
if A = B
   then  FLAG := TRUE
   else   FLAG := FALSE;
```

with a simple assignment to boolean variable FLAG,

```
FLAG := A = B ;
```

The Pascal Compiler may have difficulty recognizing a compound boolean expression. Thus if the expression

P or Q and A = B

is evaluated in two parts,

P or Q

A = B

both parts must be TRUE in order for (P or Q) and (A=B) to be TRUE. But,

P or Q and A = B

is ambiguous, while

(P or Q) and (A=B)

is clear. When in doubt use parentheses to group boolean subexpressions together.

Character Expressions

The character set of most microcomputers obeys the standard ASCII-7 definition, but one cannot always be sure. Therefore, it is best to view the character set as a gigantic scalar type,

```
type
    CHAR = ( '+', '–', ...... 'A', 'B', ...... 'Z', '0', '1', .....
```

This is *not* acceptable Pascal form, of course, but merely a way to think of characters in Pascal. This conceptualization explains why it is possible to convert from characters to integers using the *order* function, ord.

To get a numbering from either the alphabet or numerals (where C:char),

$$ord(C) - ord('A')$$

produces an integer K:0..25 for character C:'A'..'Z'. Also, when C:'0'..'9',

$$ord(C) - ord('0')$$

produces K:0..9 instead. This interpretation also leads to a *lexicographical* ordering of characters. Thus the boolean value TRUE results when characters A and B are compared;

'A' < 'B'   is TRUE if ord('A') < ord('B')
'A' = CH   is TRUE if ord('A') = ord(CH)
CH1 > CH2   is TRUE if ord(CH1) > ord(CH2)

Also note the effects of pred and succ on these simulated scalars.

pred('A') equals chr(ord('A') - 1)
succ('A') equals chr(ord('A') + 1)

where chr(J) is the *inverse* of the ord function, that is,

chr(ord ('A')) equals 'A'.

Set Expressions

We have previously encountered the type **set** whose variables take on one value from a total of $2 \wedge N$ possible values of a scalar, given N scalar values. We can "add", "subtract", and "test" sets, as illustrated in the following examples.

A set *constructor* [] is used to form sets inside an expression. For set variables A and B,

A := ['A'..'Z','0'..'9']

constructs a value for A, while the expression

B := ['A', 'E', 'I', 'O', 'U']

constructs a value for set B. Then,

A := A - B ;

removes the elements of B from set A, and

A := A − ['0' .. '9'] ;

removes the numerals from A, leaving the set of consonants.
We can add the vowels back into A by set *union*, as follows:

A := A + B ;

We could also eliminate all members of A that are not also members of B with
the *intersection* operator, * .

A := A * B ;

This leaves A and B with the same set of characters.
The test

'M' in B

is true if 'M' is in the set B, and FALSE otherwise. Two sets are equal if they
contain the same elements and no other elements.

A = B .

If some elements are (completely) contained within another set, then set
inclusion is TRUE. For example, the following tests are all TRUE:

['A', 'B'] <= ['A', 'B', 'C']

[1, 3, 5, 7, 11] >= [3, 5, 7]

[ ] <= [RED]

An illustration of the versatility of sets and strings is given in many later
examples. Until then, here are a few things to remember about sets.

A. Sets cannot be output via the WRITE procedure, but a set may be PUT to a
file of type **set**.

B. The *base type* of a set is equal to the type of the elements in the set. The elements must be either scalar or subrange values which are scalars.

C. All elements of a set must be of the same base type.

D. The most useful set types and examples of their declaration and use:

Declaration	*Example of Use*
1. **var** I: **set of char** ;	I := ['X', '0']

2. **type**
      S = (BLACK, BLUE) ;
   var
      T : **set of** S ;
	T := [BLACK] + [BLUE] ;

3. **var** K : **set of** 0..3 ;	K := [0,1,3] ;

E. Set operations are done by *overloading* the operators +, -, *, etc., with additional meanings of *union, removal, intersection*, etc.

4.2 MAKE UP YOUR MIND (CHOICE)

The second fundamental statement type needed to write structured Pascal programs is the collection of *choice* or *conditional statements*. In Pascal, we have three forms to choose from:

I. **if – then**, e.g.,
```
if A=B
   then writeln( 'A=B' ) ;
```

II. **if – then – else**, e.g.,
```
if A=B
   then writeln( 'A=B' )
   else writeln( 'A< >B' ) ;
```

III. **case**, e.g.,
```
case SWITCH of
   0 : writeln( 'zero' ) ;
   1 : writeln( 'one' )
end
```

Beware of the placement of the semicolon in the **if** statements. In particular, do not place a semicolon after the **then** clause in form II above.

In addition, Pascal allows the experienced user to employ a GOTO statement when in dire need of an uncontrolled branch. The **goto** may be enabled with the (*G+*) compiler option (see Chapter 10 for an example).

The **if** statements above are permitted to make a conditional branch to either the **then** or **else** clause based on the outcome of the **boolean** expression evaluation.

Examples:

if A< >B
if A **in** [1,2,5]
if (A+B)=(A-B)

```
if odd (A)
if pred (J) >K
if (A in [1,3,5])
      and
   ( not (A in [3,7,9]))
if not (A and B)
if (0<=X)
      and
   (X<= 100)
if FLAG
```

The boolean expression within an **if** statement is sometimes called a *predicate*. Each of these predicates can be used in either of the two forms of the **if** statement.

Often the logic of a program demands a collection of *nested* **if–then–else** statements. For instance, when choosing an action based on one of several conditions, the **tree** of choices becomes a tangle of **if–then–else** statements. The tree of Figure 4.1 shows how an action is decoded from the set of values, [1,5, 11,15]. The corresponding jungle of **ifs** is:

```
if X in [1,5,11,15]
   then
       if X=1
          then ACTION (1)
          else
             if X=5
                then ACTION (2)
                else
                   if X=11
                      then ACTION (3)
                      else ACTION (4);
(* end of the if-mess *)
```

Fortunately, Pascal has a very brief structure to handle this kind of structure. The **case** statement allows n-way branding. Instead of the if-mess, above, we can use the **case** statement to write the same thing.

```
case X of
  1:  ACTION (1);
  5:  ACTION (2);
 11:  ACTION (3);
 15:  ACTION (4);      (* semicolon is optional *)
end
```

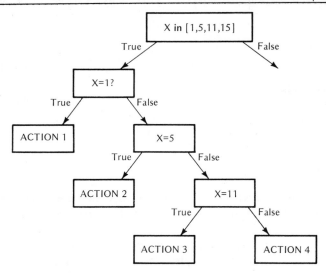

Figure 4.1.   Decision Tree for Variable X

This form is certainly a victory for clarity and conciseness. When X=5, ACTION(2) is executed followed by the **end** statement. If X **in** [1,5,11,15] is FALSE, then none of the case clauses are executed and control skips over the **case .. end** grouping.

The data type of the case selector and the cases must match, that is, both must be either a subrange scalar, integer, or character. Here are some examples:

```
var CH : char ;

case CH of
    'A'    :   writeln( 'A' ) ;
    'B'    :   begin
                   writeln( 'B' ) ;
                   readln ( CH ) ;
               end ;
    'C'    :   X := A + B
    end ;
```

Note the use of **begin** and **end** keywords to group several constructs into one *compound* statement. A compound statement is one beginning with the keyword **begin,** containing one or more other simple or compound statements, and terminating with an **end** keyword.

Another example:

var C : (RED, WHITE, BLUE) ;

```
case C of
    RED :        writeln( 'RED' ) ;
    WHITE:       (* null case *);
    BLUE :       writeln( 'BLUE' )
end ;
```

We can also label clauses with an entire list of values as shown in this next illustration.

```
case C of
    RED              :  writeln( 'RED' ) ;
    WHITE, BLUE      :  writeln( 'WHITE AND BLUE' ) ;

end ;
```

We will have ample opportunity to use the if and case statements in the following examples, also. Remember, the main features of these *choice* constructs in Pascal.

A. Beware of the placement of semicolons in the if – then and if – then – else statements.

B. Compound begin .. end statements may be used in the if – then, if – then – else, and case statements.

C. The if – then and if – then – else statements operate (make decisions) on boolean expressions called *predicates.*

D. The clauses of a case statement must match the type of the case selector variable (and they must be scalars).

E. Case clauses may be labeled with a *list* as well as a singleton.

F. If no matching case label is found, all clauses are skipped.

4.3 COUNT THE WAYS (LOOPING)

The third statement type needed in structured programming is called the *repetitive*, or *iterative*, statement. This statement causes a simple or compound statement to be executed many times. It is this collection of statements that causes programs to *loop.*

There are three kinds of loop, or iteration, statements in Pascal. They are:

I. **for**, e.g.,   **for** I:=1 **to** N **do**
        or   **for** I:=N **downto** 1 **do**
II. **while**, e.g.,   **while** X < Y **do**
III. **repeat**, e.g.,   **repeat** .. **until** X < Y ;

The **for** loop (counting loop) is useful for indexing a simple or compound statement as well as controlling iteration. The loop is executed *zero* or more times, each time with the loop *counter* either incremented or decremented by one. Here is an example for entering N values into array X:

```
for I := 1 to N do
   readln( X[ I ] ) ;
```

Notice the placement of the elusive semicolon again. This example causes a single statement to be repeated. Assume, however, that several statements are to be repeated as a group.

```
for I := 1 to  M do
   begin
      readln ( X[ I ] ) ;
      writeln( sqr( X[ I ] ) ) ;
   end ;                              (* for *)
```

The compound **begin** .. **end** brackets are used to define a group of repeated statements.

The counting loop can also be used to enumerate the elements of a scalar. In such a case the **for** loop "increments" the scalar by selecting the next scalar in sequence. Study the following illustration carefully.

```
type
   COLORS = (RED,WHITE,BLUE,BLACK);
var
   SHADE :  COLORS
   PICT   :  array [COLORS] of integer;
begin
   for SHADE := RED to BLACK do
      PICT [SHADE] :=0;
```

This powerful technique employs several new ideas in programming. First, the array structure PICT is indexed by scalar values, RED, WHITE, BLUE, and BLACK. The order of these scalar values is:

ord:	0	1	2	3
scalar:	RED	WHITE	BLUE	BLACK

So, we could have written the equivalent, but more cumbersome, code:

```
const
   RED    =  0;
   WHITE  =  1;
   BLUE   =  2;
   BLACK  =  3;
var
   PICT : array [0..3] of integer;
begin
   for SHADE := 0 to 3 do
      PICT [SHADE] :=0;
```

Thus, the **for** loop is useful for indexing over a collection of integers and scalars. If we want to iterate a statement over a range of reals or some other condition, we must turn to the conditional loops, **while** and **repeat- until**.

The **while** loop executes *zero* or more times, but the **repeat- until** loop executes at least once. Here are some examples to illustrate when to use each form.

Suppose we define the data chunks

```
var
PRIMES :  set of 0..10 ;
X      :   0 .. 10 ;
```

for both versions of looping code. In the first version we employ the **repeat-until** loop to read a number, X, and display its square only if the number is a prime less than ten. When the first non-prime number is input, the loop stops.

```
PRIMES := [ 2, 3, 5, 7 ] ;
   repeat

      readln ( X ) ;
      if ( X in PRIMES )

         then writeln( sqr( X ) ) ;
   until not ( X in PRIMES ) ;
```

Now, here is the same program written in the **while** loop form. Notice the greater degree of conciseness and clarity.

```
PRIMES := [2,3,5,7] ;
readln (X);
   while (X in PRIMES) do
```

```
begin
    writeln ( sqr (X) ) ;
    readln (X);
end;
```

This example favored the **while** loop, but there are perhaps as many instances when the **repeat** loop is preferred. The rule is to use the form that results in the most clarity and conciseness. Consider the following example, where it is *always* necessary to execute the loop at least once.

```
I := 0;
repeat
    I := I + 1;
until  ( LIST [I] = KEY )
              or
          ( I = N ) ;
```

Obviously, this loop searches a list of elements stored in LIST[I..N] for a matching KEY. If the KEY is found, the repeating code is terminated, leaving the value of I equal to the location of the match with KEY. If the KEY is not to be found, the loop stops when I reaches N.

Suppose we convert this loop into its **while** loop form. At first glance, the following loop looks like it does the same job, but with perhaps more style.

```
I := 1;
while    ( LIST [I] <> KEY )
              and
          ( I <= N )
    do
        I := I + 1 ;
```

This loop has a subtle error in it! The list is searched until LIST[I] = KEY for some I. If a matching KEY is found, the loop behaves as it should; but notice what happens when the KEY is not to be located. On the last iteration, I = (N+1), and the loop predicate becomes

```
(LIST [N+1] <> KEY)
    and
( N+1 <= N )
```

This would terminate the loop because I has exceeded N. Instead, the *program* is abnormally terminated because of subscript range error in computing LIST [N+1]! Furthermore, altering the predicate to remove this problem usually makes the loop even more erroneous.

The **repeat** loop should be used in cases where the program *must* execute the loop at least once. The **while** loop is used whenever it is possible that *no* execution of the loop body is required. In either case, clarity and correctness are the guiding principles to be applied.

These statements will also be used throughout the succeeding chapters; so keep in mind the following points concerning iteration.

A. The **repeat** statement executes at least once; the **while** executes *zero* or more times.

B. The **while** and **for** loop statements demand a **begin .. end** compound statement if more than one simple statement is to be iterated; the **repeat**, on the other hand, does *not* require a **begin .. end**.

For example,

```
repeat                    while I < N do
  I := I + 1;               begin
  writeln(I);                 I := I + 1;
until I = N;                  writeln ( I );
                          end
```

C. The **for** loop is used to enumerate scalars, integers, and (sometimes) characters, but never reals.

D. Most programming errors are in logic; most logic errors are in booleans; most boolean expressions are in loop and **if – then – else** statements.

TWENTY QUESTIONS

1. Who is buried in Charles Babbage's grave?
2. Can := be replaced by = in Pascal?
3. What do we mean by a well-formed expression?
4. What is the difference between **div** and / ?
5. Can the abs intrinsic be used on reals and integers?
6. Can J:=J-1; be replaced by J:=pred(J)?
7. What do we mean by A *coerces* B?
8. What two errors are caused by X in the array subscript operation A[X] ?
9. Given X=4, what is sqrt(X) and sqr(X)?
10. Given P is TRUE and Q is FALSE, what is (1) P **or** Q, (2) P **and** Q, (3) **not** P, (4) ord (P)?

11. Given

    type
        X = 1..3;
        Y = '1'..'3';
    var
        M : **set of** X;
        T : **set of** Y;

which of the following are illegal in Pascal?
(1) M:=['2','3'],   (2) T:=['3']
(3) M:=[ ],   (4) T:=['1'..'3'] ;
(5) T:= M + T

12. What is A + B, A − B, and A * B, given A:=[RED, BLUE] and B:= [BLUE]?

13. Which one of these is illegal?

    (1) **var**
                N : **set of integer**;

    (2) **var**
                N : **set of** −32767..32767;

14. Why is this incorrect?

    if A = B
       then A := A − B;
       else A := B − A;

15. What values can A take on in order always to execute the following **then** clause?

    if A in [1,2,5]
       then SAT:=[] ;

16. What is a predicate?

17. Write a **case** statement to handle the three actions needed in the decision tree for "X **in** [−1,0,1] ".

18. How many times is a **repeat** loop executed?

19. How many times is a **for** loop executed?

20. Is the following legal?

```
var
    ANIMALS: (ANTS, DOGS, CATS, SHEEP);
begin
    for ANIMALS:=DOGS to CATS do
```

ANSWERS

1. Who writes these questions?

2. No. The := "assigns" a value; the = "compares" values.

3. It obeys rules of grammar. In a right-hand expression, the expression is well-formed if it is in infix notation.

4. The **div** is for integers, and the / **is** for reals.

5. Yes, this is one of the anomalies of Pascal.

6. Oddly, yes.

7. A changes the type of B by converting B.

8. X must be an integer expression; X must evaluate to the subrange of [X].

9. 2 and 16, respectively.

10. (1) TRUE, (2) FALSE, (3) FALSE, (4) 1.

11. 1 and 5 because the base types do not match.

12. A + B gives [RED,BLUE], A–B gives [RED], and A * B gives [BLUE].

13. (1) because sets can be made up of finite scalars or subranges and not "infinite" base types.

14. There should be *no* semicolon after A := A–B.

15. A must be one of the values in the set of integers, e.g., 1, or 2, or 5.

16. A boolean expression found in an **if, while,** etc.

17. **case** X **of**
    ```
    -1 : ACTION(1);
     0 : ACTION(2);
     1 : ACTION(3);
    ```
    end

18. At least once.

19. Zero or more times.

20. Yes, thank heavens.

Chapter 5

Money, Money, Money! (Financial Applications)

OLD JOKE: *"Ya wanna know how to make a million dollars in the stock market?"*

"Yeah, how do you make a million in the stock market?"

"Start with 2 million!"

5.1 HOME MORTGAGE PAYMENTS

John and Suzanne had saved their money for five years so they could make a down payment on a new home.

"I saw a new house on Oak Street that looks like it will be finished in a few days," John said as he hurried through the kitchen door. The old house had been good to them, but both husband and wife were ready to move into a comfortable new house with a nursery room.

"Oh! Is it the green one I noticed yesterday when I took little Dory to her piano lessons?" Suzanne brought a tray of cookies from the oven as John shouted from the living room.

"It must be the same one. I stopped to ask the price, but nobody was around. I guess it was after five o'clock."

John called the realtor after supper and got the price. It was $100,000! The next day he talked to the loan officer at his credit union about financing. Money was tight and interest rates at a peak, but he could burrow up to 85% of the purchase price at 15% annual interest. If he paid the debt in 30 years, his monthly payments would be $1074.78. How did John's loan officer compute this payment?

A *monthly* interest rate of INTEREST fractional points produces a finance charge of VALUE dollars if computed on the balance remaining at the end of each monthly payment.

$$\text{VALUE} = (\text{INTEREST} + 1) \wedge \text{MONTHS}$$
MONTHS = Term of the loan in months.

In a crude sense, (VALUE − 1) is the amount of interest paid on AMOUNT dollars in MONTHS time. When combined with the formula for computing both principle and interest, the formula for monthly payment becomes:

$$\text{PAYMENT} = \text{INTEREST} * \text{VALUE} * \text{AMOUNT} / (\text{VALUE}-1)$$

where,

$$\text{INTEREST} = \text{ANNUAL INTEREST RATE} / 1200$$

Notice that 12 mo/yr times 100 fractional points/percentage point gives 1200. To convert from an annual rate to a monthly rate we divide by 1200.

We can now design a high-level abstraction for the MORTGAGE program. This design is given in pseudocode:

MORTGAGE PSEUDOCODE

1. Enter the parameters:

        PRICE   (* purchase price of new house *)
        PERCENT   (* percent to finance *)
        INTEREST   (* interest rate as a percent *)
        YEARS   (* term of loan *)

2. Convert to monthly values, given the annual values.

        MONTHS   := 12 * YEARS
        AMOUNT   := PERCENT * PRICE/100.0
        INTEREST := INTEREST / 1200.0

3. Compute the monthly payment from the formula.

        VALUE   := (INTEREST + 1) ∧ MONTHS
        PAYMENT := INTEREST * VALUE * AMOUNT / (VALUE-1)

4. Compute the finance charge:

        TOTALINTEREST := MONTHS * PAYMENT - AMOUNT

5. Output the values of:

        AMOUNT
        PAYMENT
        TOTAL $
        TOTAL INTEREST

6. Repeat the calculations for as long as the user wants to input values.

The pseudocode algorithm is nearly ready to be used as a guide to writing the Pascal program. First, however, we note a slight problem; Pascal is unable to compute an exponential term as designated with an upward arrow, ∧. The way around this problem is to *extend* Pascal using a **function** module that simulates exponentiation by repeatedly multiplying. Here is a function to compute the *power* of BASE ∧ EXPO.

```
function POWER (BASE : real ;
                EXPO : integer) : real;
```

This function definition statement tells the Pascal Compiler to translate a module called POWER. The *formal parameters* BASE and EXPO are defined as *input*, only, parameters. The first input is a real number, BASE. The second input is an integer, EXPO. They are passed by value.

The result, or *output*, from POWER is assigned to POWER itself. Thus, POWER can take on real values only. POWER is subsequently used in an expression like any other variable name.

POWER is a module that accepts BASE and EXPO as inputs and produces POWER as output. In addition, POWER contains *local* variables which *only* POWER can access.

```
var
    COUNTER :   integer;
    PRODUCT :   real;
```

Keep in mind that *internal* **procedure** and **function** modules can access global variables, local variables, and formal parameter variables. In this case, POWER uses local and formal parameter variables only. The module returns zero if EXPO is negative or zero (error flag), or the product as shown below.

```
begin
    if EXPO <= 0
        then POWER := 0.0
        else
            begin
                PRODUCT := 1.0;
                    for COUNTER := 1 to EXPO do
                        PRODUCT := PRODUCT * BASE;
                    POWER := PRODUCT;
            end;
```

We could have implemented this section of code in a slightly more relaxed fashion. For instance, knowing that the **for** loop is executed *zero* or more times:

```
begin
   PRODUCT := 1.0;
      for COUNTER := 1 to EXPO do
         PRODUCT := PRODUCT * BASE;
      POWER := PRODUCT;
end;
```

This version is superior in some sense because 1.0 is returned when EXPO is zero. It is inferior in the sense that it depends on the **for** loop to test EXPO.

The MORTGAGE program of Figure 5.1 shows how we enclose the POWER module inside the program. The listing also reveals two other functions — one for TAB, and another for CR (carriage return).

The TAB function skips over SPACES in a line. The CR function skips over LINES in the console screen. These two modules may cause machine dependency problems because of the way they *abuse* Pascal data types. Let's study them in detail.

```
function CR (LINES:integer) : char;
   var
      ROW : integer;
   begin
      for ROW := 2 to LINES do
            writeln;
         CR := chr (15);
   end;
```

This module causes LINES carriage returns to be performed by repeatedly executing the writeln intrinsic. (Note, ROW :=2 **to** LINES instead of ROW := 1 **to** LINES). This is done because of the way CR is used inside a writeln:

writeln (CR (5)); (* SKIP 5 LINES *)

Four of the lines are skipped by the CR function, while one additional line is skipped by the writeln (CR (5)) statement. The function *must* return a value; thus we assign the control character chr(15) to CR. This may cause undesirable machine-dependent (console) actions, so be careful with its use.

The TAB function is similar to the CR function except spaces are output:

```
for COLUMN := 1 to SPACES do
   writeln ('   ');
TAB := chr(15);
```

Again, the nuisance result chr(15) is returned by TAB.

Why were TAB and CR designed in this fashion? First, we wanted to design them as functions so they could be used in the parameter list of the intrinsic

```
(*$L CONSOLE:*)

program MORTGAGE ;

  var
    PRICE, INTEREST, AMOUNT, PAYMENT : real ;     (* WORKING VARIABLES *)
    YEARS  : 0 .. 99 ;                            (* TERM OF LOAN      *)
    MONTHS : 0 .. 1188 ;                          (* 12 * YEARS = TERM *)
    PERCENT: 0 .. 100 ;                           (* PERCENT FINANCED  *)
    TOTALINTEREST : real ;                        (* TOTAL INTEREST PAY*)
    VALUE  : real ;                               (* VALUE OF 1 DOLLAR *)
    ANSWER : char ;                               (* DONE ? 'Y' OR 'N' *)

  function CR ( LINES : integer ) : char ;        (* CARRIAGE RETURN   *)
    var
      ROW  : integer ;
    begin
      for ROW := 2 to LINES do
        WRITELN ;
      CR   := CHR ( 15 );                         (* MUST RETURN SOMETHING *)
    end ;      (*  CR  *)


  function TAB ( SPACES : integer ) : char ;      (* TAB OVER SPACES   *)
    var
      COLUMN : integer ;
    begin
      for COLUMN := 1 to SPACES do
        WRITE ( ' ' ) ;                           (* SKIP 'SPACES' TIMES *)
      TAB  := CHR ( 15 );                         (* MUST RETURN SOMETHING *)
    end ;          (*  TAB  *)

  function POWER ( BASE : real ;
                   EXPO : integer ) : real ;      (* RAISE BASE TO EXPO  *)
    var
      COUNTER  : integer ;
      PRODUCT  : real ;
    begin
      if EXPO <= 0                                (* EXPO MUST BE > 0   *)
        then  POWER := 0.0                        (* NO SEMI-COLON  !!! *)
        else
          begin
            PRODUCT := 1.0 ;
            for COUNTER := 1 to EXPO do           (* MULTIPLY EXPO TIMES *)
              PRODUCT := PRODUCT * BASE ;
            POWER := PRODUCT ;
      end ;     (* if-then-else  *)
    end ;        (* POWER  *)

  begin
    (*  GIVEN THE PURCHASE PRICE, PERCENT TO BE FINANCED, INTEREST RATE,
        AND THE NUMBER OF YEARS TO REPAY THE AMOUNT BORROWED, COMPUTE
        THE MONTHLY PAYMENT, TOTAL REPAID, AND INTEREST COST          *)

    repeat
```

Figure 5.1. Program MORTGAGE Listing

```
WRITELN ( CR( 5 ) );                          (*  CENTER IN SCREEN *)
WRITE ( TAB(20), '[1].PURCHASE PRICE          $ ' ) ; READLN ( PRICE ) ;
WRITE ( TAB(20), '[2].PERCENT to FINANCE      : ' ) ; READLN ( PERCENT ) ;
WRITE ( TAB(20), '[3].PERCENT INTEREST RATE : ' ) ; READLN ( INTEREST) ;
WRITE ( TAB(20), '[4].YEARS to REPAY LOAN    : ' ) ; READLN ( YEARS );

MONTHS      := 12 * YEARS ;                   (* CONVERT TO MONTHS *)
AMOUNT      := PERCENT * PRICE / 100.0 ;      (* AMOUNT OF LOAN    *)
INTEREST    := INTEREST / 1200.0 ;            (* CONVERT TO MONTHLY*)

VALUE       := POWER ( ( INTEREST + 1 ), MONTHS ) ;
PAYMENT     := INTEREST * VALUE * ( AMOUNT / ( VALUE - 1 ) ) ;
TOTALINTEREST := MONTHS * PAYMENT - AMOUNT ;

WRITELN ( CR(4) )  ;                          (* LEAVE 4 BLANK LINES*)
WRITELN ( TAB(6), 'BORROWED',
          TAB(6), 'PAYMENT ',
          TAB(6), 'TOTAL $ ',
          TAB(6), 'INTEREST' ) ;              (* OUTPUT HEADINGS   *)
WRITELN ;

WRITELN ( TAB(4), '$', AMOUNT:9:2,
          TAB(4), '$', PAYMENT:9:2,
          TAB(4), '$', MONTHS * PAYMENT:9:2,
          TAB(4), '$', TOTALINTEREST:9:2      ) ;
WRITELN ;                                     (* OUTPUT RESULTS    *)

WRITELN ( 'DONE (Y/N) ? ' ) ; READLN ( ANSWER ) ;
until  ANSWER = 'Y' ;
end.
```

Figure 5-1. (Continued)

procedures, e.g., write, writeln. This means they *must* return a value, but we would prefer that they not return a printable value.

At first glance, the returned values could just as well have been "empty". For example, what is the result of

TAB:= ";

or

CR := ";

where " is the "empty" character. Unfortunately, this causes a compiler error because " is not a character. The type of TAB and CR must match the type of ".

Second, we could have attempted to change the type of TAB and CR to make them match the type of "; since " is of type **string**, we could attempt the (incorrect) definition:

function TAB (SPACES: **integer**): **string** [1] ;

This would certainly allow TAB and CR to take the empty value, ''. What is wrong with this approach?

Unfortunately, Pascal defines the acceptable types of a function module as either (1) scalar, (2) subrange, or (3) pointer. Since **string** is not a scalar, subrange, or pointer, the definition above generates a compiler error.

The program of Figure 5.1 also displays another interesting and useful feature of the writeln intrinsic. Study the output statement:

```
writeln ( TAB(4), '$', AMOUNT : 9:2,
          TAB(4), '$', PAYMENT : 9:2,
          TAB(4), '$', MONTHS*PAYMENT : 9:2,
          TAB(4), '$', TOTALINTEREST : 9:2);
```

Each output is separated by 4 space TABs. The *precision* of each number is :9:2. This means the output is formatted to fit into 9 columns. The real values are stuffed into 6 digits to the left of the decimal point and 2 digits to the right of the decimal point. The decimal point takes one column.

We can control the format of any output using :L for integers and :L:D for real values. The expression

MONTHS*PAYMENT

is evaluated before being stuffed into 9 columns.

As an example, suppose we enter the following values into the running program of Figure 5.1.

[1]	PURCHASE PRICE	$12000
[2]	PERCENT TO FINANCE	:80
[3]	PERCENT INTEREST RATE	:10
[4]	YEARS TO REPAY LOAN	:3

The output is,

BORROWED	PAYMENT	TOTAL $	INTEREST
$ 9600.00	$ 309.77	$ 11151.5	$ 1551.55

Notice the format of TOTAL $. Since 11151.55 is too large to fit into :9:2, the trailing digit is truncated by writeln. If we had entered the following values, the truncation would have been more severe. For example,

```
$100 000
   85
   15
   30
```

produces

$ 85 000.0 $ 1074.78 $ 386920. $301920.

while inputs of even larger values would result in a crossover to *scientific notation*, e.g.,

$ 3.6694E6

This is too long to fit into 9 columns, so E6 extends beyond the allotted format.

This example illustrates the use of function modules and output formatting. In general, remember:

A. Every function must be defined as one of three types: (1) scalar, (2) subrange, or (3) pointer. (Scalar includes **real, integer,** and **char,** but *not* **string, array,** or **record**).

B. The chr(X) intrinsic converts X: **integer** into a character code. This intrinsic is undefined for nonprintable character codes.

C. The write and writeln intrinsics allow limited output formatting, with the precisions :L:D for reals and :L for integers.

D. The reals may be output in scientific format whenever they are too large to fit into their format specification. In scientific notation En means "times ten to the n power."

John's credit union loaned the money he and Suzanne needed to buy their new house. They paid $1,074.78 each month for their loan, $150 per month for taxes, $15 per month for insurance, and lived happily ever after.

5.2 CHARTING THE STOCK MARKET

Fred was an avid follower of the stock market before he became independently wealthy. In the "good old days" of breakouts, puts, and gets, Fred's entertainment consisted mainly of holding his breath while the market took his money for a ride.

Many "systems" have been proposed for anticipating the rise and fall of stock quotations. Obviously, if an investor is able to predict a stock price rhythm before prices actually change, then a "buy" or "sell" can become a source of profit. One such system has been suggested by Joseph Granville (see *Granville's New Key to Stock Market Profits,* Prentice-Hall, Inc., 1963).

Fred developed his own system of taking profit from common stock speculation. In this section, we study several Pascal programs that can be used as a basis for an automated stock analysis package. Like Fred, we must develop a *database* of stock prices first. The *technical strength* of some preselected stock is then judged by processing the database. The kinds of information resulting from this processing varies and is the subject of controversy among stock analysts. We will only suggest a few of the better known systems in passing.

Granville criticizes the Dow Jones Average (DJA), for example, because (1) it is based on price instead of volume, (2) as a result, the price signals are late —thus a poor "sell" decision, and (3) the DJA is not applicable to individual stocks. The idea behind the DJA theory is to buy low and sell high. The roller-coaster trend shown in Figure 5.2 shows how a series of buy-and-sell decisions *may* lead to profits if the decisions are made at just the right time. It is always easier to speculate with great hindsight, but when the future is not certain, speculation becomes an exciting venture.

Granville's system is based on volume instead of price. His decision to buy or sell is based on empirical "laws" of the market which read like inviolate laws of physics (which they are not).

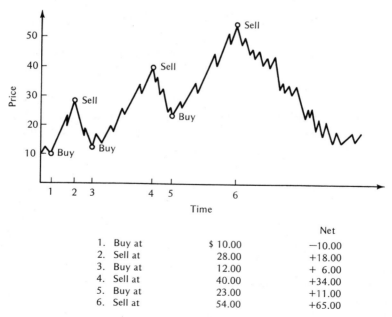

			Net
1. Buy at	$ 10.00		−10.00
2. Sell at	28.00		+18.00
3. Buy at	12.00		+ 6.00
4. Sell at	40.00		+34.00
5. Buy at	23.00		+11.00
6. Sell at	54.00		+65.00

Figure 5.2. Dow-Jones Theory of Profit

1. A stock in motion tends to stay in motion. This means that a stock usually continues to move up or down once it "breaks out" of a stable price range.

2. A stock at rest tends to stay at rest. The investor's job is to watch a stable stock and try to anticipate when it might break up or down.

3. What goes up must come down. An upside stock will eventually level off and fall back. The wise investor must be able to anticipate when a stock is about to fall.

4. It takes more energy to go up than to go down. Once the stock begins to fall, watch-out! It will fall faster than it climbed to a peak.

5. Investors flock to fill a vacuum. When a stock goes unusually high, there will be a rapid "fill in" by profit-taking investors.

We will *not* divulge any super-secret system here, but merely point the way for some experimentation. To do this, we need to learn some more about Pascal. In particular, we must know how to store a database of stock quotations on a disk device and eventually how to retrieve the individual stock quotations from the disk.

Figure 5.3 demonstrates by example the logical structure of a Pascal *file.* A file is a collection of data chunks called *records* (not the same as a **record** structure). Each access to a file is done by positioning a *window* over the appropriate file record before executing a **get** (input) or **put** (output).

Figure 5.3(b) shows how a *window pointer* is used to position a window over the desired record within the file. The window pointer is designated with an up arrow in Pascal

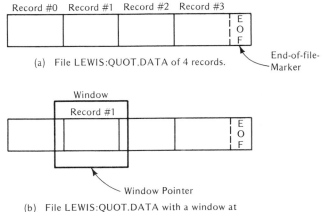

(a) File LEWIS:QUOT.DATA of 4 records.

(b) File LEWIS:QUOT.DATA with a window at Record #1. Either a get or put is allowed.

Figure 5.3. Logical Structure of a Disk File

WPOINT∧

and is moved left or right by built-in intrinsics. If the file is *sequential*, the get and put intrinsics implicitly move the window pointer after each access. If the file is *random*, the seek intrinsic moves the window pointer. We discuss sequential file structure first.

We will repeatedly use the following *model* to perform input to a sequential file in Pascal. (The file must be declared first.)

```
rewrite (FNAME, 'DATAFILE');
   repeat
      (* GET DATA FROM USER *)
         put (FNAME);
   until (* done *);
close (FNAME,OPTION);
```

This model does three critically important things: (1) *opens* the file and gives it a window name, FNAME, (2) *builds* the file by putting records in it, and (3) *closes* the file when done.

The rewrite procedure causes a diskfile to be *created* with its window *named* FNAME. For example, in the stock market program,

```
rewrite (QUOTFILE, 'LEWIS:STOCK.DATA');
```

opens a file called LEWIS:STOCK.DATA with window pointer QUOTFILE∧. Notice that .DATA is appended to the file to signify that this file is to hold data. The file is on a disk volume with prefix LEWIS:.

The rewrite intrinsic *may* automatically position the window pointer over the first (zero-th) record of the file. If the file is *typed*, the QUOTFILE∧ will point to record number zero.

We must declare all variables in Pascal; therefore, QUOTFILE must be defined in a data chunk.

```
var
      QUOTFILE : file of QUOTATIONS;
```

This defines QUOTFILE as an *external* data structure, and each file record of the external structure is defined by QUOTATIONS. What is a·QUOTATIONS?

Let's develop a program to enter stock quotations taken from the newspaper and store them on disk. This program will be designed in the image of the model above. The data is defined to accommodate a week's worth of quotations; each day of the week has an OPEN,HIGH,LOW, and CLOSING price as well as a date. Therefore, we need the following new data types.

type
   DOLLARS = real;
   WKDAYS = (MON,TUE,WED,THU,FRI);
   RANGE   = (OPEN,HIGH,LOW,CLOS);

In addition, each file record inside of file LEWIS: STOCK.DATA contains the information shown in Figure 5.4. Each record is made up of *components*, and each component is accessed by a *dot* name. To access the price of WED, see Figure 5.4.

   DAY[WED].PRICES[OPEN]
   DAY[WED].PRICES[HIGH]
   DAY[WED].PRICES[LOW]
   DAY[WED].PRICES[CLOS]

We use dot notation. This structure is defined in Pascal as follows:

type
   QUOTATIONS = **record**
             DAY: **array**[WKDAYS] **of**
               record
                 DATE: **string** [20];
                 PRICES: **array** [RANGE] **of** DOLLARS;
               end;
             AVGS : **array**[RANGE] **of** DOLLARS;
             end;

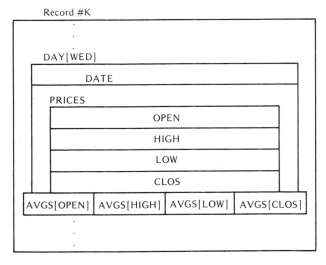

Figure 5.4. Record Structure of LEWIS: STOCK.DATA

Now we can define the window pointer as a variable that points to records with a structure like QUOTATIONS.

```
var
   QUOTFILE : file of QUOTATIONS;
```

Each access to a component of a record within QUOTFILE is made via the dot notation *and* the window pointer. To access the DATE component, we must specify which window to look into.

```
QUOTFILE∧.DAY [DAYS]. DATE
```

We have used an up arrow to indicate a window pointer which points to a *single* record in the file. The record has several components, so we must specify the DAY[DAYS] component. Within DAY, the choice is between DATE and PRICE. We must use an additional dot to specify which component within DAY[DAYS] to access.

The dot notation can be cumbersome to repeat every time an access to a window component is made. Therefore, Pascal allows the use of a WITH construct that eases this burden.

```
with ⟨prefix name⟩ do
   ⟨statement⟩ ;
```

The ⟨prefix name⟩ is a window pointer or component name, while ⟨statement⟩ can be a compound (**begin .. end**) statement which references components within ⟨prefix name⟩. In the example, we would specify QUOTFILE∧ as the prefix name.

```
with QUOTFILE∧ do
   begin
      (* any non-modifying reference to a window variable *)
   end;
```

The stocks can be input now using things we have learned about files and structures. Remember, the *first* access to a window is automatically performed by the rewrite intrinsic, because QUOTFILE is a *typed* file.

```
with QUOTFILE∧ do
   begin
      for DAYS := MON to FRI do
         begin
            readln (DAY[DAYS].DATE);
               for PRICE :=OPEN to CLOS do
```

```
                        begin
                            readln (DAY[DAYS].PRICES[PRICE]);
                        end;
                end;
            end; (* WITH *)
```

This piece of code enumerates the components of each record of QUOT-FILE structure. Now we need only **put** this structure into LEWIS:STOCK. DATA as follows:

put (QUOTFILE);   (* store it and advance the window *)

When the last file record has been output sequentially, we can close the file and lock it in place.

close (QUOTFILE,LOCK);

In general, the close intrinsic performs either a LOCK, PURGE, CRUNCH, or NORMAL option on the file.

These options are useful for a number of later activities:

A. LOCK. Causes the file to become permanent and remain on the disk even after the program terminates.

B. PURGE. The opposite of LOCK—causes the file to be removed from the disk when the program terminates.

C. CRUNCH. Causes the file to be LOCKed and keeps the window over the last record so that subsequent additions are appended to the end of the file.

D. NORMAL or Null. This results in the file being removed if it is a disk file opened with the rewrite intrinsic.

The complete (modified) input program is shown in Figure 5.5. Notice the use of line prompts DAYPROMPT and PRICEPRPT to help the user while inputting the stock quotations. This was necessary in program ENTRSTOCKS because scalars cannot be written out in Pascal.

Study the program of Figure 5.5 and run it with the following stock data. The averages of each column for each week are computed "on-the-fly" and stored in the disk file along with the row data.

Date	Open	High	Low	Close
MONDAY: Jan 5, 1959	40.00	40.00	39.00	39.00
TUESDAY: Jan 6, 1959	38.75	39.00	38.25	38.63
WEDNESDAY: Jan 7, 1959	38.38	39.38	38.38	38.75
THURSDAY: Jan 8, 1959	38.75	40.38	38.75	40.25
FRIDAY: Jan 9, 1959	40.88	41.00	40.13	40.38

```
program  ENTRSTOCK ;

   type
      DOLLARS     = real ;                 (* CALCULATE DOLLARS & CENTS  *)
      WKDAYS      = ( MON, TUE, WED,
                      THU, FRI     ) ;     (* WORK-DAYS, ABBREVIATED      *)
      RANGE       = ( OPEN, HIGH,
                      LOW, CLOS    ) ;     (* PRICE RANGE of STOCK QUOTS *)
      QUOTATIONS = record
                      DAY  : array[ WKDAYS ](* EACH DAY OF THE WEEK HAS ..*)
                             of record     (* .. A DATE AND 4 QUOTS      *)
                               DATE  : string[ 20 ] ;
                               PRICES: array[ RANGE ] of DOLLARS ;
                             end ;          (* DAILY QUOTES *)
                      AVGS : array[ RANGE ] of DOLLARS ;
                      end ;

   var
      QUOTFILE   : FILE of QUOTATIONS ;    (* DISK FILE IS SEQUENTIAL    *)
      DAYS       : WKDAYS  ;               (* COUNT THE DAYS OF THE WK   *)
      PRICE      : RANGE  ;                (* COLLECT THE QUOTES         *)
      DAYPROMPT  : array[ WKDAYS ] of string[ 10 ] ;  (* MENU PROMPTS   *)
      PRICEPRPT  : array[ RANGE ] of string[ 5 ] ;    (* MENU PROMPTS   *)
      ANSWER     : char ;                  (* USER RESPONSE (Y/N)        *)


   begin

      DAYPROMPT [ MON ] := 'MONDAY' ;  PRICEPRPT[ OPEN ] := 'OPEN' ;
      DAYPROMPT [ TUE ] := 'TUESDAY';  PRICEPRPT[ HIGH ] := 'HIGH' ;
      DAYPROMPT [ WED ] := 'WEDNESDAY';PRICEPRPT[ LOW ]  := 'LOW' ;
      DAYPROMPT [ THU ] := 'THURSDAY' ;PRICEPRPT[ CLOS ] := 'CLOSE' ;
      DAYPROMPT [ FRI ] := 'FRIDAY' ;

   REWRITE ( QUOTFILE, 'LEWIS:STOCK.DATA' ) ;

   repeat                                  (* ENTER AS MANY WEEKS AS YOU WANT *)

     for PRICE := OPEN to CLOS do
        QUOTFILE^.AVGS [ PRICE ] := 0 ;  (* INITIALIZE WEEKLY AVERAGES *)

     (*   ENTER EACH DATE, 4 QUOTATIONS, AND AVERAGE THEM FOR EACH WEEK *)
     WRITELN ( 'ENTER STOCK QUOTATIONS ONE WEEK AT A TIME :' ) ;
     with QUOTFILE^ do
        begin
          for DAYS := MON to FRI do
             begin
                WRITE ( DAYPROMPT[ DAYS ], '[1] DATE    : ' ) ;
                READLN( DAY[ DAYS ].DATE ) ;
                for PRICE := OPEN to CLOS do
                   begin
                      WRITE( PRICEPRPT[ PRICE ], ' $ ' ) ;
                      READLN( DAY[ DAYS ].PRICES[ PRICE ] ) ;
                      AVGS[ PRICE ] := AVGS[ PRICE ]
                                     + DAY[ DAYS ].PRICES[ PRICE ] / 5.0 ;
                   end ;                          (* for PRICE *)

             end ;                        (* for DAYS  *)

        end ;                             (* with QUOTFILE  *)

     PUT ( QUOTFILE ) ;                    (* WRITE THE WEEK TO DISK file *)

     WRITE ( 'DONE (Y/N) ? ' ) ;
     READLN ( ANSWER ) ;

   until ANSWER = 'Y' ;                    (* ARE YOU DONE ENTERING STOCKS ? *)

   CLOSE ( QUOTFILE , LOCK ) ;            (* LOCK FILE INTO PERMANENT PLACE *)
   end.
```

Figure 5.5. Listing Of Program ENTRSTOCKS

The quotations can be accumulated and used in a "system" of your choosing.

Now we can study the reverse of file output: input. Suppose we want to open the LEWIS:STOCK.DATA file, read it into the QUOTFILE window, and display the values on the CONSOLE.

Clearly, the data definitions will be the same for both input and output programs.

We employ the following *model* of a sequential file input routine.

```
reset (QUOTFILE, 'LEWIS:STOCK.DATA');
   repeat
     if not EOF ( QUOTFILE )
       then
          (* read each record *)
        get (QUOTFILE ) ;
     until EOF ( QUOTFILE ) ;
   close ( QUOTFILE, LOCK);
```

The piece of Pascal code does three of the most critical steps of file access: (1) *opens* the file and reads the first record into the window QUOTFILE; (2) repeatedly *accesses* the window variables as long as the end-of-file mark is not read, so we must test the EOF boolean to see if the file window is over the end-of-file mark as shown in Figure 5.6; and (3) *closes* the file when done.

We can use the model above to derive the following piece of Pascal code for accessing the records one after another. Notice how we have assumed that the first get intrinsic was performed automatically by the reset intrinsic. This is always true if the file type is not **interactive**, except when using rewrite.

```
reset ( QUOTFILE, 'LEWIS:STOCK.DATA');
;
   with QUOTFILE∧ do
     repeat
       if not EOF (QUOTFILE)
         then
             begin
               write (DAY[DAYS].DATE)
                 for PRICE:=OPEN to CLOS do
                   write (DAY[DAYS].PRICES[PRICE] ;
           end; (* IF-THEN *)
       until EOF (QUOTFILE);
```

We could have prefixed the inner part of this piece of code with a *nested* **with** statement. For example,

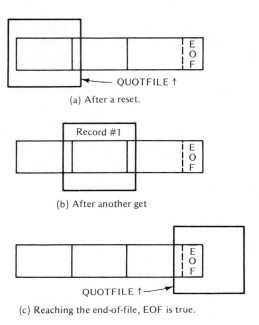

(a) After a reset.

(b) After another get

(c) Reaching the end-of-file, EOF is true.

Figure 5.6.   Moving the Window Over a Sequential File

```
with DAY[DAYS] do
    begin
        write ( DATE);
            for PRICE := OPEN to CLOS do
                write (PRICES [PRICE]);
    end;
```

We ended up with the full program shown in Figure 5.7. This program be-gins at record #0 and reads the entire file until reaching the EOF marker. What happens when this program attempts to read an empty file?

Finally, lets see if we can convert the program of Figure 5.7 into a *random file* program. A *random access file* is any file in which records may be accessed at random rather than in sequence. The LEWIS.STOCK.DATA file containing the stock QUOTATIONS is converted into a random file by using the seek in-trinsic of Pascal.

```
seek ( FNAME,RECORD#);
```

This procedure positions the FNAME∧ window over the RECORD#

```
program  DISPSTOCK ;

   type
      DOLLARS     = real ;                    (* CALCULATE DOLLARS & CENTS  *)
      WKDAYS      = ( MON, TUE, WED,
                      THU, FRI    )  ;        (* WORK-DAYS, ABBREVIATED     *)
      RANGE       = ( OPEN, HIGH,
                      LOW, CLOS   )  ;        (* PRICE RANGE of STOCK QUOTS *)
      QUOTATIONS  = record
                      DAY  : array[ WKDAYS ](* EACH DAY of THE WEEK HAS ..*)
                             of record        (* .. A DATE AND 4 QUOTS      *)
                                DATE  : string[ 20 ] ;
                                PRICES: array[ RANGE ] of DOLLARS ;
                                end ;         (* DAILY QUOTES *)
                      AVGS : array[ RANGE ] of DOLLARS ;
                      end ;

   var
      QUOTFILE   : file of QUOTATIONS ;  (* DISK FILE IS SEQUENTIAL    *)
      DAYS       : WKDAYS  ;             (* COUNT THE DAYS OF THE WK   *)
      PRICE      : RANGE  ;              (* COLLECT THE QUOTES         *)
      DAYPROMPT  : array[ WKDAYS ] of string[ 10 ] ;  (* MENU PROMPTS *)
      PRICEPRPT  : array[ RANGE ] of string[ 5 ] ;    (* MENU PROMPTS *)
      ANSWER     : integer ;            (* USER RESPONSE record #     *)

   begin

      DAYPROMPT [ MON ] := 'MONDAY' ;  PRICEPRPT[ OPEN ] := 'OPEN' ;
      DAYPROMPT [ TUE ] := 'TUESDAY';  PRICEPRPT[ HIGH ] := 'HIGH' ;
      DAYPROMPT [ WED ] := 'WEDNESDAY';PRICEPRPT[ LOW ]  := 'LOW' ;
      DAYPROMPT [ THU ] := 'THURSDAY'; PRICEPRPT[ CLOS ] := 'CLOSE' ;
      DAYPROMPT [ FRI ] := 'FRIDAY' ;

      RESET ( QUOTFILE, 'LEWIS:STOCK.DATA' ) ;

      WRITELN ( ' STOCK QUOTATIONS LISTED ONE WEEK AT A TIME :' ) ;

      with QUOTFILE^ do
        repeat
          if not EOF ( QUOTFILE )
            then
              begin
                for DAYS := MON to FRI do
                  begin
                    WRITE ( DAYPROMPT[ DAYS ], ' DATE   : ' ) ;
                    WRITE ( DAY[ DAYS ].DATE ) ;
                    WRITELN ;
                    for PRICE := OPEN TO CLOS do
                       begin
                         WRITE( ' ', PRICEPRPT[ PRICE ], ' $ ' ) ;
                         WRITE( DAY[ DAYS ].PRICES[ PRICE ]:7:2 ) ;
                         end ;             (* for PRICE *)
                    WRITELN ;
                    end ;                   (* for DAYS  *)
                WRITELN( '           AVERAGES FOR THIS WEEK') ;
                for PRICE := OPEN to CLOS do
                  WRITE ( ' ', PRICEPRPT[ PRICE ], ' $ ', AVGS[ PRICE ]:7:2 ) ;
                WRITELN ;
                WRITELN( 'STRIKE <RETURN> WHEN READY TO CONTINUE' ) ;
                READLN ( ANSWER ) ;

              end ;                         (* if-then   *)

          GET ( QUOTFILE ) ;               (* FETCH THE NEXT RECORD *)
          until EOF ( QUOTFILE ) ;

      CLOSE ( QUOTFILE , LOCK ) ;          (* LOCK FILE INTO PERMANENT PLACE '

end.
```

Figure 5.7. Listing Of Program DISPSTOCKS

record of the file. So, in Figure 5.6 (b) we could directly access the second record of a sequential file by executing the intrinsic procedure,

>   seek (QUOTFILE, 1);

and we could *fill* this window with the values stored in record #1 by immediately executing the input intrinsic:

>   get (QUOTFILE);

>   Any attempt to access a record that does not exist is ignored by seek, that
is,

>   seek (QUOTFILE, 1000);
>   seek (QUOTFILE, –10);

are ignored when the file contains fewer than 1000 records. In both cases, the
previous valid seek will remain in force. *Remember, a get or put must be executed between two seeks.* Failure to do so will cause nasty errors.

>   In Figure 5.8 we have modified the DISPSTOCK program to do random
accesses on the file of QUOTATIONS. This program incorporates a new use (and
type) for variable ANSWER and no longer relies upon EOF to cause it to halt.

>   The model used to design random access programs is shown below.

```
reset   ⎫
        ⎬  either one
rewrite ⎭

repeat
    (* for more than one access *)
    readln ( RECNUMBER);
    seek ( FNAME, RECNUMBER);
    get (FNAME);
    (* OTHER STUFF *)
until (* done *);
close ( FNAME, OPTION);
```

A very simple random access program would permit only one file record to be
accessed:

```
reset
readln    (RECNUMBER);
seek      (FNAME, RECNUMBER);
get       (FNAME);
close     (FNAME);
```

```
program  RANDSTOCK ;
   type
    DOLLARS     = real ;                   (* CALCULATE DOLLARS & CENTS  *)
    WKDAYS      = ( MON, TUE, WED,
                    THU, FRI    ) ;        (* WORK-DAYS, ABBREVIATED      *)
    RANGE       = ( OPEN, HIGH,
                    LOW, CLOS   ) ;        (* PRICE RANGE OF STOCK QUOTS *)
    QUOTATIONS = record

                    DAY   : array[ WKDAYS ](* EACH DAY of THE WEEK HAS ..*)
                            of record      (* .. A DATE AND 4 QUOTS      *)
                              DATE  : string[ 20 ] ;
                              PRICES: array[ RANGE ] of DOLLARS ;
                            end ;          (* DAILY QUOTES *)

                    AVGS : array[ RANGE ] of DOLLARS ;
                 end ;
   var
    QUOTFILE   : file of QUOTATIONS ;      (* DISK file IS SEQUENTIAL     *)
    DAYS       : WKDAYS  ;                 (* COUNT THE DAYS OF THE WK    *)
    PRICE      : RANGE  ;                  (* COLLECT THE QUOTES          *)
    DAYPROMPT  : array[ WKDAYS ] of string[ 10 ] ;  (* MENU PROMPTS      *)
    PRICEPRPT  : array[ RANGE ] of string[ 5 ] ;    (* MENU PROMPTS      *)
    ANSWER     : char ;                    (* USER RESPONSE (Y/N)         *)

   begin

    DAYPROMPT [ MON ] := 'MONDAY' ;  PRICEPRPT[ OPEN ] := 'OPEN' ;
    DAYPROMPT [ TUE ] := 'TUESDAY';  PRICEPRPT[ HIGH ] := 'HIGH' ;
    DAYPROMPT [ WED ] := 'WEDNESDAY';PRICEPRPT[ LOW ]  := 'LOW' ;
    DAYPROMPT [ THU ] := 'THURSDAY' ;PRICEPRPT[ CLOS ] := 'CLOSE' ;
    DAYPROMPT [ FRI ] := 'FRIDAY' ;
    RESET ( QUOTFILE, 'LEWIS:STOCK.DATA' ) ;

    WRITELN ( ' STOCK QUOTATIONS RANDOMLY ACCESSED BY NUMBER' ) ;

    with QUOTFILE^ do
      repeat
        WRITE ( 'ENTER RECORD NUMBER : ' ) ;
        READLN( ANSWER ) ;
        if ANSWER >= 0
          then
           begin
            SEEK ( QUOTFILE, ANSWER ) ;          (* INDEX INTO file  *)
            GET ( QUOTFILE ) ;                   (* FILL WINDOW      *)
            for DAYS := MON to FRI do
              with DAY[ DAYS ] do
                begin
                 WRITE ( DAYPROMPT[ DAYS ], ' DATE    : ' ) ;
                 WRITE ( DATE ) ;
                 WRITELN ;
                 for PRICE := OPEN to CLOS do
                   begin
                    WRITE( '  ', PRICEPRPT[ PRICE ], ' $ ' ) ;
                    WRITE( PRICES[ PRICE ]:7:2 ) ;
                   end ;                         (* for PRICE *)
                 WRITELN ;
                end ;                            (* for DAYS  *)
            WRITELN( '          AVERAGES FOR THIS WEEK') ;
            for PRICE := OPEN to CLOS do
              WRITE ( '  ', PRICEPRPT[ PRICE ], ' $ ', AVGS[ PRICE ]:7:2 ) ;
            WRITELN ;
            WRITELN( 'STRIKE <RETURN> WHEN READY TO CONTINUE' ) ;
            READLN ( ANSWER ) ;

           end ;                                 (* if-then   *)

        GET ( QUOTFILE ) ;                       (* FETCH THE NEXT RECORD *)
      until EOF ( QUOTFILE ) ;

    CLOSE ( QUOTFILE , LOCK ) ;                  (* LOCK FILE INTO PERMANENT PLACE *)

   end.
```

Figure 5.8. Listing Of Program RANDSTOCKS

A final note — the get and put intrinsics should always be used to access files. The readln and writeln procedures *may* be used only in files of types **text** or **interactive**. We discuss these topics in a later chapter.

We can also copy the window variable components into an ordinary variable by assignment. This may be necessary in applications where several records are needed simultaneously in main memory. To make a second copy of a window:

```
seek  ( QUOTFILE, ANSWER);
get    ( QUOTFILE);
TEMP := QUOTFILE∧;
```

where

```
var
   TEMP : QUOTATIONS;
```

is the same type as every file record. Notice that the window pointer is used with an up arrow in the assignment. Here is a piece of code which reads ten records from QUOTFILE and stores them in a memory array.

```
var
   TEMP    :  array[1..10] of QUOTATIONS;
   I       :  0..9;
begin
   reset (QUOTFILE, 'LEWIS:STOCK.DATA');
      for I:=0 to 9 do
         begin
            seek (QUOTFILE,I);
            get (QUOTFILE);
            TEMP [I] := QUOTFILE∧;
         end;
end.
```

The file structures of Pascal are built around the concept of sequential and random access. All files must first be opened with either a reset or rewrite intrinsic. All files must be accessed through a window pointer, and all pointer values are changed using implied updates (sequential) or the seek intrinsic.

The venturesome stock speculator can now begin exploring the many systems available to increase his or her wealth. These systems must process a database of quotations as illustrated by these fundamental file access programs. We turn now to more ways to make money with Pascal programs.

5.3 REAL ESTATE CASH FLOW ANALYSIS

Deb always wanted to be financially independent, even from the time she was a 3-year old in Los Angeles. She worked on this goal for years; she studied finances in high school, majored in business in college, and opened her own clothing store before she was 21 years old. Then, Deb discovered real estate and the concept of *pyramiding* to wealth.

Albert Lowry taught Deb how to become financially independent through his book, *How You Can Become Financially Independent by Investing In Real Estate* (Simon and Schuster, New York). Deb practiced what she learned and realized her goal in five short years of ambitious speculation. The first thing Deb bought with her profits from investing in apartments, rental houses, and land was a computer to help her analyze investment cash flow. This section explores the cash flow analysis program used by Deb to decide when to buy a new apartment or rental house.

Also in this section, we learn some new Pascal programming techniques. In particular, we learn how to *overlay* modules of a very large program. The *segment* structure of Pascal is used to *fold* large programs into small overlays; each overlay occupies the same main memory space, but at different times. This allows the Pascal System to run a large program in a small memory. Figure 5.9 illustrates this concept.

For example, the Pascal program we develop here consists of over 7100 characters of Pascal text. When it is compiled into P-code, it produces over 2700 bytes of P-code, uses 570 words of symbol table, and maintains 66 words of data values. If the main memory is too small to hold this size of program (in addition to the P-code simulator), then the program must be segmented so the P-code simulator can dynamically overlay parts of it during execution. The largest segment is 1150 bytes long; the smallest is 190 bytes long.

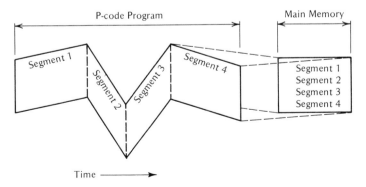

Figure 5.9. Pascal Segments are Folded

When investing in real estate it is best to consider both the soundness of the investment and its effects on the investor's income taxes. A loss due to expenses, loan interest, etc., may actually be an advantage if it saves the investor money normally paid to taxes. Therefore, we will consider the investment's potential as a (1) tax shelter, (2) inflation fighter, and (3) profit center.

The net operating expenses may result in a profit immediately.

$$NET := GROSS - EXPENSES;$$

The gross operating income of investment property is based on the percent of occupancy and the rental income:

$$GROSS := 12 * RENT * OCCUPANCY / 100.00;$$

It also costs the owner money to keep an apartment maintained, rented, and away from the tax man. These are called expenses:

$$EXPENSES := 12* (ADVERTISING$$
$$+ REPAIRS$$
$$+ UTILITIES$$
$$+ MANAGER) + PROPTAXES;$$

The owner must place ads in the newspaper, pay all repair bills, often pay for garbage collection, electric utilities, etc., and pay a manager to help run the apartment. The county will also demand a yearly property tax based on the assessed valuation of the property.

The NET income from investment property is offset by the costs associated with borrowing money to buy the property. This can often become a tax advantage if the interest on the loan exceeds the net operating expense. We can accumulate the yearly interest and principle paid by the owner as follows.

```
INTEREST := 0 ; PRINCIPLE :=0;
   for MONTH := 1 to 12 do
      begin
         INT := IRATE * BALANCE / 1200.0;
         BALANCE := BALANCE + INT - PAYMENT;
         INTEREST := INTEREST + INT;
         PRINCIPLE := PRINCIPLE + PAYMENT - INT;
      end;
```

The interest rate IRATE and running BALANCE are used to compute the yearly totals of INTEREST as well as PRINCIPLE paid.

We can use the same formula derived in section 5.1 to compute the monthly payments. This is made into a module which returns the PAYMENT as VALUE.

```
IRATE  := IRATE / 1200.0 ; (* monthly interest *)
TIME   := 12 * TIME ;        (* convert to months *)
POWER := 1.0;
   for MONTHS := 1 to TIME do
      POWER:= POWER * ( IRATE + 1.0 ) ;
VALUE := IRATE * POWER * AMOUNT / ( POWER - 1.0 ) ;
```

The interest rate is converted into a monthly rate by dividing by 1200. The exponential form

$$(IRATE + 1.0) \wedge TIME$$

is computed by repeated multiplication since Pascal does not have an exponentiation operator. Actually, we could have used the intrinsics LOG or PWROFTEN:

```
POWER := EXP ( TIME * LN ( IRATE + 1) ) ;
```

The LN and EXP functions are included in the translation by specifying

uses TRANSCEND ;

This must be included in the program (as the second statement right after the **program** statement). Returning to the cash flow analysis problem, we calculate the taxable income

$$TAXABLE := NET - INTEREST ;$$

and the difference between annual depreciation of the property and the taxable income after finance charges gives the depreciation overflow.

$$OVERFLOW := DEPRECIATION - TAXABLE ;$$

We must consult the IRS rulings on the depreciation rate and length of term in order to compute DEPRECIATION above. For simplicity, let's assume a *straight-line* method computed over TERM years. If the salvage value of the property is given as SALVAGE after TERM years, then

$$DEPRECIATION := (COST - SALVAGE) / TERM ;$$

This is called the straight-line method of depreciation because it assumes a constant rate of depreciation each year of the term.

The OVERFLOW from taxable income and depreciation must be included in the owner's tax return. The amount of OVERFLOW paid to the IRS depends on the owner's tax bracket.

$$TAXADVANTAGE := OVERFLOW * BRACKET / 100.0 ;$$

Obviously, a tax savings results when OVERFLOW is a negative value. This occurs whenever depreciation is greater than the taxable income left after expenses and loan interest.

We can now compute the cash flow and return on investment,

$$CASHFLOW := TAXABLE - PRINCIPLE ;$$

$$RETURNED := APPRECIATION + TAXADVANTAGE$$
$$+ CASHFLOW$$
$$+ PRINCIPLE ;$$

where, $$APPRECIATION := INFLATION * COST / 100.0 ;$$

and INFLATION is the rate of inflation for the year.

These calculations are carried out in part by the input routines and in part by the output routine. Since the resulting program is lengthy (not necessarily complicated), the Pascal modules must be small and *segmented*. A **segment** is a function or procedure that is overlaid into main memory *only when it is being used*. When not in use a segment remains on disk, thus not taking up main memory space.

Figure 5.10 contains a complete listing of the segmented Pascal program for calculating cashflow and return on investment. The INPUT module was divided into INPUTA and INPUTB because of its size. These two modules handle the data-entry chores.

The TABLE module is overlaid during outputting of the cashflow table. It is held in memory with the main program body, global data, and function VALUE. Each overlay cuases a slight pause in the program's execution while the disk is being read.

Deb put CASHFLOW to work one spring day in 1980 and made $ 8029.82 that first year. Here is what she did. A triplex cost Deb $100,000 to buy with a 90% loan. So with a $10,000 investment in 1980, Deb made $8029.82 and ended up owning a triplex also.

COST	$100,000
FINANCED	: 90 %
TIME	: 25 years
IRATE	: 12 % per year
RENT	$ 740 per month
OCCUPANCY	: 80 % expected
ADS	$ 20 per month (expected)
UTILITIES	$ 20 per month (expected)
REPAIRS	$ 30 per month (expected)
MANAGER	$ 0 Deb does this, herself
PROP. TAX	$ 800 per year
SALVAGE	$ 10,000

```
(*$L CONSOLE:*)
program  CASHFLO ;

   type
      DOLLARS      = real ;
      PERCENT      = real ;
      YEARS        = 1 .. 40 ;

   var                                   (* MORTGAGE INFORMATION            *)
      COST, AMOUNT  : DOLLARS ;          (* PURCHASE, LOAN AMOUNT           *)
      FINANCED      : PERCENT ;          (* PERCENT FINANCED                *)
      TIME          : YEARS   ;          (* TERM OF LOAN                    *)
      IRATE         : PERCENT ;          (* INTEREST RATE OF LOAN           *)
                                         (* OPERATING INCOME INFORMATION    *)
      RENT          : DOLLARS ;          (* MONTHLY RENTAL INCOME           *)
      OCCUPANCY     : PERCENT ;          (* RATE OF OCCUPANCY               *)
                                         (* OPERATING EXPENSE INFORMATION   *)
      ADVERTISING,                       (* MONTHLY NEWSPAPER ADS           *)
      REPAIRS,                           (* MONTHLY EXPECTED BILLS          *)
      UTILITIES,                         (* MONTHLY ESTIMATED BILLS         *)
      MANAGER       : DOLLARS ;          (* MONTHLY MANAGER FEE             *)
      PROPTAXES     : DOLLARS ;          (* YEARLY PROPERTY TAX BILL        *)
                                         (* DEPRECIATION INFORMATION        *)
      SALVAGE       : DOLLARS ;          (* SALVAGE VALUE OF BUILDING       *)
      TERM          : YEARS   ;          (* LIFE OF BUILDING                *)
      YEAR          : 1980 .. 2100 ;     (* STARTING YEAR ...               *)
                                         (* APPRECIATION INFORMATION        *)
      INFLATION     : PERCENT ;          (* YEARLY RATE OF INFLATION        *)
                                         (* CALCULATIONS                    *)
      DEPRECIATION,
      APPRECIATION  : DOLLARS ;
      GROSS, NET    : DOLLARS ;          (* INCOME                          *)
      EXPENSES      : DOLLARS ;          (* TOTAL EXPENSES                  *)
      BALANCE,
      PRINCIPLE,
      INTEREST, INT,
      PAYMENT       : DOLLARS ;          (* LOAN VALUES                     *)
      BRACKET       : PERCENT ;          (* INCOME TAX BRACKET              *)
      TAXABLE,                           (* TAXABLE INCOME                  *)
      OVERFLOW,                          (* TAXABLE - DEPRECIATION          *)
      TAXADVANTAGE,                      (* BRACKET * OVERFLOW / 100        *)
      CASHFLOW,                          (* TAXABLE - PRINCIPLE             *)
      RETURNED      : DOLLARS ;          (* TOTAL CASH FLOW RETURN          *)
                                         (* OTHER                           *)
      MONTH         : 1 .. 12 ;
      I             : 1 .. 24 ;          (* LOOP COUNTER TO CLEAR CRT       *)
      ANSWER        : char    ;          (* USERS RESPONSE (Y/N) ?          *)

   segment procedure INPUTA ;
      begin
         WRITELN( 'C A S H F L O W    A N A L Y S I S' ) ;
         WRITELN ;
         WRITELN( '           MORTGAGE INFORMATION' ) ;
         WRITELN ;

         WRITE  ( '[ 1]. PURCHASE PRICE         $ ' ) ; READLN( COST ) ;
         WRITE  ( '[ 2]. PERCENT FINANCED       % ' ) ; READLN( FINANCED ) ;

         AMOUNT  := FINANCED * COST / 100.0 ;
         BALANCE := AMOUNT ;
         WRITE  ( '[ 3]. YEARS TO REPAY LOAN    : ' ) ; READLN( TIME ) ;
         WRITE  ( '[ 4]. INTEREST RATE ON LOAN % ' ) ; READLN( IRATE ) ;
         WRITELN( '          OPERATING INCOME INFORMATION' ) ;
         WRITE  ( '[ 5]. MONTHLY RENTAL INCOME $ ' ) ; READLN( RENT ) ;
         WRITE  ( '[ 6]. PERCENT OCCUPANCY      : ' ) ; READLN( OCCUPANCY ) ;

         GROSS  := 12 * RENT * OCCUPANCY / 100.0 ;

      end ;                              (* INPUTA                          *)
```

Figure 5.10. Program CASHFLO Listing

```
segment procedure INPUTB ;
  begin
    WRITELN( '               OPERATING EXPENSE INFORMATION' ) ;
    WRITE   ( '[ 7]. MONTHLY ADVERTISEMENT   $ ' ) ; READLN( ADVERTISING ) ;
    WRITE   ( '[ 8]. MONTHLY REPAIR BILLS    $ ' ) ; READLN( REPAIRS ) ;
    WRITE   ( '[ 9]. MONTHLY UTILITY BILLS   $ ' ) ; READLN( UTILITIES ) ;
    WRITE   ( '[10]. MONTHLY MANAGER FEE     $ ' ) ; READLN( MANAGER ) ;
    WRITE   ( '[11]. YEARLY PROPERTY TAXES   $ ' ) ; READLN( PROPTAXES ) ;

    EXPENSES:= 12 * ( ADVERTISING
                    + REPAIRS
                    + UTILITIES
                    + MANAGER ) + PROPTAXES ;

    WRITELN( '               DEPRECIATION INFORMATION' ) ;
    WRITE   ( '[12]. SALVAGE VALUE OF BLDG  $ ' ) ; READLN( SALVAGE ) ;
    WRITE   ( '[13]. LIFE OF BUILDING       $ ' ) ; READLN( TERM ) ;
    WRITE   ( '[14]. STARTING YEAR (19??)   : ' ) ; READLN( YEAR ) ;

    DEPRECIATION:= ( COST - SALVAGE ) / TERM ;

    WRITELN( '               APPRECIATION INFORMATION' ) ;
    WRITE   ( '[15]. YEARLY INFLATION RATE  % ' ) ; READLN( INFLATION ) ;

    APPRECIATION:= INFLATION * COST / 100.0 ;

  end ;                              (* INPUTB                    *)

segment procedure TABLE ;
  begin
    WRITELN( '               YEAR : ', YEAR:5 ) ;
    WRITELN;
    WRITELN( '(+) GROSS SCHEDULED INCOME       $ ', GROSS:12:2 ) ;
    WRITELN( '(-) OPERATING EXPENSES           $ ', EXPENSES:12:2 ) ;

    NET     := GROSS - EXPENSES ;

    WRITELN( '(=) NET OPERATING INCOME         $ ', NET:12:2 ) ;
    WRITELN ;
    WRITELN( '(-) INTEREST ON LOAN             $ ', INTEREST:12:2 ) ;

    TAXABLE:= NET - INTEREST ;

    WRITELN( '(=) TAXABLE INCOME               $ ', TAXABLE:12:2 ) ;
    WRITELN ;
    WRITELN( '(-) DEPRECIATION, ST. LINE       $ ', DEPRECIATION:12:2 ) ;

    OVERFLOW:= TAXABLE - DEPRECIATION ;

    WRITELN( '(=) OVERFLOW                     $ ', OVERFLOW:12:2 ) ;
    WRITELN( '    INCOME TAX BRACKET           % ', BRACKET:12 ) ;

    TAXADVANTAGE:=BRACKET * OVERFLOW / 100.0 ;

    WRITELN( '(+) PRINCIPLE PAID               $ ', PRINCIPLE:12:2 ) ;

    CASHFLOW:=TAXABLE - PRINCIPLE ;

    WRITELN( '(+) CASH FLOW AMOUNT             $ ', CASHFLOW:12:2 ) ;

    APPRECIATION:=INFLATION * COST / 100.0 ;

    WRITELN( '(+) APPRECIATION IN VALUE        $ ', APPRECIATION:12:2 ) ;

    RETURNED:=APPRECIATION
            + TAXADVANTAGE
            + CASHFLOW
            + PRINCIPLE ;

    WRITELN( '(=) RETURN ON INVESTMENT         $ ', RETURNED:12:2 ) ;
    WRITELN ;
    WRITE   ( 'WANT ANOTHER YEAR (Y/N)          ? ' ) ;
    READLN ( ANSWER ) ;

  end ;                              (* TABLE                     *)
```

Figure 5-10. (Continued)

```
function VALUE ( IRATE : PERCENT ;
                 AMT   : DOLLARS ;
                 TIME  : integer ): DOLLARS ;
  var
    POWER  : real ;
    MONTHS : integer ;

  begin
    IRATE  := IRATE / 1200.0 ;         (* CONVERT TO MONTHLY RATE    *)
    TIME   := 12 * TIME ;              (* CONVERT TO MONTHS          *)

    POWER  := 1.0 ;                    (* SAME AS IF ..              *)
    for MONTHS := 1 to TIME do         (* ..PWROFTEN( TIME * LOG (   *)
     POWER := POWER * ( IRATE + 1.0 );(*    IRATE+1 )) ;             *)

    VALUE  := IRATE * POWER * AMT / ( POWER - 1.0 ) ;

  end ;                                (* VALUE                      *)


begin

  for I := 1 to 24 do WRITELN ;        (* CLEAR THE CRT SCREEN       *)

  INPUTA ; INPUTB ;                    (* OVERLAY SEGMENTS           *)

  PAYMENT:= VALUE ( IRATE, AMOUNT, TIME ) ;

  repeat

    INTEREST := 0 ;  PRINCIPLE := 0 ; (* START ANEW EACH YEAR       *)
    for MONTH := 1 to 12 do
      begin
        INT       := IRATE * BALANCE / 1200.0 ;
        BALANCE   := BALANCE + INT - PAYMENT ;
        INTEREST  := INTEREST + INT ;
        PRINCIPLE:=PRINCIPLE + PAYMENT - INT ;
      end ;                            (* for MONTH                  *)
    TABLE ;                            (* ROLL IN OUTPUT PROC        *)

    YEAR   := YEAR + 1 ;

  until ANSWER = 'N' ;
end.
```

Figure 5-10. (Continued)

TERM   : 20 years
START   : 1980
INFLATION   : 10 % per year (expected)
BRACKET   : 34 %

The CASHFLOW program showed Deb how a loss in taxable income could be turned into a gain from taxes and value appreciation. The results:

Gross operating income	$ 7,104
Expenses	$ 1,640
Net income	$ 5,464
Interest paid on loan	$ 10,767
Taxable income	$ −5,303

The negative taxable income is where Deb shows a *loss*, but wait!

Depreciation	$ 4,500
Overflow	$ 9,803
Tax advantage	$ 3,333

The tax advantage almost makes up for the taxable income loss. When the principle and the appreciation in value are included, we see the payoff.

Principle	$ 607
Cash flow	$ -5,910
Appreciation	$ 10,000
Return on investment	$ 8,029

The actual return on investment is nearly equal to the down payment. This is called *leverage* in the real estate business and is the secret to pyramiding. By 1990, Deb would be enjoying an annual return of $8952 without further investments (but still needing a cash flow influx of $450 each month to make loan payments, etc.).

Deb repeated this strategy every six months or so until she owned property worth a million dollars. By the ripe old age of 29, Deb had retired in Hawaii.

We are now prepared to study more sophisticated features of Pascal, but first, we can summarize the important features demonstrated in this chapter.

A. Pascal does not have an exponentiation operator. As a result, the intrinsics LN and EXP must be used.

B. **For** loops are executed *zero* or more times, **repeat** loops are executed *one* or more times.

C. Functions *must* return a single value, but procedures return no values (they may have side effects, however).

D. Functions can be typed as scalar, subrange, or pointer, but *never* as **string, set, record**, or any structured type.

E. Output formats :L and :L:D define the precision of integers and reals (inside the writeln intrinsic).

F. File access is either sequential or random.

G. A file window is positioned over only one file record at a time. Therefore, only one file record can be accessed at a time, i.e., the window record.

H. Files are accessed through a window using get and put; for random files we also must use seek.

I. Files are created and opened with the rewrite intrinsic, opened with the reset intrinsic, and closed with the close intrinsic.

J. Pascal modules are overlaid into a small memory by segmenting the internal functions and procedures. A segment is a function or procedure prefixed with the word **segment**.

K. To make a million dollars you need two million dollars or a clever computer!

TWENTY QUESTIONS

1. How is 10.5235 output as 10.52?

2. Is this legal? **function** X : **set of** 1..10 ;

3. What is a local variable?

4. How many times is this loop executed?
   for I := 10 **to** 9 **do** ;

5. What is chr(65) ?

6. Why is it incorrect to assign the empty token to a variable typed as **char**, e.g., TAB := ' ' ; ?

7. What is 3.6E–2?

8. What is QUOTFILE∧?

9. Can sequential files be accessed at random?

10. What happens if a file is opened a *second* time using rewrite instead of reset?

11. Can read and write be used on Pascal files?

12. Could we have defined RANGE = (OPEN, HIGH, LOW, CLOSE) ; in the stock analysis program?

13. How can we ease the burden of dot notation?

14. Write a file close statement with a NORMAL option.

15. What happens when a seek is out of range (the index is beyond the file)?

16. What does **segment** do?

17. What is PWROFTEN (3)?

18. What does **uses** TRANSCEND ; do?

19. What is the disadvantage of **segment** modules?

20. How is a new data file created?

ANSWERS

1. Use :6:2 format in the write statement.

2. No, a function can be typed as scalar but not as a set.

3. A variable that can be accessed by its function or procedure only.

4. Zero times.

5. In ASCII code, it is the letter 'A'.

6. The empty token is *not* an character, so the assignment mixes types. The variable must be typed **string**[1].

7. Scientific notation for 0.036.

8. The window pointer of file QUOTFILE.

9. Yes, use the seek intrinsic.

10. You risk losing the entire file.

11. Yes, only on **interactive** or **text** files.

12. No, because close is the name of the close intrinsic in Pascal.

13. Use the **with** statement to prefix the structure name.

14. You can use close (FNAME) ; or close(FNAME, NORMAL) ; .

15. It is ignored.

16. Causes overlay code to be compiled.

17. 1000.

18. Copies the transcendental functions from SYSTEM.LIBRARY.

19. The program runs slower because of disk activity.

20. Use the rewrite intrinsic and the name of a window variable.

Chapter 6

For the Drow Pundit (Text Processing)

They climbed over a crumbling plastic wall and walked down a devastated hall. A pile of rubble forced them to one side of the narrow passageway.

"What do you make of it?" Cyben vibrated in a cautious tone. The two archeologists simultaneously spotted the upturned bookshelf at their feet.

"I believe these ancient ones employed a form of recording called 'script' as a means of recalling detail," Elec said as he bent forward to bring one of the torn volumes into view. The crumbling book reflected the sun's dull red glow as Elec opened it with a tractor beam.

'It must be some kind of code," was Cyben's guess. They studied the lines of text on page 40. Cyben drew the volume closer and touched its cover.

"Wait a centron," they both vibrated. Elec brushed away layers of dust and increased the magnification on camera B.

"I can almost see a design that looks a lot like ancient lettering now".

"Yes, I see it also."

"What does it mean?"

"P. A. S. C. A. L.   U. S. E. R. S.   M. A. N. U. A. L.   A. N. D.   R. E.- P. O. R. T."

6.1 STICKS AND STONES

Of course, *drow* is *word* spelled backwards. Curiously, many words also spell their drow. For example, DAD is spelled the same as its drow, DAD. In such rare occurrences, we call the word and its drow a *palindrome*. Unfortunately for the palindrome pundit, the drow of palindrome makes no sense at all: semordnilap.* But some palindromic sentences do indeed make sense.

---

*Wallechinshy Wallace and Wallace, *The People's Almanac: The Book Of Lists.* (New York: William Morrow and Co., 1977), pp. 138–139.

The first palindromic sentence seems to have been "lewd did I live, evil I did dwel." The first and last words are palindromes, and the second and second-to-last are palindromes, etc. Apparently the palindrome pundit thinks nothing at all of misspelling a drow in order to lay claim to the longest, most intricate, or outright humorous palindrome.

While it cannot be verified, someone claimed that the first palindromic sentence spoken was "Madam I'm Adam." Of course the answer was also a palindrome — "Eve."

The history of palindromes seems to follow civilization like a bad joke. Napoleon was afflicted also, when he first saw his new home: "Able was I ere I saw Elba". Perhaps the real estate agent forgot to mention a lack of indoor plumbing. But Napoleon was no worse off than the politician who proclaimed, "A man, a plan, a canal; Panama."

Palindromes are full of good advice. For example, programmers should always remember, "never odd or even," and the owner of a domesticated panther will agree that, "step on no pets" is a good policy. We can envision Anna and Otto arguing over a slight difference of opinion when they uttered this palindrome full of drows, "Anna: 'did Otto peep?', Otto: 'did Anna?'"

Unfortunately, the list of palindromic phrases goes on and on. The pundit who really wants to find palindromes is faced with countless hours of experimentation and drow beating. The modern pundit, however, knows enough to use a computer in search of drows; so we begin with the task of finding single-word palindromes in a sentence.

Consider the following top-level pseudocode design for **program** PALINDROME.

1. Input a sentence containing words separated by spaces.
2. Examine each character one at a time:
   2.1 If the m-th character is a letter, then it must be part of a word.
   2.2 Copy the letters of an individual word into a separate string called "word".
   2.3 The first non-letter encountered after the first letter of each word is used to designate an end-of-word. Also, we must stop when we reach the end of the sentence.
   2.4 Reverse the word and store it in a string called "drow".
       2.4.1   If the word equals drow, then it must be a palindrome.
       2.4.2   Print the palindrome.
3. Continue step 2 until the sentence has been checked, character by character.

The first step in composing **program** PALINDROME is to develop the data chunk. We actually developed several versions of the data chunk before we derived the final version shown below.

```
const
    N = 80; (* max. length of sentence *)

type
    LETTERS = 'A' .. 'Z' ;
    LINE = string [ N ] ;
```

The two types above will be used to define the alphabet and a sentence string S, a word string WORD, and a drow string DROW.

```
var
    S, WORD, DROW    :    LINE ;
    ALPHABET         :    set of LETTERS ;
    P, Q, M          :    0 .. N ;
```

The ALPHABET contains every possible combination of the letters from A to Z. But we will only need one combination — the set containing all A to Z.

Later on we will discover a need for three working indexes, P, Q, and M. P is used to count the number of characters in each word and drow. The number Q is used to count from one up to P when reversing WORD to make DROW. The counter M is used to keep track of the M-th character in sentence, S.

Here is a snapshot of the PALINDROME program in action:

S = THE DEED WAS DID.

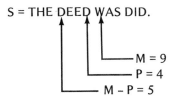

The essence of the program is in locating a word, counting its length, and then reversing the word by copying it from M=9 backwards to M–P=5. First we must initialize the strings and prompt the user for input.

ALPHABET := ['A' .. 'Z'] ;

This statement assigns the set of letters to ALPHABET. Note the square brackets used to signify a set value.

The strings S, WORD, and DROW are processed using intrinsics for **string** data. We can visualize each string as an array of characters, but we must use the intrinsics to modify the array. For example, the sentence S is thought of as an array.

S[1]	S[2]	S[3]	S[4]	S[5]	S[6]	S[7]	S[8]
T	H	E		C	A	T	

Initially, the sentence is cleared to make a clean start.

DELETE (S, 1, N);

The DELETE intrinsic removes N characters from S beginning in character position 1. In general, the intrinsic deletes LENGTH characters from STRING beginning at location START.

DELETE (STRING, START, LENGTH);

We must input the sentence S and immediately check for a terminating period. The period is used as an end-of-string mark. If no period exists, we put one there.

if POS('.', S) = 0
    then INSERT ('.', S, LENGTH(S) + 1);

This statement uses two very useful string intrinsics. First, the POSition function returns an integer equal to the index of the pattern '.'. In other words, S is searched for the first occurrence of a period. If no period is found, a zero is returned. The general form of the POS function shows how to call it with a STRING and a search PATTERN.

0 <= POS (PATTERN, STRING) <= LENGTH (STRING)

The INSERT intrinsic is used to insert a substring pattern into another string at the location indicated by the 3-rd parameter. Thus, '.' is inserted into string S at location LENGTH(S) + 1. This *concatenates* a period to the tail of S. We could have used the CONCAT function to do the same thing, that is, S := CONCAT (S, '.'). In general, the INSERT procedure operates on a PATTERN and STRING by insertion of PATTERN into STRING at LOCATION.

INSERT (PATTERN, STRING, LOCATION) ;

At this point in the program's development we have a punctuated sentence in string S. How do we (1) isolate a word at a time and (2) reverse the words to see if they are palindromes? Let's start with character M=1 and repeat the search for palindromes until M exceeds the LENGTH(S).

M:=1;
repeat
  P := 0 ;
  DELETE(WORD,1,LENGTH(WORD)) ;

This segment of code initializes the sentence index, M, the word length counter, P, and clears-out all characters in WORD.

```
while (M < LENGTH (S))
        and
    (S[M] in ALPHABET)
    do
```

This loop test considers both possible loop conditions: either the sentence has been examined a character at a time until M = LENGTH(S), or the M-th character of S is not to be found in the set ALPHABET. The set operation **in** is used to search for a matching character. We could have been more careful about accessing string S by using the COPY intrinsic.

```
COPY (S, M, 1) ;
```

Indeed, the Pascal manual warns against direct access of characters in any string. "Only string functions or full string assignments should be used to alter strings". Since S[M] is not *altered*, the abuse is tolerated.

The body of the **while** loop is used to count the characters in each word.

```
begin
    P  := P + 1 ;
    M  := M + 1 ;
end
```

The program will have found a word of length P at this point. Thus, if P <> 0, the word can be compared with its drow.

```
if P <> 0
    then
        begin
            INSERT (COPY(S, M–P, P),WORD, 1);
            DELETE (DROW, 1, LENGTH (DROW)) ;
```

This segment of the program copies the P characters at location M–P from the sentence and stores them in string WORD. In preparation for building the DROW, the previously constructed drow is then erased.

```
for Q := 1 to P do
    begin
        INSERT (COPY(WORD, P–Q + 1, 1), DROW, Q) ;
    end ;
```

This loop copies each character in WORD into string DROW, but in reverse order. The index P–Q+1 computes the starting location (tail) of WORD. The index Q indicates where to insert the character into DROW.

The complete Pascal program is shown in Figure 6.1. It employs all string intrinsics except CONCAT and STR. Careful study of this program will enable the reader to use these intrinsics for other programming projects that employ strings.

Summary Of String Intrinsics

    0 <= LENGTH (STRING)
    0 <= POS (PATTERN, STRING) <= LENGTH (STRING)
    STRING := CONCAT(STRING1,STRING2, .., STRINGK)

    STRING := COPY(STRING,LOCATION,LENGTH)

    DELETE (STRING, START, LENGTH)

    INSERT (PATTERN, STRING, LOCATION)

    STR (LONG INTEGER, STRING)

We can also access characters in a string by carefully specifying the subscript corresponding with a character. The following pair of accesses are identical.

    STRING [M] , .VS. COPY (STRING, M, 1) ;

    STRING := ' ' ; .VS., DELETE (STRING, 1, LENGTH(STRING));

The casual observer must be cautioned about the use of strings. Apple Pascal (UCSD) is an extension of standard Pascal, and type **string** is actually a packed array of characters:

    string : **packed array** [1..80] **of char** ;

This means that we must be careful about how we alter the characters within the packed array. In particular, note the following treacherous features.

    read (stringvariable1) ;
    readln (stringvariable2) ;

The first statement, above, reads a string of *indefinite* length since no "ln" is indicated. This means that the second statement has no useful function. If the user inputs two strings separated by a carriage return

```
(*$L CONSOLE:*)
program PALINDROME ;

 const
  N = 80 ;                          (* MAX. LENGTH OF SENTENCE  *)

  type
   LETTERS   = 'A' .. 'Z' ;         (* THE ALPHABET IS MADE OF LETTERS *)
   LINE      = string [ N ] ;       (* MAX SIZE OF ANY WORD OR SENTENCE *)
 var
  S          : LINE ;               (* THE INPUT SENTENCE *)
  WORD       : LINE ;               (* THE ISOLATED WORD  *)
  DROW       : LINE ;               (* THE REVERSED WORD  *)
  ALPHABET   : set of LETTERS ;     (* HAS 2^26 POSSIBLE VALUES *)
  P, Q, M    : 0 .. N ;             (* WORKING COUNTERS   *)


 begin

  ALPHABET := [ 'A' .. 'Z' ] ;
  DELETE ( S, 1, N ) ;             (* CLEAR OUT S [ 1..N ] *)

  WRITE ( 'SENTENCE ? ' ) ; READLN ( S ) ;

  if POS ( '.' S, ) = 0           (* GUARANTEE AN END-OF-SENTENCE *)
     then  INSERT ( '.', S, LENGTH ( S ) + 1 ) ;

  M := 1 ;                         (* LOOK AT CHAR M IN SENTENCE *)
    repeat
     P := 0 ;                      (* COUNT SIZE OF WORD  *)
     DELETE ( WORD, 1, LENGTH ( WORD ) ) ;   (* CLEAR OUT PREVIOUS WORD *)
     while ( M < LENGTH ( S ))
              and
          ( S[ M ] in ALPHABET )
         do
          begin                    (* ISOLATE THE WORD *)
           P := P + 1 ;
           M := M + 1 ;
           end ;                   (* while *)

      if P <> 0                    (* FOUND A WORD ? *)
         then                      (* YES ..         *)
          begin
           INSERT ( COPY ( S, M - P, P ), WORD, 1 ) ;
           DELETE ( DROW, 1, LENGTH ( DROW ) ) ;

           for Q := 1 to P do      (* REVERSE WORD *)
            begin
             INSERT ( COPY ( WORD, P - Q + 1, 1 ), DROW, Q ) ;
            end ;                  (* for LOOP *)

           if DROW = WORD
             then WRITELN ( 'PALINDROME IS ', DROW ) ;

          end ;                    (* if P<>0  *)
      M := M + 1 ;
     until M > LENGTH ( S ) ;      (* repeat  *)
 end.
```

Figure 6.1. Program Palindrome Listing

STRING1 (carriage return)
STRING2

the values input to the computer are actually

stringvariable1 is assigned STRING1
stringvariable2 is null

The (carriage return) is ignored by the first read but terminates the second
readln before the second string is entered!

Another example of carelessness can cause distress in a programmer who is
unaware of the side effects of string intrinsics. Suppose we want to copy a substring of length LONG into another string. We might write this as:

FIELD := COPY (TEMP, 1, LONG) ;

Here, FIELD and TEMP are strings, and the idea is to copy LONG characters
from positions 1 through LONG into FIELD. Now suppose TEMP contains only
LONG-1 characters. Perhaps the programmer miscalculated or else was under
the impression that the partial substring of length LONG-1 would be copied anyway. Untrue! The result is garbage.

Finally, be careful to type functions as scalars. Since a **string** is really a
character **array**, we *cannot* do this:

function SCAN : **string** ;

We will have an opportunity to test our new knowledge of strings in the
next section. Let's turn now to the problem of text files, CRT screen formatting,
and pressing the use of the string intrinsics.

6.2 MAY I SEE THE MENU, PLEASE?

In some applications of microcomputers to large-scale systems the programmer is faced with installing large programs in relatively small main memories. One way to do this, as we have seen in an earlier chapter, is to segment the
procedures of a program. The segment procedures remain on disk until needed
by the executing program. Overlaying is a means of fitting large programs into
small memories.

A second approach is to remove much of the text from a program and put
it on disk. The program must fetch the text from disk, display it, and then dis-
card it. This reduces the size of the program by eliminating prompt lines, menus,
etc., from write and writeln commands, for example.

The next series of programs demonstrates a method used in software development tools. A *software tool* is a system of programs used to develop other
programs. An editor is a software tool. An application development tool usually

```
[1]. LAST NAME        :  _ _ _ _ _ _ _ _ _ _ _
[2]. FIRST NAME       :  _ _ _ _ _ _ _ _ _ _ _
................................................................
[3]. SOC. SEC. NO.    :  _ _ _    _ _    _ _ _ _
[4]. TELEPHONE NO. :  (_ _ _)    _ _ _    _ _ _ _
[5]. COMMENTS         :  _ _ _ _ _ _ _ _ _ _ _
     _ _ _ _ _ _ _ _ _ _ _ _ _ _ _ _ _ _ _
```

Figure 6.2.   Sample Screen Format

goes beyond source program text editors to such aids as screen formatting for inputting data, etc.

Three programs are needed to build a screen format, display and capture the input data fields, and then recall the values input. The EDITCRT program allows a system developer to input a form containing prompts, blanks, and instructions. The form in Figure 6.2 is an example of *input* to EDITCRT. The sample form incorporates prompting in the form of phrases or titles for each *field* and broken lines showing the location and size of each input value. Notice that fields may be placed anywhere in the screen and be separated by text or blank spaces.

Program FILLFORM is used whenever a user is to be prompted by the form entered earlier. FILLFORM fetches the screen format from disk, displays the form, accepts field values at each designated location of the form (the ——— fields), and stores the field values back on disk. FILLFORM should be flexible enough to display any screen format, and accept any field values as input. It is a generalized input routine which can be used over and over again in numerous systems.

The third program we will discuss in this section is called GETFIELD. It is a short program for merely retrieving the field values written to disk by FILL-FORM. We can use GETFIELD to display the field values only, or in modified form as a routine to fetch the field values and input them into a processing program.

We will use the special intrinsic function, GOTOXY, heavily. This routine is employed by the Pascal System to position the screen *cursor* upon *every* reference to CONSOLE: output. Figure 6.3 shows the layout of an 80-column, 24-line CRT screen. We can think of the screen as an array of 24 strings; each string is up to 80 characters long [0..79].

```
var
    SCREEN : array [YAXIS] of string [limit] ;
```

The cursor is positioned at location X,Y by moving it x columns to the right and Y lines down. Thus, no matter where the cursor currently is located, it will be positioned to X,Y after execution of the statement:

```
GOTOXY(X,Y) ;
```

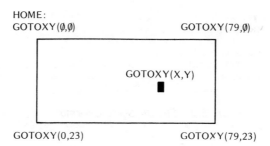

```
HOME:
GOTOXY(∅,∅)                          GOTOXY(79,∅)


                    GOTOXY(X,Y)
                        ■


GOTOXY(0,23)                         GOTOXY(79,23)
```

Figure 6.3.   Dimensions of CRT Screen

The three programs for building a CRT screen format will assume a single character (line) margin around the top, left, and bottom of the screen. Therefore, we will use the following data chunk throughout.

```
const
   XORIGIN  =   1;  XLIMIT   = 79 ;
   YORIGIN  =   1;  YLIMIT   = 22 ;
   UPPER    =   0;  LEFT     =  0 ;
   FIELDS   =  20;  SPACE    = '        ' ;
```

This defines a HOME square at location

GOTOXY (LEFT,UPPER) ;

and the four corners of the screen format at locations (clockwise from the origin at top, left side):

```
GOTOXY (XORIGIN, YORIGIN) ;
GOTOXY (LIMIT, ORIGIN) ;
GOTOXY (XLIMIT, YLIMIT) ;
GOTOXY (XORIGIN, YLIMIT) ;
```

Each field entry is stored in a record containing the character string value, FIELD, its GOTOXY location XPOS, YPOS, and its size, LONG.

```
type
   XAXIS    = XORIGIN .. XLIMIT ;
   YAXIS    = YORIGIN .. YLIMIT ;
   ENTRIES  = record
                 FIELD   :   string [XLIMIT] ;
                 XPOS    :   XAXIS ;
                 YPOS    :   YAXIS ;
                 LONG    :   XAXIS ;
              end ;
```

```
var
    SCREEN   :  array [YAXIS] of string [XLIMIT] ;
    ENTRY    :  array [1..FIELDS] of ENTRIES ;
    ANS      :  file of ENTRIES ;
```

The field values are stored in a working array ENTRY until all corrections have been made by the data entry user. They are then written to a file, ANS. The screen form is stored on a disk in file, FORM, which is a file of type character. In Apple Pascal (UCSD), we abbreviate text files as **text**.

```
FORM  :  text ; (* file of char *)
```

The disk file name is

```
DISKFILE :  string [31] ;
```

and the size of each field is designated

```
SIZE :  0 .. XLIMIT ;
```

The EDITCRT program shown in Figure 6.4 has a simple structure. Its pseudocode design is as follows:

1. Clear the screen.

2. Move cursor to HOME square.

3. Prompt user to enter screen format.

4. Enter each line, one line at a time.

5. Allow user to correct any line

    5.1 If no corrections, store form on disk.

    5.2 If corrections, re-enter lines and then store corrected form on disk.

Several pieces of program EDITCRT need mentioning. First, it is important to use

```
readln (SCREEN [Y]) ;
```

instead of read, because the (carriage return) must be sensed in order to terminate the input after each line.

The statement

```
write ( 'FINISH UP' ) ;
```

merely warns the user of the last line in the screen.

Each prompt which is not part of the screen form is written to the top line; thus,

```
program  EDITCRT ;

const
   XORIGIN    = 1  ;    XLIMIT  = 79 ;   (* WIDTH OF SCREEN WITH MARGIN *)
   YORIGIN    = 1  ;    YLIMIT  = 22 ;   (* LENGTH OF SCREEN, & MARGIN  *)
   UPPER      = 0  ;    LEFT    = 0  ;   (* UPPER LEFT HAND CORNER CRT  *)
   BLANK      ='                                                        '  ;

type
   XAXIS      = XORIGIN .. XLIMIT ;      (* COUMNS OF EACH LINE         *)
   YAXIS      = YORIGIN .. YLIMIT ;      (* EACH LINE                   *)

var
   SCREEN     : array[ YAXIS ] of string[ XLIMIT ];
   LINE       : YAXIS ;
   Y          : 0 .. YLIMIT ;
   DISKFILE   : string ;
   FORM       : text ;                   (* type text=file of char ;    *)
   OK         : char ;


begin
   for Y := UPPER to YLIMIT do
      WRITELN ;                          (* CLEAR FORM AREA             *)
   GOTOXY ( LEFT, UPPER ) ;              (* MOVE CURSOR TO TOP of SCREEN*)
   WRITELN( 'ENTER SCREEN FORM :' ) ;    (* PROMPT USER TO START FORM   *)
   GOTOXY ( XORIGIN, YORIGIN ) ;         (* START AT THE BEGINNING      *)

   for Y := YORIGIN to YLIMIT - 1 do    (* READ EACH LINE, ONE A TIME  *)
      begin
         READLN( SCREEN[ Y ] )      ;    (* END for Y LOOP              *)
         GOTOXY ( XORIGIN, Y + 1 ) ;     (* MOVE DOWN A LINE            *)
      end ;

   WRITE  ( 'FINISH UP' ) ;              (* WARNING TO USER             *)
   GOTOXY ( XORIGIN, YLIMIT ) ;          (* OVERWRITE WARNING LINE      *)
   READLN ( SCREEN[ YLIMIT ] ) ;         (* READ LAST LINE IN SCREEN    *)

   repeat
      GOTOXY ( UPPER, LEFT ) ;           (* ANY CORRECTIONS ??          *)
      WRITE  ( 'ENTER ZERO TO STOP,',
      'OR LINE NUMBER TO CHANGE : ' ) ;
      READLN ( LINE ) ;

      if LINE > 0
         then
            begin
               GOTOXY ( XORIGIN, LINE ) ; (* MOVE CURSOR TO BAD LINE    *)
               READLN ( SCREEN[ LINE ] ) ; (* REPLACE IT WITH NEW LINE  *)
               GOTOXY ( LEFT, UPPER ) ;   (* MOVE CURSOR TO HOME        *)
            end ;                         (* END if-then CLAUSE         *)
   until LINE <= 0 ;
   GOTOXY ( LEFT, UPPER ) ;
   WRITELN ( BLANK ) ;                   (* ERASE LINE AT TOP OF CRT    *)

   repeat
      GOTOXY ( LEFT, UPPER ) ;
      WRITE  ( 'ENTER DISK FILE NAME : ' ) ;
      READLN ( DISKFILE ) ;
      GOTOXY ( LEFT, UPPER ) ;
      WRITE  ( 'IS THIS NAME OK (Y/N)? ' ) ;
      READLN ( KEYBOARD, OK ) ;          (* NON-ECHO KEYBOARD !!        *)
   until OK = 'Y' ;

   REWRITE ( FORM, DISKFILE ) ;          (* OPEN THE file               *)

   for Y := YORIGIN to YLIMIT do
      WRITELN ( FORM , SCREEN[ Y ] );    (* WRITE EACH LINE TO DISK     *)
   GOTOXY ( LEFT, UPPER ) ;
   WRITELN ( BLANK ) ;                   (* ERASE LINE AT TOP OF CRT    *)
   GOTOXY ( LEFT, UPPER ) ;
   WRITE    ( 'FORM IS SAVED IN ', DISKFILE ) ;

   CLOSE  ( FORM, LOCK ) ;               (* MAKE FILE PERMANENT         *)

end.
```

Figure 6.4. Program EDITCRT Listing

GOTOXY (LEFT, UPPER) ;

is used throughout the program in order to reposition the screen cursor. A previously written line is erased by writing blanks over the top of it.

writeln (BLANK) ;

An important new feature is shown in the last part of EDITCRT:

for Y := YORIGIN **to** YLIMIT **do**
    writeln (FORM, SCREEN [Y]) ;

Note: *all* file I/O must be performed by get and put intrinsics, except for files of type **text** and **interactive**. Since FORM is a **text** file, we can use writeln instead of the put intrinsic. This exception is a useful one because it allows the user to redirect output without rewriting the program.

Also, note another (sneaky) feature of program EDITCRT. The pair of statements

write ('IS THIS NAME OK (Y/N)?') ;
readln (KEYBOARD, OK) ;

allows a prompted input to be made without echo checking back to the CRT screen. The text file KEYBOARD is a pseudo-file that takes its data from the console keyboard. Therefore, data entry through keyboard strokes does *not* cause a corresponding output to the console screen.

The two statements above will allow the user to enter either 'Y' or 'N' without it appearing on the CRT screen. This method of input is more clever than necessary in this case, but it is useful for entering *passwords* which must be kept secret.

Finally, the statement

close (FORM, LOCK) ;

causes the output to be locked permanently in the disk directory. Without the LOCK option, the results would be lost.

Now we are prepared to use the form stored in the file FORM. The pseudocode version of FILLFORM is:

1. Read the CRT form from disk file FORM.

2. Display the form.

3. For each line of form:

    3.1 While a field remains empty in the line:

        3.1.1   Locate a field.

        3.1.2   Count the number of '-'s in the field.

3.1.3   Position CRT cursor at the beginning of the field, and read the field value into a string variable.

4. Make any changes requested by field number:

4.1 Get field number.

4.2 Reposition cursor to field.

4.3 Input new value.

4.4 Repeat until all changes have been made.

5. Write the field values to disk file ANS:

5.1 Create file ANS.

5.2 Output array of field values.

5.3 Lock file in place.

The program design can be refined into another level of concreteness, as follows.

The Shape of the Processing Program

```
GETFORM ;                          (* read form *)
;
N := 0                             (* fill-in fields *)
   for Y := YORIGIN to YLIMIT do
     begin
        X := POS ('-', SCREEN [Y]) ;
        while                 (X > 0)

                          and

        (X <= LENGTH(SCREEN[Y]))
     do
     begin
        (* Measure the size of the field *)
        (* Read the field value *)
        (* Update the position of column X *)
     end ;
```

The section of pseudocode above accomplishes steps 1, 2, and 3 of the design. The POS function returns the location of the *first* '-' in the Y-th line of the form. If no '-' exists in the line, the **while** loop is skipped.

If a form field exists $(X > 0)$ and the column counter X has not reached the end of the line $(X <= \text{LENGTH (SCREEN [Y]})$, the program begins sizing up the field to enter the field value. We can refine this section into greater detail.

To Find the Size of a Field
```
DONE   := FALSE ;
SIZE    := 0;
  while ((X + SIZE ) <= LENGTH (SCREEN [Y])
                  and
                ( not DONE)
       do
          if SCREEN [Y] [X + SIZE] = '-'
            then SIZE := SIZE + 1
            else DONE := TRUE ;
```

This section of the program contains some interesting information. The reference to column [X + SIZE] of line [Y] is shown as

SCREEN [Y] [X + SIZE] .

This is proper grammar in Pascal. If this column of SCREEN contains a '-', the size is increased by one, SIZE := SIZE + 1. Otherwise, the end-of-field must have been reached. The DONE flag indicates the state of "doneness," which may result because a field has been measured (SIZE > 0) or because the end-of-line has been reached (DONE=FALSE). Thus, we must know which is the case before attempting to input a value.

To Read the Field Value
```
if SIZE > 0
   then
      begin
        N := N + 1 ;
        GETFIELD (X-1, Y, SIZE, N) ;
        X := X + SIZE ;
      end
   else
        X := X + 1 ;
```

If a field was found, then SIZE >0, and we can input the N-th field value. The cursor must be positioned to location

GOTOXY (X-1, Y)

and the column counter X must be updated to skip over the field of length, SIZE. Otherwise, no field was found and X:= X + 1 moves the column counter to the next character in the line.

The FILLFORM routine also must allow repairs to the input (step 4 of the design plan). If the user enters a field number M > 0, then this field is replaced by a newly input value.

Make Repairs

```
if M > 0
    then
        with ENTRY [M] do
            GETFIELD (XPOS, YPOS, LONG, M) ;
```

The **with** clause is used to abbreviate the actual parameters XPOS, YPOS, and LONG. In general, be careful when passing record parameters to a procedure. Remember,

Warning 1. The procedure cannot change the structure ENTRY [M],

Warning 2. The actual parameters must be passed by value, *not* passed by reference (no **var** parameters).

We have used GETFIELD twice now. Figure 6.5 contains the entire program listing, but let's examine GETFIELD more closely. It does two things:

A. Remembers the location and value of the input field.

B. Copies of the first SIZE character into the ENTRY[Y].FIELD value.

The first step is accomplished by the assignment statements:

```
with ENTRY [N] do
    begin
        XPOS    := XX ;
        YPOS    := YY ;
        LONG    := SIZE;
```

Step B is accomplished in a roundabout manner that requires some explanation.

```
readln (TEMP) ;
    if LENGTH (TEMP) > LONG
        then
            FIELD := COPY(TEMP, 1, LONG)
        else
            FIELD := TEMP ;
```

Why is it not possible simply to write:

```
readln (FIELD) ;
```

```
program  FILLFORM;

  const
    XORIGIN    = 1  ;     XLIMIT   = 79 ;   (* WIDTH OF SCREEN WITH MARGIN *)
    YORIGIN    = 1  ;     YLIMIT   = 22 ;   (* LENGTH OF SCREEN, & MARGIN  *)
    UPPER      = 0  ;     LEFT     =  0 ;   (* UPPER LEFT HAND CORNER CRT  *)
    FIELDS     =20  ;     SPACE    ='                                        ' ;

  type
    XAXIS      = XORIGIN .. XLIMIT ;        (* COUMNS OF EACH LINE         *)
    YAXIS      = YORIGIN .. YLIMIT ;        (* EACH LINE                   *)
    ENTRIES    = record
                   FIELD : string[ XLIMIT ] ;
                   XPOS  : XAXIS ;
                   YPOS  : YAXIS ;
                   LONG  : XAXIS ;
                 end ;

  var
    SCREEN     : array[ YAXIS ] of string[ XLIMIT ] ;
    X          : 0 .. XLIMIT ;
    Y          : 0 .. YLIMIT ;
    DISKFILE   : string[ 31 ] ;
    FORM       : text ;
    ANS        : file of ENTRIES ;
    SIZE       : 0 .. XLIMIT ;
    DONE       : boolean ;                  (* end-of-LINE SWITCH          *)
    ENTRY      : array[ 1..FIELDS ] of ENTRIES ;
    N , M      : 0 .. FIELDS ;

procedure GETFIELD( XX, YY, SIZE, N : integer ) ;

  var
    TEMP       : string[ XLIMIT ] ;

  begin
    GOTOXY( LEFT, UPPER ) ;  WRITELN( SPACE ) ;
    GOTOXY( LEFT, UPPER ) ;  WRITE( 'ENTER :' );

    with ENTRY[ N ] do
      begin
                  GOTOXY ( XX, YY ) ;
                  XPOS  := XX ;
                  YPOS  := YY ;
                  LONG  := SIZE ;           (* REMEMBER WHERE FIELD IS     *)
        READLN( TEMP );
        if LENGTH( TEMP ) > LONG
          then  FIELD   := COPY( TEMP, 1, LONG )
          else  FIELD   := TEMP ;           (* TRUNCATE IF TOO LONG FOR FLD *)
        end ;                               (*       with ENTRY            *)
      end ;                                 (*         GETFIELD            *)

procedure GETFORM ;

  begin

        WRITELN( 'ENTER FORM FILE NAME : ' ) ;
        READLN ( DISKFILE ) ;
        RESET  ( FORM, DISKFILE ) ;
    for Y := YORIGIN to YLIMIT do
      begin
        READLN( FORM, SCREEN[ Y ] ) ;
        WRITELN( SCREEN[ Y ] ) ;
      end ;                                 (* READ DISK AND DISPLAY FORM  *)
    CLOSE ( FORM, lock ) ;
  end ;                                     (*         GETFORM             *)

procedure PUTANS ;

  var CH:char;
```

Figure 6.5.   Program FILLFORM Listing
(Continued next page)

```
         begin
               GOTOXY( LEFT, UPPER ) ;  WRITE( SPACE ) ; WRITE ( SPACE ) ;
               GOTOXY( LEFT, UPPER ) ;  WRITE(
               'ENTER DISK FILE NAME FOR ANSWERS : ');
               READLN ( DISKFILE ) ;
               REWRITE( ANS, DISKFILE ) ;
         for M := 1 to N do
           with ENTRY[ M ] do
               begin
                 ANS^.FIELD := FIELD ;
                 ANS^.XPOS  := XPOS  ;
                 ANS^.YPOS  := YPOS  ;
                 ANS^.LONG  := LONG  ;
                 PUT( ANS ) ;
               end ;
         CLOSE ( ANS , lock ) ;

         for Y := YORIGIN to YLIMIT do
           WRITELN( SCREEN[ Y ] )  ;              (* DISPLAY ONE FINAL TIME  *)
         end ;                                    (*        PUTANS           *)


begin
   GETFORM ;                                      (* GET CRT FORM FROM DISK     *)
   N := 0 ;
   for Y := YORIGIN to YLIMIT do
      begin
      X := POS( '-',SCREEN[ Y ] ) ;
         while    (    X > 0        )
                          and
                 ( X<=LENGTH( SCREEN[ Y ] ) )
             do
              begin
                 SIZE := 0 ;
                 DONE := FALSE;
                 while ( ( X+SIZE ) <= LENGTH( SCREEN[ Y ] ) )
                                  and
                              ( not DONE )
                    do
                       if SCREEN[ Y ] [ X+SIZE ] = '-'
                          then  SIZE := SIZE + 1
                          else  DONE := TRUE ;     (* end of while-if-then-else *)

                    if SIZE > 0
                       then
                          begin
                          N      := N + 1 ;
                          GETFIELD( X-1 , Y , SIZE , N ) ;
                          X      := X + SIZE ;
                          end

                    else X     := X + 1 ;
       end ;                          (*         while           *)
      end ;                           (*         for Y           *)

   repeat
         GOTOXY( LEFT, UPPER ) ;  WRITE( SPACE ) ;
         GOTOXY( LEFT, UPPER ) ;  WRITE(
         'ENTER ZERO to STOP,OR NUMBER OF FIELD TO CHANGE : ' ) ;
      READLN ( M ) ;                           (* CHANGE FIELD #M          *)
      if M > 0
         then
           with ENTRY[ M ] do
              GETFIELD( XPOS, YPOS, LONG, M ) ;
   until M <= 0 ;

   PUTANS ;                                    (* SAVE ANSWERS ON DISK, TOO *)
end.
```

Figure 6-5. (Continued)

This would fail to truncate the input to fit within SIZE characters, but it would work correctly for an input of length less than or equal to SIZE characters.

Why not simply use

```
readln (TEMP) ;
FIELD := COPY (TEMP, 1, LONG);
```

This fails whenever the input, TEMP, contains fewer than LONG characters. This is an example of some of the unspecified actions which can take place in Pascal whenever the conditions differ slightly from what the Pascal intrinsics expect.

Another devastating and yet nearly impossible error to detect is the possible slip-up in string input:

```
read (TEMP) ;
```

This causes *all* subsequent inputs to be skipped! So, remember to use the "ln" form when inputting strings.

Finally, Figure 6.5 contains an output procedure, PUTANS, which opens a newly created file, ANS; transfers each ENTRY [M] into the file *window* ANS∧, one at a time, and *puts* them in the file. The put intrinsic *must* be used here, because ANS is not a **text** or **interactive** file. As a parting courtesy, the PUTANS routine displays the blank form, again, to show the user that all fields have been sent to disk.

Now we can study the GETFIELD program. This program simply retrieves the field values previously stored on disk by PUTANS and displays them on the screen for convenience. Instead of merely displaying them, we could modify GETFIELD to send the field values to a processing program.

Figure 6.6 shows GETFIELD. The shape of this program is:

1. Reset the input file

2. While **not** end-of-file **do**

    2.1 **with** window ANS∧ **do**

        2.1.1 output a row of field value parameters

        2.1.2 get another record into ANS∧.

3. Close the file.

Note: the reset intrinsic *pre-fetches* the first record into window ANS∧. Thus, the first get command is done for you by the reset. *This is always true of typed files other than* **text** *or* **interactive**.

The main difference between **text** and **interactive**, and other files is:

Achtung.1: All **text** and **interactive** files are accessed by readln and writeln, or read and write.

```
program  GETFIELD;

   const
      XORIGIN    = 1    ;   XLIMIT    = 79 ;
      YORIGIN    = 1    ;   YLIMIT    = 22 ;

   type
      XAXIS      = XORIGIN .. XLIMIT ;
      YAXIS      = YORIGIN .. YLIMIT ;
      ENTRIES    = record
                      FIELD  : string[ XLIMIT ]   ;
                      XPOS   : XAXIS    ;
                      YPOS   : YAXIS    ;
                      LONG   : XAXIS    ;
                      end ;

   var
      DISKFILE   : string ;
      ANS        : file of ENTRIES ;


   begin
           WRITE ( 'ENTER DISK FILE NAME FOR FIELDS : ' ) ;
           READLN ( DISKFILE ) ;
           RESET  ( ANS, DISKFILE ) ;
   WRITELN( ' LINE    COL   SIZE    FIELD ' ) ;
   while not EOF( ANS )´do
       with ANS^ do
         begin
             WRITELN( YPOS:6, XPOS:6, LONG:6,'    ', FIELD ) ;
             GET ( ANS ) ;
           end ;      (* WITH AND WHILE LOOP  *)
   CLOSE ( ANS , lock ) ;

   end .
```

Figure 6.6.   Program GETFIELD Listing

Achtung.2: All other files are accessed by put and get.

Achtung.3: No pre-fetch is done when opening **text** and **interactive** files.

Achtung.4: A pre-fetch is always done when opening all files other than **text**
            and **interactive**.

Try these programs and observe how the GOTOXY works and how the field values are captured by FILLFORM. Also, it is important to understand the differences between files as illustrated here.

We can turn now to an interesting application of information retrieved. The next section describes a system for translating French (or any other language) into English.

6.3 PARLEZ-VOUS FRANÇAIS?

As a final example of text processing, strings, and file input/output, suppose we develop a set of programs for translating French words into their English equivalents. These programs constitute a kind of electronic dictionary that allows their user to retrieve an English word when given a French word.

This same idea can be used in many information retrieval systems. Another example would be to retrieve phonetic spellings of English for output to a speech synthesizer. Further applications would be in recalling a client's records from a database of information used by a small business. The client's record is accessed by the name of the client, customer identification number, or some similar "key" unique to the information.

These programs will also provide an opportunity to study some new features of Pascal. We will be introduced to

    long integers

    truncation

    seek and *random access*

    hash coding

    nested procedures

    boolean assignment statements

    the EXIT statement.

So, watch for these coming attractions! Now, we need some background for the technique we will use. This is called *hash coding.*

Suppose we create a file containing the components shown in Figure 6.7.

	ENGLISH	FRENCH	FLAG
0			EMPTY
1	CAT	CHAT	FULL
2			EMPTY
3			EMPTY
4			EMPTY
5	WAITER	GARCON	FULL
6	DOG	CHIEN	FULL

Figure 6.7. Logical Organization of the French-English Concordance

The file is *sequential* because one record follows another and each record is numbered from zero to LNGTH = 6. The first component is the ENGLISH word, the second component contains the FRENCH equivalent, and the last component contains a FLAG. The FLAG indicates whether the record is FULL (has a word pair) or EMPTY.

In Pascal, we describe this structure as follows:

```
const
    EMPTY = 'EMPTY' ;
    FULL  = 'FULL'  ;          (* string constants *)
    N     = 16      ;          (* word length, max *)

type
    CONCORDANCE   =    record
                            ENGLISH  :    string [N] ;
                            FRENCH   :    string [N] ;
                            FLAG     :    string [5] ;
                       end ;
    TABLE         =    file of CONCORDANCE ;

var
    DICTIONARY   :  TABLE ;
    LNGTH        :  integer ;
```

The file is initialized to BLANK entries by the program in Figure 6.8(a). We can also read the file with the program in Figure 6.8(b).

The peculiar thing about the dictionary shown in Figure 6.7 is that it is sparse. Some of the entries are purposely blank, that is, we design the file always to contain some EMPTY records. This has to do with the way we will *randomly* access the file.

Suppose we enter the word pair (CAT, CHAT) into the dictionary. One way to do this is simply to store this pair in the first available location of the table. Then, when we are given CHAT, we read the file from "top" to "bottom" looking for CHAT. When CHAT is found, we exchange it for CAT. The Pascal segment for doing this would look like the following:

```
RESET (DICTIONARY, 'DICTIONARY.DATA') ;
    for I := 0 to LNGTH-1 do
        if DICTIONARY∧.FRENCH = TEMPFR
            then WRITELN (DICTIONARY∧.ENGLISH)
            else GET (DICTIONARY) ;
```

The problem with this section of code is (1) the loop is *always* executed LNGTH times, thus using LNGTH accesses to the file (slow) and (2) even if we

```
program MAKEDICTIONARY ;

  const
    EMPTY    = 'EMPTY' ;
    FULL     = 'FULL ' ;
    BLANK    = '
    N        = 16 ;

  type
    CONCORDANCE = record
                    ENGLISH  : string[ N ] ;
                    FRENCH   : string[ N ] ;
                    FLAG     : string[ 5 ] ;
                  end ;
    TABLE       = file of  CONCORDANCE ;

  var
    DICTIONARY  : TABLE ;
    LENGTH      :  integer ;
    I           :  integer ;
    ENTRY       : CONCORDANCE ;
    HEADER      : file of  integer ;

  begin

    WRITELN( 'ENTER SIZE OF DICTIONARY ( # WORDS ) : ' ) ;
    READLN ( LENGTH ) ;

    REWRITE( HEADER, 'HEADER.DATA' ) ;
    HEADER^  := LENGTH ;
    PUT ( HEADER ) ;
    CLOSE( HEADER, lock ) ;

    ENTRY.ENGLISH := BLANK ;
    ENTRY.FRENCH  := BLANK ;
    ENTRY.FLAG    := EMPTY ;

    REWRITE( DICTIONARY, 'DICTIONARY.DATA' ) ;
    DICTIONARY^   := ENTRY ;
    for I := 0  to  LENGTH - 1  do
      PUT( DICTIONARY )  ;

    CLOSE( DICTIONARY, lock ) ;
    WRITELN( 'READY' ) ;

  end.
```

Figure 6.8 (a)   Program MAKEDICTIONARY Listing

could overcome the first objection we would still require an average of LNGTH/2 accesses to locate one word pair only. In other words, this *sequential search* is too slow. We need a faster, more direct method of accessing the disk file than the tape-like sequential search method.

Instead of searching the entire file to find one match we can use the key

```
program READDICTIONARY ;

   const
      EMPTY    = 'EMPTY' ;
      FULL     = 'FULL ' ;
      BLANK    = '            ;
      N        = 16 ;

   type
      CONCORDANCE = record
                        ENGLISH  : string[ N ] ;
                        FRENCH   : string[ N ] ;
                        FLAG     : string[ 5 ] ;
                     end ;
      TABLE       = file  of  CONCORDANCE ;

   var
      DICTIONARY : TABLE ;
      LENGTH     : integer ;
      I          : integer ;
      ENTRY      : CONCORDANCE ;
      HEADER     : file  of   integer ;

   begin
RESET   ( HEADER, 'HEADER.DATA' ) ;
LENGTH  := HEADER^ ;
CLOSE( HEADER, lock ) ;

WRITELN( 'READING DICTIONARY OF ', LENGTH:5, ' WORDS' ) ;

RESET   ( DICTIONARY, 'DICTIONARY.DATA' ) ;
for I := 0  to   LENGTH - 1  do
  begin
    WRITELN(DICTIONARY^.ENGLISH,
            DICTIONARY^.FRENCH,
            DICTIONARY^.FLAG  ) ;
    GET( DICTIONARY )  ;
  end ;

CLOSE( DICTIONARY, lock ) ;
WRITELN( 'READY' ) ;

end .
```

Figure 6.8 (b)   Program READDICTIONARY Listing

word CHAT as a clue to tell us where it is located in the file. Many methods exist to do this, but they all fall under the name of *hashing.* We will *hash* CHAT into a table location. This location is directly accessed using the SEEK intrinsic in Pascal.

The French word CHAT can be converted into a number by replacing its letters by their equivalents. An 'A' is replaced by zero, a 'B' by one, and so on. The letter 'Z' is replaced by 25. In Pascal this is done using the order intrinsic.

ORD(WORD[LETTER]) – ORD('A')

Here, the LETTER-th letter of WORD is accessed by a subscript. Thus, CHAT becomes,

```
C  H  A  T
2  7  0  18
```

Unfortunately, 2+7+0+18 is also the same as 7+0+2+18, or 18+2+7+0, or any other permutation of the letters in CHAT. We want something unique for CHAT so we won't confuse it with HATC, etc. Suppose we weight the numbers as follows.

$$2*25^0 + 7*25^1 + 0*25^2 + 18*25^3$$

or in other words,

$$2 + 25\ (7+ 25\ (0 + 25(18))).$$

This gives a unique number for every word that we might convert into a number. In this case CHAT is converted into 1,968,752.

As you can see, the numerical equivalent of the four-letter word is quite large. On a microcomputer with wordsize of 15 bits, the large number 1,968,752 will overflow the normal **integer** variable. Fortunately, a special case exists for *long integer*. Here is how it works.

var

KEY : **integer**[36] ; (* 36-digit integer *)

procedure CONVERT (WORD : **string**);

var

LETTER : I .. N ;

begin

KEY :=0;

for LETTER :=I to LENGTH (WORD) do
KEY :=25*KEY+ORD(WORD[LETTER])–ORD('A');

end;

This section of program converts any string of letters into a long integer. The integer must be 36 digits or less in precision, since we defined KEY as a 36-digit integer. We could have defined KEY as a 25 digit, 12 digit, etc. precision integer, but 36 is the largest length possible in UCSD Pascal.

This routine certainly helps to solve the problem of large numbers, but we have several more problems to worry about. First, the file is only LNGTH records long. How do we use 1,968,572 to directly access a word inside the dictionary if it only contains 500 words? Here is where hashing comes to the rescue.

If we reduce KEY to a number between zero and LNGTH–1, then we can use KEY, directly, to access the entries in the dictionary. We can do this by converting KEY into its remainder after dividing KEY by LNGTH.

KEY := KEY **mod** LNGTH

This statement produces a value between zero and (LNGTH – 1), but unfortunately, Pascal will *not* accept this because **mod** fails to work on long integers. So we need the equivalent statement:

KEY := KEY – LNGTH * (KEY **div** LNGTH) ;

In Figure 6.7, LNGTH is 7; so we get KEY reduced to a remainder of 4. Look in the table of Figure 6.7. CHAT is *not* stored in location (record) 4 of the table!

When we compare CHAT with the BLANK in record 4, we know right away that an additional *probe* is needed to find CHAT. Where do we look next?

Suppose we add an offset, OFSET, to 4 in order to try again. Let the offset be equal to the length of the word (it can be most anything, but this gives a certain uniqueness to the offset).

OFSET := LENGTH (FRENCH);

This offset is added to the KEY, and we try the comparison again.

(4+4) **mod** LNGTH =1

This time we get a match in record 1. The French word CHAT has been located in 2 accesses to disk instead of 7 accesses. This is the main advantage of hash coding. It speeds direct access to random files. In general, if the file has K FULL records, then the *average* number of accesses needed to locate any record is given by

$$\# = \frac{\text{LNGTH}}{\text{LNGTH} - \text{K}}$$

Obviously, if K is very nearly equal to LNGTH, this method becomes very slow,

too. The reason we purposely keep some of the records empty is to keep the retrieval speed as high as possible. For example, if we use 3/4 of the file and leave
1/4 of the records empty, we can expect the average number of accesses to be 4
seeks per retrieval. *This is true regardless of the size of the file*, LNGTH.

We are now ready to put together a search routine which uses hash coding
both to insert word pairs into the dictionary and retrieve them when given a
French word, TEMPFR. Here is the heart of the routine (see Figure 6.9 for the
complete listing).

First we must convert the French word TEMPFR into a numerical key as
discussed before. We then use the number to hash the file.

```
CONVERT (TEMPFR); (*computes KEY *)
FINDSPACE := (-1); (* means it failed *)
OFSET := LENGTH (TEMPFR);

if OFSET :=0 then OFSET :=1;

for I :=1 to LNGTH do
    begin
        SEEK (DICTIONARY, TRUNC (KEY));
        GET (DICTIONARY);

        if DICTIONARY ∧. FLAG = FULL

            then
                KEY := (TRUNK (KEY) + OFSET ) mod LNGTH
            else begin
                FINDSPACE := TRUNC (KEY);
                EXIT (FINDSPACE);
                end;
    end;
```

This code has several interesting features worth mentioning. First, it loops
over all records of the file if necessary. The dictionary may *not* contain a matching French word. If this is true, then we must search the entire file to find out.
(A slight modification to this loop will prevent a full search by stopping on the
first EMPTY record.)

Second, this section of code is used to find an EMPTY space for the purpose of inserting a new French-English word pair. If a record is already FULL,
the offset is used to compute another KEY value.

Next, notice how TRUNC is used to convert KEY into an ordinary integer.
This is needed to allow arithmetic with other (short) integers.

Finally, we have used a new statement in Pascal to overcome the problem mentioned earlier. EXIT (FINDSPACE) causes the FINDSPACE routine to be terminated. In general, EXIT will terminate any **function** or **procedure**. The statement EXIT (PROGRAM) will cause termination of the program.

We will modify this code to handle the problem of retrieval by changing the text:

> **if** DICTIONARY ∧. FRENCH <> TEMPFR
> > **then**
> > > KEY := (TRUNC(KEY) + OFSET) **mod** LNGTH
> > **else**
> > > . . .

This gives us a method for insertion into the dictionary and retrieval from the same file. The marvelous hashing function solves two problems for the price of one.

```
program ADDICTIONARY ;

   const
     EMPTY   = 'EMPTY' ;
     FULL    = 'FULL ' ;
     N       = 16 ;

   type
     CONCORDANCE = record
                     ENGLISH  : string[ N ] ;
                     FRENCH   : string[ N ] ;
                     FLAG     : string[ 5 ] ;
                     end ;
     TABLE       = file  of  CONCORDANCE ;

   var
     DICTIONARY  : TABLE ;
     LNGTH       : integer ;
     HEADER      : file  of    integer  ;
     INDEX       : integer ;
     KEY         : integer[ 36 ] ;
     TEMPFR,
     TEMPENG     : string[ N ] ;
     I           : 1 .. N ;

   function FINDSPACE  :  integer ;

     var
       OFSET     : integer ;

     procedure CONVERT( WORD : string )  ;

       var
         LETTER  : 1 .. N ;

       begin
         KEY  := 0 ;
```

126

```
      for LETTER := 1 to LENGTH( WORD ) do
        KEY:= 25 * KEY + ORD( WORD[ LETTER ] ) - ORD( 'A' )   ;
      KEY := KEY - LNGTH * ( KEY div LNGTH ) ;
    end ;                      (* CVT *)

begin
  CONVERT( TEMPFR ) ;
  FINDSPACE := ( -1 ) ;
  OFSET     := LENGTH ( TEMPFR ) ;
  if OFSET = 0 then OFSET := 1 ;
  for I := 1 to LNGTH do
    begin
      SEEK( DICTIONARY, TRUNC( KEY ) ) ;
      GET ( DICTIONARY ) ;
      if DICTIONARY^.FLAG = FULL
        then  KEY := ( TRUNC( KEY ) + OFSET ) mod LNGTH
        else
          begin
            FINDSPACE :=TRUNC(  KEY ) ;
            EXIT ( FINDSPACE ) ;
          end ;    (* if-then-else *)
    end ;
end ;                      (* FINDSPACE  *)


function MOREWORDS  :  boolean ;

  begin
    WRITELN( 'ENTER A FRENCH WORD : ' ) ;
    READLN ( TEMPFR ) ;
    WRITELN( 'ENTER THE ENGLISH TRANSLATION : ' ) ;
    READLN ( TEMPENG ) ;
    MOREWORDS :=not ( ( TEMPFR = '.' ) and ( TEMPENG = '.' ) )   ;
  end ;              (* MOREWORDS *)

begin
  RESET ( HEADER, 'HEADER.DATA' ) ;
  LNGTH  := HEADER^ ;
  CLOSE( HEADER, LOCK ) ;


  WRITELN('ENTER A FRENCH WORD FIRST, FOLLOWED BY THE ENGLISH TRANSLATION' );
  WRITELN('       ( ENTER ''.'' TO STOP ENTERING )' ) ;

  RESET ( DICTIONARY, 'DICTIONARY.DATA' ) ;
  while MOREWORDS do
    begin
      INDEX  := FINDSPACE ;
      if INDEX >= 0
        then
          begin
            SEEK ( DICTIONARY, INDEX ) ;
            DICTIONARY^.FLAG := FULL ;
            DICTIONARY^.FRENCH := TEMPFR ;
            DICTIONARY^.ENGLISH:= TEMPENG;
            PUT ( DICTIONARY ) ;
          end              (* THEN *)
        else WRITELN( 'DICTIONARY IS FULL' ) ;
    end ;                  (* WHILE LOOP *)

  CLOSE( DICTIONARY, LOCK ) ;
end.
```

Figure 6.9. Program ADDICTIONARY Listing

```pascal
program FINDWORD ;

  const
    EMPTY   = 'EMPTY' ;
    FULL    = 'FULL ' ;
    N       = 16 ;

  type
    CONCORDANCE = record
                    ENGLISH  : string[ N ] ;
                    FRENCH   : string[ N ] ;
                    FLAG     : string[ 5 ] ;
                  end ;
    TABLE      = file  of  CONCORDANCE ;

  var
    DICTIONARY : TABLE ;
    LNGTH      : integer ;
    HEADER     : file  of   integer ;
    INDEX      : integer ;
    KEY        : integer[ 36 ] ;
    TEMPFR,
    TEMPENG    : string[ N ] ;
    I          : 1 .. N ;

  function FINDSPACE  :  integer ;

    var
      OFSET      : integer ;

    procedure CONVERT( WORD : string )  ;

      var
        LETTER  : 1 .. N ;

      begin
        KEY  := 0 ;
        for LETTER := 1 to LENGTH( WORD ) do
          KEY:= 25 * KEY + ORD( WORD[ LETTER ] ) - ORD( 'A' )  ;
        KEY := KEY - LNGTH * ( KEY div LNGTH ) ;
      end ;                    (* CVT *)

    begin
      CONVERT( TEMPFR ) ;
      FINDSPACE := ( -1 ) ;
      OFSET      := LENGTH ( TEMPFR ) ;
      if OFSET = 0 then OFSET := 1 ;
      for I := 1 to LNGTH do
        begin
          SEEK( DICTIONARY, TRUNC( KEY ) ) ;
          GET ( DICTIONARY ) ;
          if DICTIONARY^.FRENCH <> TEMPFR
            then  KEY := ( TRUNC( KEY ) + OFSET ) mod LNGTH
            else
              begin
                FINDSPACE :=TRUNC(  KEY ) ;
                EXIT ( FINDSPACE ) ;
              end ;     (* if-then-else *)
      end ;
  end ;                        (* FINDSPACE  *)
```

```
function  MOREWORDS  :  boolean ;

  begin
    WRITELN( 'ENTER A FRENCH WORD : ' ) ;
    READLN ( TEMPFR ) ;
    MOREWORDS := not ( TEMPFR = '.' ) ;
  end ;                     (* MOREWORDS *)


begin
  RESET   ( HEADER, 'HEADER.DATA' ) ;
  LNGTH   := HEADER^ ;
  CLOSE( HEADER, lock ) ;

  RESET   ( DICTIONARY, 'DICTIONARY.DATA' ) ;
  while MOREWORDS do
    begin
      INDEX   := FINDSPACE ;
      if INDEX >= 0
        then
          begin
            SEEK ( DICTIONARY, INDEX ) ;
            TEMPENG := DICTIONARY^.ENGLISH ;
            WRITELN( 'THE ENGLISH WORD IS ', TEMPENG ) ;
          end                     (* THEN *)
        else WRITELN( 'THE FRENCH WORD IS NOT IN THIS DICTIONARY' ) ;
    end ;                     (* WHILE LOOP *)

  CLOSE( DICTIONARY, lock ) ;
end.
```

Figure 6.10.   Program FINDWORD Listing

The retrieval program in Figure 6.10 contains the same routines and variables as the earlier programs (with minor changes). Notice the simplicity of the main body of FINDWORD.

```
INDEX :=FINDSPACE;
  if INDEX >= 0
    then
      begin
        SEEK (DICTIONARY, INDEX);
        TEMPENG := DICTIONARY ∧.ENGLISH;
        WRITELN ('THE ENGLISH WORD IS', TEMPENG);
      end
    else
        WRITELN ('THE FRENCH WORD IS NOT HERE');
```

We summarize the hash coding method so that it can be applied in other retrieval problems.

1. Convert the key to a number
2. Reduce the number to the subrange of zero to one less than the length of the file.
3. Seek the record.
4. If the keys do not match, add an offset to the key.
5. If the new key (old key plus offset) is outside the subrange 0..LNGTH −1, then reduce it to this subrange using the **mod** operator.
6. Continue to add the offset to the new key until a match is found or until the entire file is searched.

This recipe works for insertion if the routine looks for an EMPTY record. It works for lookup if the match is between the retrieval key and the contents of the record. The retrieval routine can stop as soon as it (1) finds the matching key, (2) runs into an EMPTY record (no match will be made because the key is not in the file), or (3) has searched LNGTH records. These rules apply to insertion and lookup but *not* to deletion. When a hash-coded file allows deletion of records, the problem is a little more difficult to handle.

The program listings can be studied now. The MOREWORDS routine has an interesting boolean assignment statement in it.

MOREWORDS := **not** (TEMPFR ='.') **and** (TEMPENG='.'));

This assigns either TRUE or FALSE to the variable.

The CONVERT procedure is a *nested* procedure because it is inside function FINDSPACE, which is in turn inside of the main program. This is perfectly acceptable, but be careful that you do not try to access CONVERT from some other procedure. You will get an "undeclared variable" error if a name is used outside of the nested routine containing the name.

Let's summarize the main points of this section. First, long integers allow up to 36 digits of precision by defining variables as type **integer**[K], where 4 <= K<=36. We can mix long integers with other variables if we assume that expressions will be converted to long or we use the TRUNC intrinsic.

We can make random access to a sequential file using the SEEK intrinsic. The actual parameters of SEEK must fall within the file boundaries; otherwise it is ignored.

SEEK (filename, record number)

The record numbers are enumerated from zero to (LENGTH OF FILE − 1). When SEEK is combined with hash coding, we can reduce the time it takes to retrieve records from a file by reducing the number of accesses to the file.

When the problem dictates, we can use the EXIT statement to leave a procedure, function, or program. The EXIT statement can even be used to leave several (nested) routines in one jump to the outermost level.

The advanced programmer will want to read the chapter on file structures to learn more ways to organize data for fast access, but hashing is a very valuable and frequently used technique found in many applications.

TWENTY QUESTIONS

1. Who cares about palindromes anyway?
2. What happens in COPY (STRING1, 1, LONG) whenever LONG > LENGTH [STRING1]?
3. What is a **string**?
4. If a zero is returned by POS, what does it mean?
5. What is a software tool?
6. Who is Cyben?
7. What happens when GOTOXY (81,25)?
8. Which is best: read (STRING1) or readln (STRING1)?
9. Is this legal? **function** X: **string**;
10. Does reset fetch the window?
11. What does LOCK do in CLOSE (F,LOCK)?
12. Is this legal? SCREEN [Y] [X].
13. What does the **with** clause do?
14. What do you have to be careful *not* to do when passing record structures?
15. What is ANS∧?
16. What is the difference between **text** files and typed files?
17. Can all files be accessed with the read and write intrinsics?
18. How long is the largest integer?
19. What is wrong with a sequential search?
20. What does TRUNC do to a long integer?

ANSWERS

1. Hardly anyone.
2. Who knows? Usually a null copy is made.
3. **Type string** is a **packed array of char.**
4. The pattern could not be found.
5. A system of programs for developing other programs.
6. A cyborg citizen of the 21st Century.

7. The same thing when GOTOXY (79,23).

8. Always use readln.

9. No, functions are scalars, not structured types.

10. Yes. Reset and rewrite get the first record, unless they work on **interactive** or **text** files.

11. Locks the file in the directory so it stays after the program goes away.

12. Yes. It is an alternate way to access two-dimensional arrays.

13. It allows the programmer to abbreviate names.

14. Pass by value, not pass by reference.

15. A file window for file ANS.

16. A typed file record zero is fetched into the window when it is opened, while text files are not. Also, text files can store text only. Typed files can store anything.

17. No! Only **text** or **interactive** files.

18. 36 digits.

19. It is kind of slow.

20. Converts it to a short integer.

Chapter 7

Programming in the Large

*Once upon a time three little people left the farm to seek their fortune.
The first little person studied hard, was an ambitious employee, and took the
advice of her elders — "Here have the mighty fallen", and "It can't be done!"
And the first little person believed what her elders said.*

*The second little person also studied hard and pursued a career with great
ambition. He barely noticed the failure around him and cared not if the "race is
not to the swift, nor the battle to the strong."*

*The first person never found her fortune or happiness. The second person
succeeded because he didn't know it couldn't be done. What happened to the
third little person? She became a computer programmer — that sealed her fate.*

7.1 THE GAMBLER

Is it possible to write big programs on little computers? If we use some
advanced features of Pascal, the answer is "yes". But exactly what do we mean
by a big program?

A computer program is big if it requires:

1. Large amounts of data

2. Large amounts of program memory space

3. Large numbers of modules

The first definition actually applies to the data rather than the program,
but nonetheless it is a concern in many applications where large arrays of data
values must be processed. In this case we can resort to file structures on disk as a
means of accommodating the large amount of data. We have discussed several
ways of accessing data on disk files in previous chapters.

The second and third definitions of "big" pose a more difficult obstacle to
overcome. No matter how large a computer we might use, there is always a problem too large to fit on such a computer. In fact, the Pascal System places certain
restrictions on the programmer:

Maximum size of:	UCSD Limitation:
Procedure or function	1200 bytes of object P-code
Data chunk in a module	16,383 words per procedure/function
Characters in a string	255 characters
Elements in a set	512 elements
Segment modules per program	7 user segments
Modules within a unit	127 procedures or functions

We were able to overcome the object code limitation (1200) earlier using **segment** modules instead of ordinary **procedure** or **function** modules. The solution to the second problem defined above is to overlay code segments onto a (smaller) main memory. We will develop this idea in greater detail later.

The size problem not only causes trouble when we run out of memory space, but it also causes problems in management of the software development process. We may be faced with large program text to edit (causing a burden on the editor) and time-consuming compiles of large programs. Fortunately, there is a way around these management problems.

We can employ two techniques to aid in program development of very large programs. Both techniques are mere conveniences and *do not* solve the problem of large object code. If the resulting P-code is too large to fit into main memory, we must use **segments** anyway; but we will return to that problem in the final section of this chapter.

The first method of managing large programs is to edit the modules into separate text files. The files can then be merged together by the compiler during translation. This is done using the include directive.

        (*$Ifilename*)

This directive must be placed in the text of the program exactly where you want to insert *filename*. It also must appear without blanks between $Ifilename, etc. Suppose we compose three pieces of Pascal text and store them in files P1.TEXT, P2.TEXT, and P3.TEXT. If we want to include these in another program, we must insert the compiler directive in the same place in the text where we want these files to be inserted.

```
program BIG;
   (*IP1.TEXT*)
   (*IP3.TEXT*)
   (*IP2.TEXT*)
end.
```

Perhaps file P1.TEXT contains the global data chunk, P3.TEXT contains the functions and procedures, and P2.TEXT contains the main body of the program. Thus, we can "divide and conquer" by individually editing each file and perhaps using it over and over again in similar programs.

This is a handy way to manage large programs, but it does not solve the problem associated with time consuming compiles. The three files, above, must be re-compiled every time they are used as shown. If they never change, then why not compile them once, and *link* their object P-code to the main program P-code after the main program has been translated? This is indeed a good practice, because it avoids lengthy compiles.

The Pascal System employs this technique itself. For example, if we use the pre-compiled functions for graphics, simulation, analog controls, or making music, we *must* include the Pascal units containing them. Figure 7.1 lists several pre-compiled **unit** names and the modules they contain.

Recall from Chapter 3 that the shape of a Pascal program that uses precompiled units is:

```
program NAME ;
    uses MODULES ;
    const
        (* constants *)
    type
        (* types *)
    var
        (* data variables *)
    procedure
        (* procedure modules *)
    function
        (* function modules *)
    begin
        (* main body of program *)
    end.
```

The **uses** MODULES; statement causes the definition statements of every procedure and function contained within the **unit** MODULES to be inserted into this program. After the program is compiled, its P-code is linked together with the procedures and functions defined in MODULES. Since MODULES contains a collection of pre-compiled P-code modules, it is *not* necessary to compile them again. This avoids a lengthy compile by requiring a short **link** step.

We demonstrate this idea using APPLESTUFF in the following application example. Suppose we derive a program for playing Blackjack or some other card game. The first step in simulating most card games is to start with a shuffled deck of cards. Therefore, we must randomize a deck of cards using the random number generator pre-compiled and stored in the unit named APPLESTUFF. See Figure 7.1.

(a) **uses** TURTLEGRAPHICS
  INITTURTLE ; (* initialize graphics *)
  TEXTMODE ; (* change to text mode *)
  GRAFMODE ; (* change to graphics mode *)
  VIEWPORT ; (* restrict the screen *)
  PENCOLOR ; (* set color of pen *)
  FILLSCREEN ; (* solid color *)
  MOVETO ; (*
  TURNTO ; drawing commands
  MOVE ;
  TURN ;   *)
  TURTLEX ; (*
  TURTLEY ;   find out where turtle
  TURTLEANG ;   is on the screen
  SCREENBIT ;   *)
  DRAWBLOCK ; (* send an array to screen *)
  WCHAR ; (* output characters or
  WSTRING ; string to screen *)
  CHARTYPE ; (* set type of display *)

(b) **uses** APPLESTUFF ;

  RANDOMIZE ; (* initialize RANDOM *)
  RANDOM ; (* random number generator *)
  PADDLE ; (*
  BUTTON ;   analog input/output
  TTLOUT ;   *)
  NOTE ; (* musical sound *)

(c) **uses** TRANSCEND ;

  ATAN ; (* arctangent *)
  SIN ; (* sine *)
  COS ; (* cosine *)
  EXP ; (* exponential *)
  LN ; (* log base e *)
  LOG ; (* log base 10 *)
  SQRT ; (* square root *)

Figure 7.1. Pre-Compiled Units

Our program for shuffling a deck of 52 cards *must* specify APPLESTUFF in the statement immediately following the **program** statement.

    program CARDSHUFFLE;
      uses APPLESTUFF;

If we also wanted to use TRANSCEND, we would have to include its name in the same **uses** statement (only one is allowed per program).

    uses APPLESTUFF,TRANSCEND;

Now we can write the program just as before, including calls to the modules contained within APPLESTUFF. Suppose we use scalars to define the deck of cards.

```
type
   SUITS    = (CLUBS, HEARTS, DIAMONDS, SPADES);
   VALUES   = (ONE, TWO, THREE, FOUR, FIVE, SIX, SEVEN,
               EIGHT, NINE, TEN, JACK, QUEEN, KING, ACE);
   CARDS    = record
              SUIT      :    SUITS;
              VALUE     :    VALUES;
              end;

var
   DECK   :   array [1..N] of CARDS;
```

The deck of cards is simulated in the CARDSHUFFLE program by representing each card as a record in an array of CARDS. Each card has a suit and a face value.

Now we need a method of randomizing that disorders the array of CARDS. How do we randomize a list?

A pseudocode design for a card shuffle algorithm is given below. The idea is simple: pick a card at random, exchange it with the last card in the deck, and then repeat the random selection over again using a shortened deck.

Design of Shuffle

1. Initialize the deck of cards by listing them in some (arbitrary) order.
2. Repeat until the deck is shortened to one card:
   2.1. Randomly select a card from the deck.
   2.2. Exchange the card with the last card in the deck.
   2.3. Shorten the deck by ignoring the last card.
3. Deal the cards from the top of the deck.

We are going to need the RANDOMIZE procedure and RANDOM function from the pre-compiled unit APPLESTUFF. RANDOMIZE selects a random starting value for the RANDOM function. RANDOM returns an integer from zero to 32767 (the largest short integer possible).

First, we must initialize the deck:

```
DEAL :=0
  for TS := CLUBS to SPADES do
    for TV := ONE to ACE do
      begin
        DEAL := DEAL +1;
        DECK [DEAL].VALUE := TV;
        DECK [DEAL].SUIT := TS;
      end;
```

This assigns a suit and value to each element of the array from DEAL=1 to DEAL=N. Notice how the components of this structure are accessed in dot notation. The alternate expression is *not* equivalent:

```
DECK.VALUE [DEAL]
```

Be careful to avoid this oversight. Also, notice how the two **for** loops are *nested*. Next, we initialize the random number generator and produce a random integer in the range 1..N by reducing the interval 0..32767 to 1..52:

```
I := RANDOM mod N + 1;
```

This produces the required subrange value when N=52. The remaining main program carries out the exchange and shortens the deck as prescribed.

```
RANDOMIZE;
J := N;
  repeat
    I := RANDOM mod N + 1;

  EXCHANGE (I, J);
  J := J – 1;
  until J = 1;
```

The complete program is shown in Figure 7.2.

The DISPLAY module is particularly interesting because it uses the **case** statement.

```
program  CARDSHUFFLE ;

  uses APPLESTUFF ;

  const
    N            = 52 ;

  type
    SUITS        = ( CLUBS, HEARTS, DIAMONDS, SPADES ) ;
    VALUES       = ( ONE, TWO, THREE, FOUR, FIVE, SIX,
                     SEVEN, EIGHT, NINE, JACK, QUEEN,
                     KING, ACE ) ;
    CARDS        = record
                     SUIT  : SUITS ;
                     VALUE : VALUES ;
                   end ;
    SUBS         = 1 .. N ;

  var
    DECK         : array[ SUBS ] of CARDS ;
    I, J         : SUBS ;
    TS           : SUITS ;
    TV           : VALUES ;
    DEAL         : integer ;

  procedure EXCHANGE ( MID, LAST : SUBS ) ;

    begin
      TS                 := DECK[ MID ].SUIT ;
      DECK[ MID ].SUIT   := DECK[ LAST ].SUIT ;
      DECK[ LAST ].SUIT := TS ;
      with DECK[ MID ] do
        begin
          TV               := VALUE ;
          VALUE            := DECK[ LAST ].VALUE ;
        end ;          (* with *)
      DECK[ LAST ].VALUE:= TV ;
    end;             (* EXCHANGE *)

procedure DISPLAY ;

  var
    CH          : char ;

  begin
    for I := 1 to N do
      begin
        J := ORD( DECK[ I ].VALUE ) + 1 ;   (* CONVERT TO NUMBER   *)
        if J <= 9
          then  WRITE( J:4 )
          else
            case DECK[ I ].VALUE of
            JACK   : WRITE( 'JACK' ) ;
            QUEEN  : WRITE( 'QUEEN' ) ;
            KING   : WRITE( 'KING ' ) ;
            ACE    : WRITE( 'ACE ' ) ;
            end  ;  (* case *)
```

Figure 7.2. CARDSHUFFLE
(Continued next page.)

```
         case DECK[ I ].SUIT of
            CLUBS     : WRITELN( ' OF CLUBS ' ) ;
            HEARTS    : WRITELN( ' OF HEARTS' ) ;
            DIAMONDS : WRITELN( ' OF DIAMONDS' ) ;
            SPADES    : WRITELN( ' OF SPADES ' ) ;
         end ;            (* case *)
         if I mod 5 = 0
            then
               begin
                  WRITELN( 'HIT ? ' ) ;
                  READLN( CH ) ;      (* WAIT for USER *)
               end ;
     end ;             (* for I *)
   end ;               (* DISPLAY *)
begin                (* M A I N *)
   DEAL   := 0 ;
   for TS := CLUBS to SPADES do
      begin
         for TV := ONE to ACE do
            begin
               DEAL             := DEAL + 1 ;
               DECK[ DEAL ].VALUE := TV ;
               DECK[ DEAL ].SUIT  := TS ;
            end ;
      end ;            (* for TS *)
   WRITELN( 'BEGIN SHUFFLING' ) ;
   RANDOMIZE ;
   J   := N ;
   repeat
     I   := RANDOM mod N + 1 ;
     EXCHANGE( I, J ) ;                         (* FLIP TWO CARDS IN DECK *)
     J   := J - 1 ;
   until J = 1 ;
   WRITELN( 'DONE SHUFFLE' ) ;
   DISPLAY ;
end.
```

Figure 7-2. (Continued)

```
case DECK[I].VALUE of
     JACK   :  WRITE ('JACK');
     QUEEN :  WRITE ('QUEEN');
     KING   :  WRITE ('KING');
     ACE    :  WRITE ('ACE');
   end;
```

The statement selects the JACK clause when DECK[I].VALUE = JACK, the QUEEN clause when DECK[I].VALUE = QUEEN, etc. Since Pascal prevents direct output of a scalar, we must translate the value of DECK[I].VALUE in this manner.

The boolean values TRUE and FALSE are scalars, as we saw in Chapter 4. We cannot output them directly, but we *could* output their order, ORD(DECK[I].VALUE), for example.

We must do the same for the suits of each card.

```
case DECK[I].SUIT of
    CLUBS       :  WRITELN ('OF CLUBS');
    HEARTS      :  WRITELN ('OF HEARTS');
    DIAMONDS    :  WRITELN ('OF DIAMONDS');
    SPADES      :  WRITELN ('OF SPADES');
end;
```

Remember that each clause of the case statement is executed independently. The other clauses are shipped over. If the switch variable, DECK[I].SUIT, fails to match one of the clause labels, the case statement is ignored.

The reader should compile this program with the list option:

(*$L CONSOLE:*)

or

(*$L PRINTER:*)

and study the procedure definitions inserted into the listing by **uses** APPLE-STUFF. Compare these procedure names with the list in Figure 7.1.

Before we move on to an example of user created **units** in the next section, remember these important lessons:

Achtung #1. Include files aid in the management of large programs, but they do not reduce compile time.

Achtung #2. Segments are used strictly for overlaying P-code sections into a small main memory. Segments cannot be used in a unit; they must be compiled in the main program.

Achtung #3. A program may contain one **uses** statement immediately following the **program** statement. One or more **units** may be defined in this way. A **unit** is a collection of pre-compiled procedures and functions which are linked to the main program after translation into P-code.

Now we turn to the more difficult problems of forming **units**, storing them in the SYSTEM.LIBRARY, and linking their modules to other (separately compiled) programs.

7.2 THE LINK EXPERT

Fred owned a shoe store in downtown San Francisco. He decided to use a small computer to keep track of his accounts: accounts receivable for billing his charge customers, payroll for paying his employees, and inventory for keeping up his warehouse and shoe orders. Fred purchased a Pascal system and began writing programs to do these chores. It was not too long before he noticed how often certain functions were used over and over again. For example, he repeatedly used the GOTOXY routine to position the screen cursor before writing a prompt line to the screen. He often needed a way to tab over to a certain line on the screen and begin the prompt.

These repeated and highly useful modules began to take time to compile each time they appeared in the application programs, and they monopolized memory space due to their redundant use. Fred decided to include these modules as pre-compiled entries in the SYSTEM.LIBRARY. Here is Fred's story.

The AT function moves the screen cursor to a line and column just like the GOTOXY intrinsic. But the AT function is easier to use because it can appear in a write or writeln statement. Here is what Fred did to implement AT.

```
function AT (X : COLUMN;
             Y : ROW): char
  begin
    GOTOXY ( X, Y);
    AT := EMPTY;
  end;
```

When AT is executed, an "empty" character is returned (one that means nothing), and the cursor is moved to coordinates (X,Y). The following statement prompts in line 8, column 10.

```
WRITE ( AT ( 10, 8), '[1]. ACCOUNTS RECEIVABLE!);
```

Next, Fred implemented a SKIP function that skips over several columns of a line. This function also returns an "empty" character to the CONSOLE:. Here is the simple routine to output blank spaces.

```
function SKIP ( c : COLUMN): char;
  var
    I : COLUMN;
  begin
    for I :=1 to C do
    WRITE (SPACE);
    SKIP:= EMPTY;
  end;
```

These two routines were used so frequently that Fred decided to include them as pre-compiled modules in the SYSTEM.LIBRARY. To do this, Fred must *encapsulate* these functions within a **unit**. The general form of a Pascal **unit** is as follows.

Note the three major parts of a unit:

1. An interface containing public data accessible to the unit modules as well as any other modules that use the unit;
2. The implementation part containing the two (or more) functions; and
3. The executable initialization code which is executed before any other code in the program.

General Form of a Unit

unit NAME

    interface
        (* public, global data chunk *)
        (* function, procedure definitions *)

    implementation
        (* data chunk for the unit modules *)
        (* modules to be compiled *)

    begin
        (* initialization code *)

    end; (* unit *)

The completed unit in Figure 7.3 contains an interface part which describes the data chunk local to the unit's modules. It also defines the functions AT and SKIP along with their parameter lists. If the program which uses this unit is compiled with the list option turned "on", the interface part will be displayed along with the main program statements.

(*$L CONSOLE:*)

The implementation part contains the modules described earlier. Notice how Fred has dropped the parameter list and type from the definition of AT and SKIP in this part. It is not necessary to repeat the parameters and type again.

The unit global variable EMPTY is common to both functions, but *not* accessible by any other functions. All variables appearing in the interface part are accessible by other modules, however.

The initialization code

begin
    EMPTY :=CHR(0);
end.

```
unit  FORMAT ;

  interface

    type
      COLUMN   = 0 .. 79 ;
      ROW      = 0 .. 23 ;

    function AT ( X : COLUMN ;
                  Y : ROW  ) : char ;

    function SKIP ( C : COLUMN ) : char ;

    implementation

    const
      SPACE    = ' ' ;

    var
      EMPTY    : char ;

    function AT ;
      begin
        GOTOXY ( X, Y ) ;
        AT := EMPTY ;
      end ;

    function SKIP ;
      var
        I   : COLUMN ;
        begin
          for I := 1 to C do
            WRITE( SPACE ) ;
          SKIP := EMPTY ;
        end ;

    begin
      EMPTY := CHR( 0 ) ;
      end .                      (** UNIT **)
```

Figure 7.3. Unit Format

is executed first, even before the main program which uses the modules in FOR-
MAT. Thus, EMPTY is assigned a null character which will be ignored by the
CONSOLE: device.

Suppose we look at a small version of Fred's main program to see how
these unit modules are used. This program merely displays a menu in the middle
of the screen. Note the **uses** statement.

```
program MAIN;

uses FORMAT;

var
    N : integer;

begin
    WRITE ( AT(10,8), '[1].ACCOUNTS RECEIVABLE.');
    WRITE ( AT(10,9), '[2].PAYROLL.');
    WRITELN ( AT(10,10), '[3].INVENTORY.');
    WRITELN;
    WRITE (SKIP (10), 'ENTER A NUMBER',SKIP(5));
    READLN (N);
end.
```

Now that Fred has a unit named FORMAT and a program named MAIN stored on disk, he can compile and link them as follows.

STEPS IN INSTALLING AND USING A UNIT

1. Design and write the external modules you want to pre-compile for repeated use.

2. Insert these modules into a unit according to the general format described above. Also see the example in Figure 7.3.

3. Compile the unit and store its P-code in a code file. The external modules are now pre-compiled and *never* need to be compiled again.

4. If the unit happens to use external procedures or functions itself, then they will have to be linked into the unit's P-code file together with the modules inside the unit. The Linker will be needed to do this, as we will demonstrate for unit FORMAT in the following example.

5. Install the pre-compiled unit in the SYSTEM.LIBRARY using the LIBRARY. CODE (sometimes called the LIBRARIAN) program. See the following example for details on how to do this.

6. Now, any program may use the modules in the installed unit. Suppose we design and write a program which uses the unit (like MAIN). Be sure to include the name of the unit in MAIN:

    uses UNITNAME;

7. Compile the (MAIN) program containing the **uses** statement.

8. Next, use the Linker to connect the unit modules and the other modules already contained in MAIN. (If you work from the SYSTEM.WRK.CODE file you may not need to do this explicitly.)

Well, Fred did all this, and here is what happened. The unit FORMAT compiled and went to UNIT.CODE. The MAIN program compiled and went to MAIN.CODE. The big hurdle facing Fred was step 5: the LIBRARIAN. The unit must be installed *before* we compile MAIN because MAIN must have access to the interface part of all units in uses; so Fred received a compiler error when he attempted to compile MAIN before installing the FORMAT unit in SYSTEM. LIBRARY.

The general idea of LIBRARIAN is as follows. Copy all units from one library file into another. If new units are to be added to an existing file, then copy the unit from one file into the existing file. During the use of the LIBRARIAN an "I/O error #7" may occur, which simply means that a file name could not be located, is misspelled, etc. Fred used the LIBRARY.CODE program to add FORMAT to SYSTEM.LIBRARY, as the following dialogue shows.

eXecute LIBRARY.CODE

Output code file -> NEW.LIBRARY

Link code file -> SYSTEM.LIBRARY

At this point in the dialogue, Fred has told the LIBRARIAN that he wants to create a new library called NEW.LIBRARY using units to be taken from the old SYSTEM.LIBRARY. At this point, the contents of SYSTEM.LIBRARY will be displayed on the screen. They will appear as follows:

Slot Number		(Sequent Number)	Unit Name	Size
0	–	(30)	LONGINTI	2452
1	–	(31)	PASCALIO	1238

The slot number will be used as the number we refer to in the remaining dialogue. All inputs are one of the following:

= copy all units into NEW.LIBRARY
? copy one unit at a time, selectively
N request a new unit to be added to the NEW.LIBRARY
"number" copy this one to NEW.LIBRARY.

Fred typed "=" to get all SYSTEM.LIBRARY units copied into NEW. LIBRARY. After this is done, the new FORMAT unit is installed in NEW. LIBRARY by typing N for new:

Link code file -> UNIT

This opens the code file for FORMAT and causes its slot table to be displayed. They will all be empty, except for one:

7 - (7) FORMAT   100

Thus FORMAT is installed in slot 7 of the P-code of UNIT.CODE. We must move it from this slot into some empty slot of NEW.LIBRARY. This is done as follows:

7
Segment to link into ? 6

This causes slot 7 containing FORMAT to be copied into slot 6 of NEW. LIBRARY. The display will be updated to show this result.

To exit from the LIBRARIAN, Fred typed Q. To abort an entry he would have typed A. The final input is some kind of comment such as a note.

NOTICE ? FORMAT ADDED JAN 10, 1980.

Fred is not yet done. The newly installed unit is not known to the Pascal System until NEW.LIBRARY is copied into old SYSTEM.LIBRARY. We must transfer from the NEW.LIBRARY to SYSTEM.LIBRARY. Since the new library may be larger than the old one, it may be necessary to Krunch the disk and make more space available for the new SYSTEM.LIBRARY.

Fred can compile MAIN now and link the new unit modules into MAIN. CODE. If we tried to execute MAIN.CODE without linking the pre-compiled unit, the system would complain:

Must L(ink first

Before the MAIN.CODE file is executed, Fred types L and gets the following:

Host file?   MAIN
Opening MAIN.CODE
Lib file? *:SYSTEM.LIBRARY
Lib file; ⟨CR⟩

At this point in the linker, Fred has told the system that he wants a file named MAIN to be linked with routines stored in a (LIB) library file called SYSTEM.LIBRARY. If more than one library file is used, additional file names could be entered. Instead, Fred terminated this sequence by entering a carriage return. He also doesn't need a map file, so it is terminated with a carriage return (below).

Map name? ⟨cr⟩

Reading MAIN
Reading FORMAT

Output file? MAIN.CODE

That's it! Fred watched as the Linker opened and read MAIN and FOR-MAT. They were linked and the result stored back into MAIN.CODE. Notice that .CODE is specified in the output P-code file name.

Fred might have checked to make sure the linkage went smoothly. For example, if he tried to link the MAIN program again:

L
Host file? MAIN
Opening MAIN.CODE
All segs linked.

The MAIN program is linked and ready to run. A test run shows that the AT and SKIP modules work as expected. Fred continued to build large programs from smaller programs pre-compiled and installed in SYSTEM.LIBRARY. Let's summarize the sequence of events just described above.

A. The units containing external modules are compiled and their .CODE files saved on disk.

B. The SYSTEM.LIBRARY is updated by adding a new unit(s) to its segment table using LIBRARY.CODE and creating a new SYSTEM. LIBRARY file.

C. The main program is compiled with a **uses** statement which lists the unit names to be used.

D. The main program .CODE file is linked by naming the SYSTEM.LI-BRARY as the file containing external modules.

Remember, this is a software development tool that helps manage large program development. It saves time by removing the repeated compiles normally needed. It helps the programmer deal with details by removing some bookkeeping chores. It saves some space by modularizing the program, but it does not reduce the need for main memory if the program is large. We turn to that problem in the next section. Remember also, the only way to make inherently large programs run on small computers is to overlay sections of the program as needed. This is called **segmenting** and is the reason why Pascal provides the **segment** module.

7.3   SEGMENTS EVERYWHERE, BUT NOT A BYTE TO SPARE

A Pascal **segment** is a module which may reside on disk until it is called by
a running program. The running program is temporarily stopped until the segment module is copied into main memory. Next the P-code interpreter passes
control to the newly overlaid segment in main memory, and program execution
continues.

A program may consist of up to 16 segments; but because the System
uses segments also, the user program is limited to 7 segments. Segments can be
mixed with other modules (**units, function, procedure**) as long as the segment
modules are *defined before any other code generating modules.* We can define
up to seven segments in a program with the following shape:

```
program MAIN;
   uses UNIT1, UNIT2;
   procedure A ; forward;
   function B (X : integer); forward;
   segment procedure C1;
   segment procedure C2;

            ...
   segment procedure C7;
   procedure A; begin . . . end;
   function B; begin . . . end;
begin
   (* main program code *)
end.
```

Notice the shape of the program with respect to the **forward** reference
modules. Since the segments *must* be defined first, and since they *may* reference procedure A and/or function B, we *must* define these "global" modules
afterwards, as shown. The **uses** statement must be the second statement in the
program, of course, but since it does not produce P-code during the compila-
tion of the MAIN program, it does not violate the rules concerning segments.

The reader should be cautioned against a very subtle error that is often
committed when using segments. The segments may use a forward reference
module, but the module must be defined globally rather than locally in order
to result in code. The following shape will cause the system to fail to produce
P-code output from the Compiler:

```
program ERROR;
   segment procedure C1;
      procedure BAD; forward;
      begin . . . end; (* C1 *)
   procedure BAD;
      begin ... end; (* BAD *)
```

begin
   (* program ERROR will not compile *)
end.

In other words, beware of forward references from a segment to a global (MAIN) program definition of the reference.

Now, let's revisit Fred's shoe store to take a closer look at the package developed for accounting. The package consists of three parts: (1) ACCOUNTS RECEIVABLE, (2) PAYROLL, and (3) INVENTORY. Each one of these is in itself a sizable program. Thus Fred's PACKAGE is actually a collection of programs, as shown in Figure 7.4. We have shown part of the overall system only. If necessary, Fred will segment other procedures and functions in order to fit each of the subsystems into main memory.

We will abbreviate the program listing of Figure 7.5 so that the ideas are not clouded; but keep in mind that a "real-world" system would be much more complex than the one shown for Fred's PACKAGE. The shape of the PACKAGE conforms to the organization chart of Figure 7.4:

program PACKAGE;

uses FORMAT;

procedure CLEAR; **forward**

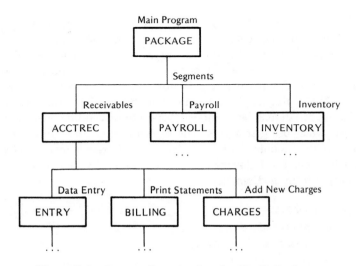

Figure 7.4. System Organization for Fred's Package

```
segment procedure ACCTREC;

        procedure ENTRY; begin . . . end;
        procedure BILLING; begin . . . end;
        procedure CHARGES; begin . . . end;
        begin

            . . .

               case J of
                  1:ENTRY;
                  2:BILLING;
                  3:CHARGES;
               end;

            . . .

        end;

segment procedure PAYROLL;
        begin . . . end;

segment procedure INVENTORY;
        begin . . . end;

begin

    . . .

    Case J of
       1:ACCTREC;
       2:PAYROLL;
       3:INVENTORY;
    end;

end.
```

Fred could have segmented the internal modules, ENTRY,BILLING, and CHARGES, if memory space dictated. In each case, the program must be copied from disk, loaded into memory, and then control passed to it before program execution can resume; therefore, the price paid for segmenting is speed.

Segmented programs run slower than non-segmented programs; therefore, the system should be designed to take advantage of natural breaks in user/system interaction. Menus are a good place to divide programs. The PACKAGE of Figure 7.5 overlays a different segment for each menu used to prompt the user. Thus the delay is barely noticed.

When PACKAGE is compiled the modules from FORMAT must be linked again. The dialogue for doing this is shown below.

```
(*$L CONSOLE:*)
program  PACKAGE ;

  uses  FORMAT ;

  var
    J   : integer ;
    NUM : set of 1 .. 3 ;
  (* THE USUAL GLOBAL DATA AND MODULES GO HERE   *)
  (* NOTE : SEGMENTS MUST BE FIRST, BEFORE OTHER MODULES *)

   segment procedure ACCTREC ;

     (* THE USUAL DATA AND MODULES GO HERE *)
     var
       CH  :  char ;

     procedure CLEAR ; forward ;

     procedure ENTRY ;

       begin
         CLEAR ;
         WRITELN( 'ENTER ACCOUNTS' ) ;
         READLN ( CH ) ;
       end ;   (* ENTRY *)

     procedure BILLING ;

       begin
         CLEAR ;
         WRITELN( 'PRINT BILLS' ) ;
         READLN ( CH ) ;
       end ;   (* BILLING *)

     procedure CHARGES ;

       begin
         CLEAR ;
         WRITELN( 'ADD NEW CHARGES' ) ;
         READLN ( CH ) ;
       end ;   (* CHARGES *)

     begin               (*   ACCTREC SUBSYSTEM   *)
       repeat
         CLEAR ;
         WRITE  ( AT( 15, 5 ), '[1]. ENTER ACCOUNTS.' ) ;
         WRITE  ( AT( 15, 7 ), '[2]. DO BILLING.' ) ;
         WRITE  ( AT( 15, 9 ), '[3]. ADD CHARGES.' ) ;
         WRITE  ( AT( 15,12 ), '[ ]?' ) ;
         WRITE  ( AT( 16,12 ) ) ;
         READLN ( J ) ;
         case J of
           1 : ACCTREC ;
           2 : BILLING ;
           3 : CHARGES ;
         end ;
       until not ( J in NUM ) ;
     end ;              (* SEGMENT ACCTREC OVERLAY *)
```

```
segment procedure PAYROLL ;

  (* THE USUAL DATA AND MODULES GO HERE *)

  procedure CLEAR ; forward ;

  var
    CH  : char ;
  begin
    CLEAR ;
    WRITE  ( AT( 30,12 ), 'BILLING', SKIP( 10 ), 'OK?' ) ;
    READLN ( CH ) ;
  end ;   (* PAYROLL *)

segment procedure INVENTORY ;

  (* DATA CHUNK GOES HERE *)
  (* INTERNAL MODULES, TOO *)

  var
    CH  :  char ;

  procedure CLEAR ; forward ;

  begin
    CLEAR ;
    WRITE  ( AT ( 30,12 ), 'INVENTORY', SKIP( 10 ), 'OK?' ) ;
    READLN ( CH ) ;
  end ;   (* INVENTORY *)

procedure CLEAR ;

  var
    I : 0 .. 23 ;
  begin
    for I := 0 to 23 do
      WRITELN( SKIP( 79 ) ) ;
  end ;  (* CLEAR *)


  begin     (* M A I N   M E N U *)
    NUM := [ 1, 2, 3 ] ;
    repeat
      CLEAR ;
      WRITE  ( AT( 20,10 ), '[1]. RECEIVABLES.' ) ;
      WRITE  ( AT( 20,12 ), '[2]. PAYROLL.' ) ;
      WRITE  ( AT( 20,14 ), '[3]. INVENTORY.' ) ;
      WRITE  ( AT( 20,17 ), '[ ]. ?' ) ;
      WRITE  ( AT( 21,17 ) ) ; READLN ( J ) ;
      case J of
        1 : ACCTREC ;
        2 : PAYROLL ;
        3 : INVENTORY ;
      end ;
    until not ( J in NUM )   ;
  end .
```

Figure 7.5. PACKAGE

L(ink

Host file? PACKAGE
Opening PACKAGE.CODE
Lib file? *: SYSTEM.LIBRARY
Lib file? ⟨cr⟩
Map file? ⟨cr⟩
Reading PACKAGE
Reading FORMAT
Output file? PACKAGE.CODE
Linking FORMAT #7
Linking ACCTREC #8
Linking PAYROLL #9
Linking INVENTOR #10
Linking PACKAGE #1

Notice the ⟨cr⟩ (carriage returns) which signal a "don't care" situation. The Map file is discarded. Be sure to specify a .CODE file as output. Hence, the PACKAGE.CODE *must* be entered, rather than PACKAGE.

The segments are linked into their slots in their respective segment tables. Thus slots 1,7,8,9,10 are linked as shown.

We can summarize the important features of this chapter as follows:

A. Include files (*$Ifilename*) can be used to merge together more than one text file during compiles. The advantage of this is the modularity and system development management tool it provides. The disadvantage is the compile time it takes.

B. Modules can be lumped together into a unit. The collective modules in the unit are compiled, stored in SYSTEM.LIBRARY, for instance, and then linked to other programs as needed. Advantage: they do not need to be compiled over and over again. Disadvantage: they must be stored in the library beforehand and linked. Also, they do not save memory space directly.

C. Modules can be segmented so that they do *not* simultaneously reside in main memory while the main program is being executed. Advantages are obvious; we can run large programs on small computers. The disadvantage is that the program runs slower.

The techniques studied in this chapter will serve application programmers well. Careful study and attention to the details will be rewarded.

7.4 BONUS FEATURES

The Apple Pascal system permits assembly language modules to be linked together with P-code modules. It also permits P-code **units** to be linked from files other than SYSTEM.LIBRARY. We give examples of how this is done in each case.

First, suppose two assembly language programs have been assembled and stored in disk file, EXTRA. Module FRED is a function, and module PETE is a procedure. In assembler language, we would define FRED and PETE as follows:

```
.PROC PETE,2   ;  TWO WORDS FOR PARAMETERS.
   . . .       ;  BODY OF PROCEDURE
.END           ;  END OF PETE.
```

Likewise, the function is defined in assembler language:

```
.FUNC FRED,1   ;  ONE WORD PARAMETER.
   . . .       ;  BODY OF FUNCTION
.END           ;  END OF FRED
```

The Pascal program must define the parameter list for each module it uses. Thus we must define PETE and FRED as **external** modules and then link them to the main Pascal program *after all modules have been translated.* Suppose we use these two modules in a Pascal program called MAIN.

```
program MAIN;
   var
      A, Y : real;

   . . .
procedure PETE (M,N; integer);
   external;
function FRED (T : real) : integer;
   external;

begin
   . . .
end.
```

The program above defines PETE and FRED as *external* modules. Notice how the Compiler marks these as undefined modules when they are encountered in the MAIN program text. It will be the linker's job to define these two external modules by linking them to the main program before it is run.

Assembly language modules can be linked into Pascal programs by (1) pre-assembling the modules (2) defining the modules in a Pascal program as **external**, and (3) linking the external modules using the system linker.

The second bonus feature of the Apple Pascal system is the "uses library option" in the Compiler. This option makes *any* pre-compiled (P-code) file a library file. Thus modules from separate .CODE files can be linked into program MAIN merely by overriding the default SYSTEM.LIBRARY file.

Since only one **uses** statement is allowed within a program, the $U option must be imbedded within the only **uses** statement.

Suppose three **units**, U1,U2,U3, stored in files U1.CODE, U2.CODE, and U3.CODE, respectively, are to be linked into MAIN. The following program might be used:

```
program MAIN
    uses  (*$U U1.CODE*) U1,
          (*$U U2.CODE*) U2,
          (*$U U3.CODE*) U3;
```

Notice the commas in the *single* statement above. The Compiler directives can be placed anywhere before the unit's name. Also, note the space between $U and the file name. Do not confuse this option with the $U+, or $U– option!

In summary, pre-compiled units can be linked into a MAIN program by first declaring them in a **uses** statement containing the $U directive, and then by linking them into the MAIN program using the linker.

```
Lib file? U1
Lib file? U2
Lib file? U3
Lib file? ⟨cr⟩
```

The linker will do the rest. A Pascal program may contain a mixture of P-code from the user's main programs, SYSTEM.LIBRARY, .CODE files, and machine code modules from preassembled .PROC and .FUNC files.

TWENTY QUESTIONS

1. What do we mean when we say a program is big?
2. How can we overcome large data problems?
3. Why can a user only use 7 segments instead of 16?
4. Write a compiler directive to merge text file NOMAD into a program during translation.
5. What is a *unit*?
6. Why don't we have to link the units of Figure 7.1 into the programs that use them?
7. The random number generator intrinsic is found in a unit. Which one?
8. A raffle program could be written to shuffle a list of tickets. If 10,000 tickets are to be randomized, can we use SHUFFLE?

9. Write a statement to generate a random integer between the values of 50 and 100.

10. Why is this illegal in Pascal?

```
var
   J : string [1] ;
begin
      READLN (J);
         case J of
         'A' : ADAM;
         'B' : BAKER;
   end;
```

11. How many **uses** statements are allowed in a program?

12. How many **units** are permitted to be used by a Pascal program?

13. What are units really designed for?

14. What are segments really designed for?

15. What are the three parts of a **unit**?

16. What does EMPTY := CHR(0); do?

17. What is the purpose of LIBRARY.CODE?

18. What is the purpose of SYSTEM.LINKER?

19. Is it necessary to restart the system every time the SYSTEM.LIBRARY is changed?

20. Can we use both units and segments in the same program?

ANSWERS

1. It takes lots of data and memory or consists of too many separate modules.

2. Use files, instead of large arrays, etc.

3. The system uses 9 of them.

4. (*$INOMAD.TEXT*)

5. A collection of modules, their data, and an initialization section of code. Units are pre-compiled.

6. Intrinsic units are automatically linked for you.

7. Applestuff.

8. Not without changing N to 10,000 and modifying the data chunk. Otherwise, the concepts are identical.

9. I := 50 + RANDOM **mod** 51;

10. The case statement works on scalars, and J is not a scalar.

11. One.

12. Seven, but they must be declared in only one **uses**.

13. To save compiling the same programs over, again.

14. To save main memory space.

15. Interface, Implementation, and Initialization sections.

16. It is a nasty, evil trick which should never be allowed in a program.

17. This is a program to insert a unit into a library.

18. To link together separate modules.

19. Yes.

20. Yes, but units may *not* contain segments themselves.

Chapter 8

Star-Spangled Graphics

"To make graphics easy for children who might have difficulty under-standing Cartesian coordinates, Papert et al. invented the idea of a 'turtle' who could walk a given distance and turn through a specified angle while dragging a pencil along."

Apple Pascal Reference Manual
Jef Raskin and Brian Howard, Eds.

8.1 PIXEL LAND

The Apple-to-TV interface consists of two separate "screen memories". The *character screen* holds all letters and numbers seen when using the keyboard. We say the screen is in TEXTMODE whenever it is used to display characters. Alternately, the *picture screen* holds line drawings, colored areas, and a limited number of character strings. We say the screen is in GRAFMODE whenever it is used to display pictures.

The picture screen is divided into 53,760 tiny dots called *pixels*. Each pixel is "colored" one of the 13 possible shades as defined by the TURTLE-GRAPHICS unit.

> **type**
> SCREENCOLOR = (NONE,WHITE, BLACK, REVERSE, RADAR,
>   BLACK1, GREEN, VIOLET, WHITE1, BLACK2,
>   ORANGE, BLUE, WHITE2);

Figure 8.1 illustrates the array of pixels, showing how they are arranged in 192 rows with 280 pixels in each row. Thus the upper left-hand corner of the picture screen is numbered row 191, column zero when in GRAFMODE (compare this with the GOTOXY designation of row zero when in TEXTMODE).

The table of Figure 8.1 (b) lists the colors available for coloring pixels. The pseudo-colors (NONE, REVERSE, and RADAR) are actually *control* colors:

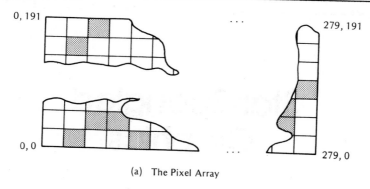

(a)   The Pixel Array

Number	Color	Complement(REVERSE)
0	NONE	
1	WHITE	BLACK
2	BLACK	WHITE
3	REVERSE	
4	RADAR	
5	BLACK1	WHITE1 (6, 7)
6	GREEN	VIOLET
7	VIOLET	GREEN
8	WHITE1	BLACK1 (6, 7)
9	BLACK2	WHITE2 (10, 11)
10	ORANGE	BLUE
11	BLUE	ORANGE
12	WHITE2	BLACK2 (10, 11)

(b)   Color Scheme

Figure 8.1.   GRAFMODE Uses Pixels of Various Colors

NONE : Causes no change to the picture screen. This is used to lift the TUR-
TLE and move him to another pixel without leaving a trail.

REVERSE :   This control color puts the GRAFMODE screen in a complement
mode. The colors are changed according to the complements
shown in Figure 8.1(b).

RADAR :   Unused. Perhaps this will be used in future versions.

Notice the absence of certain colors (e.g., RED and YELLOW are not available). This is because of the way most color televisions work internally. Also, notice the pair of numbers next to WHITE1 and WHITE2 in Figure 8.1 (b). Because of the way TV exaggerates some colors and not others, the WHITE1 pixels should be drawn next to GREEN and VIOLET (#6 and #7) pixels; the WHITE2 pixels should be drawn next to the ORANGE and BLUE pixels, etc. If

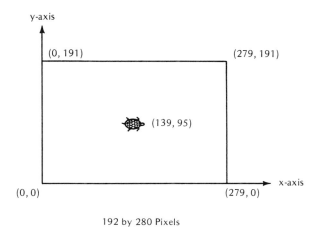

192 by 280 Pixels

Figure 8.2. GRAFMODE Picture Screen Format. Initially the turtle is at the center, facing right.

we do not do this, often the colors will appear to overlap, run over their boundaries, or appear as "clumps" rather than a thin line.

We can summarize the concepts underlying GRAFMODE as follows:

A. The GRAFMODE screen consists of 192 times 280 dots called pixels. The pixels are arranged in 192 rows of length 280 each.

B. Each pixel is colored by one of the 12 "colors", some of which may overlap unless we are careful of how they are mixed.

C. The GRAFMODE screen has its *origin* (pixel zero,zero) located at the lower left-hand corner of the TV screen.

We saw the *shape* of a graphics program in Chapter 3. Recall that the intrinsic functions for controlling the TV screen are pre-compiled and stored in unit TURTLEGRAPHICS. This is done to avoid lengthy searching every time a program is compiled (without GRAFMODE); but note that TURTLEGRAPH-ICS is an *intrinsic unit*, and it does *not* need to be linked after translation.

Every graphics program must have a *uses* statement containing TURTLE-GRAPHICS and an INITTURTLE call to initialize the graphics routines. The following program produces an *initial state* of GRAFMODE, as shown in Figure 8.2.

```
program START;
  uses TURTLEGRAPHICS;
  begin
    INITTURTLE;
  end.
```

The turtle is *never* seen in a GRAFMODE program. Neither are the boundaries of the 192 x 280 pixels. Thus the *initial state* shown in Figure 8.2 is a *virtual* image we use to imagine what will happen next. Suppose we select a small portion of the total picture from Figure 8.2 so we can work within a smaller virtual image. Say, for example, we choose to work with the rectangle defined by:

LEFT CORNER   = 100
RIGHT CORNER   = 200
BOTTOM CORNER   = 50
TOP SIDE   = 120

We can select a piece of the total GRAFMODE screen by defining a viewport to contain any drawing. Thus a *virtual box* is defined as follows:

VIEWPORT (100, 200, 50, 120);

In general, we can select any virtual region from the total screen by giving the integers which define the corners and sides:

VIEWPORT (LEFT, RIGHT, BOTTOM, TOP);

Any movements of the turtle outside this box are ignored. Any movements inside this box are recorded and displayed.

Now, let's draw a simple flag to illustrate how the viewport works with other GRAFMODE functions. Figure 8.3 shows how to lay out a collection of virtual boxes shaped like the stars-and-stripes.

The Pascal program for displaying the ORANGE, WHITE2, and BLUE flag is sketched in Figure 8.4. The WHITE2 shade is employed because it is compatible with a BLUE boundary. The ORANGE shade is used to simulate RED.

The idea behind program FLAG is quite simple; (1) define a viewport, and

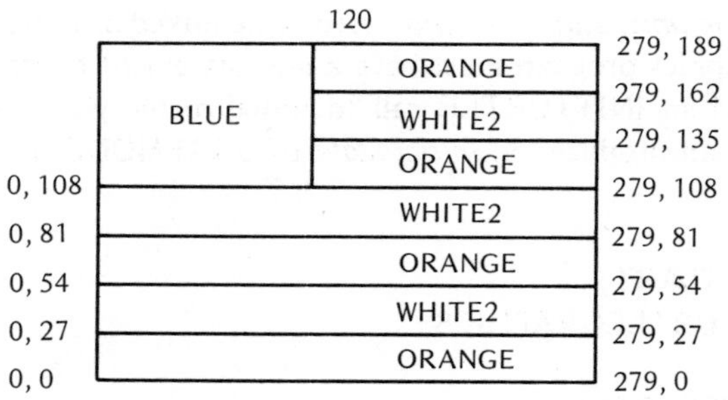

Figure 8.3. Design of Stars and Stripes

```
program FLAG ;

  uses TURTLEGRAPHICS ;

  begin

    INITTURTLE ;

    VIEWPORT( 0, 279,   0,  27 ) ; FILLSCREEN( ORANGE ) ;
    VIEWPORT( 0, 279,  27,  54 ) ; FILLSCREEN( WHITE2 ) ;
    VIEWPORT( 0, 279,  54,  81 ) ; FILLSCREEN( ORANGE ) ;
    VIEWPORT( 0, 279,  81, 108 ) ; FILLSCREEN( WHITE2 ) ;

    VIEWPORT(120, 279, 108, 135 ) ; FILLSCREEN( ORANGE ) ;
    VIEWPORT(120, 279, 135, 162 ) ; FILLSCREEN( WHITE2 ) ;
    VIEWPORT(120, 279, 162, 189 ) ; FILLSCREEN( ORANGE ) ;

    VIEWPORT( 0,  120, 108, 189 ) ; FILLSCREEN( BLUE ) ;

  end.
```

Figure 8.4.   FLAG

(2) fill the viewport with a solid color. We used another intrinsic from TURTLE-GRAPHICS to cause all pixels within the viewport to be colored. The general form of FILLSCREEN is

FILLSCREEN (colortype);

where colortype must be one of the colors selected from Figure 8.1(b).

The example above illustrates a simple method of placing squares, rectangles, and approximations to triangles, discs, etc., on the picture screen. It is *not* a very good way to draw irregular shapes, circles, or *open* figures. To do this, we can use a combination of the paddle wheels and television graphics.

8.2   THE ELECTRIC ARTIST

Suppose we want to "draw" an arbitrary figure on the picture screen. The figure may be a handwritten signature, a floor plan for a house, a model airplane sketch, or a wiring diagram.

Many special-purpose input tablets might be used for this purpose, but we can develop a low-cost solution using the paddle wheels already available. The paddle wheel intrinsics are pre-compiled in unit APPLESTUFF. Paddle wheels VERT (0) and HORIZON (1) are used in the following example.

VERT controls the angle of the turtle's path, while HORIZON controls the distance moved. Each paddle generates an integer between zero and 255, depending on the clockwise rotation of the paddle wheel.

0 <= PADDLE (VERT) <= 255

0 <= PADDLE (HORIZON) <=255

But we want to control a 360-degree angle and a viewport of up to 280 pixels (as illustrated in Figure 8.5). Therefore, we must scale-up the integer value returned by the paddle wheel setting. This is done by the following assignment to JUMP and ANGLE.

JUMP :=280.0 * PADDLE(HORIZON)/255.0;
ANGLE := 360.0 * PADDLE (VERT) /255.0;

We *coerced* the integer value returned by PADDLE into a **real** value by writing 255.0 and 360.0 instead. The real valued ANGLE and JUMP must be converted back into integers before being used by any of the GRAFMODE intrinsics (they *all* take integer parameters).

There is a flaw in the design of program STEAR so far. We cannot control *when* the computer might read (sample) the paddle wheel setting. In fact, the computer will read the settings so fast that an artist could never keep up.

We can slow the computer to an artist's pace by sampling the paddle wheel settings *only* when the paddle BUTTON is pressed. BUTTON is true when it is pressed and false at all other times. Thus we can synchronize the artist and the computer using a simple wait loop as shown.

While not BUTTON (HORIZON) **do;**
JUMP :=280.0 * PADDLE(HORIZON)/255.0;

The while loop is an *empty* loop. All it does is repeatedly test the boolean value of BUTTON. When BUTTON is **true, not** BUTTON is **false,** and the while loop terminates. When the loop terminates, the wheel setting is quickly read and used to compute JUMP.

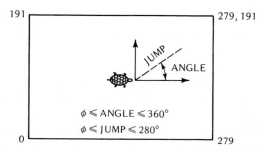

Figure 8.5. Idea Behind a Paddle-Wheel-Controlled Turtle

This same idea is used to synchronize the other paddle wheel. If we had not used this mechanism, the computer would have sampled the wheels too fast for even the paddle wheels. This would lead to a run-time error in Pascal. To avoid the run-time error, we could have put a delay in the program which merely wastes some time. For example,

for I:=1 **to** 3 **do**;

will stall long enough to let the paddle wheel catch up.

The program of Figure 8.6 uses two GRAFMODE intrinsics to move the turtle around the screen. The TURNTO intrinsic causes the turtle to point in the direction given by ANGLE.

TURNTO (DIRECTION)

DIRECTION must be an integer in the range 0..360. If DIRECTION is 0 or 360, the turtle moves horizontally to the right. If DIRECTION is 180, the turtle backs up to the left (horizontally).

We could also have used the alternate intrinsic which *adds* the current direction to the new value;

TURN (DIRECTION).

```
(*$L CONSOLE:*)
Program  STEAR ;

  uses TURTLEGRAPHICS, APPLESTUFF ;

  const
    FOREVER = FALSE;
    VERT    = 0 ;
    HORIZON = 1 ;

  var
    JUMP    : real ;
    ANGLE   : real ;

  begin
    INiTTURTLE ;
    FILLSCREEN( BLUE ) ;
    PENCOLOR( ORANGE) ;
      repeat
        while not BUTTON( HORIZON ) do ;
        JUMP := 280.0 * PADDLE( HORIZON ) / 255.0 ;
        while not BUTTON( VERT ) do ;
        ANGLE:= 360.0 * PADDLE( VERT ) / 255.0 ;
        TURNTO( TRUNC( ANGLE ) )° ;
        MOVE  ( TRUNC( JUMP ) ) ;
      until FOREVER ;
    TEXTMODE ;
  end.
```

Figure 8-6. Program STEAR Demonstrates BUTTON and PADDLE

If this is used twice in succession the turtle is turned in an increasing angle.

    TURN (100);
    TURN (80);

These two turns add up to 180 degrees.

Figure 8.6 also shows how to use the MOVE intrinsic to cause the turtle to move from its present location to some distant location.

    MOVE (DISTANCE);

The turtle leaves a trail from its current location to a spot at angle DIRECTION and distance DISTANCE. We could also have used the MOVETO (X, Y) intrinsic to cause the turtle to move to the pixel at location (X,Y) regardless of the current location. The following sequence causes the turtle to walk the boundary of the picture screen.

    MOVETO (0,0);
    MOVETO (279.0);
    MOVETO (279,191);
    MOVETO (0,191);
    MOVETO (0,0);

Next, we notice the PENCOLOR intrinsic in Figure 8.6. This simply selects which color is used by turtle when drawing a line. The parameter, COLOR, must be one of the scalars listed in Figure 8.1(b). The turtle can be moved secretly (without leaving a mark) using PENCOLOR(NONE). Thus a better version of the screen boundary is:

    INITTURTLE;
    PENCOLOR (NONE);
    MOVETO (0,0);
    PENCOLOR (WHITE2);
    MOVETO (279,0);
    MOVETO (279,191);
    MOVETO (0,191);
    MOVETO (0,0);

As a final example of a simple graphics program consider the problem of plotting a line in the x,y plane. Suppose we want to plot the function shown in Figure 8.7. The straight line is given as

    $Y = M*X + B.$

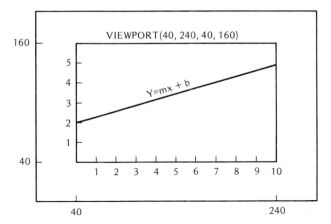

Figure 8.7.   Plotting a Function

We can plot this function on a blue background with a white border as follows:

```
VIEWPORT (30,250,30,170);
FILLSCREEN (WHITE);
VIEWPORT (40,240,40,160);
FILLSCREEN (BLUE);
```

This places the origin of the X,Y - axis coordinate system at pixel (40,40), see Figure 8.7. The actual straight line is drawn with the MOVETO intrinsic shown below.

```
PENCOLOR (BLACK2);
   for X := 1 to 10 do
      begin
         Y := M * X + B;
         MOVETO (TRUNC (20 * X + 40),
                  TRUNC (20 * Y + 40));
      end;
```

A BLUE background interacts with a BLACK line, so we use BLACK2 instead. The line is placed inside the viewport by adding 40 to each (X,Y) point. Finally, each point in the graph is worth 20 pixels on the screen, so we scale-up by a factor of 20. TRUNC is used to guarantee an integer parameter for MOVETO.

```
program  PLOT ;

  uses TURTLEGRAPHICS ;

  var
    M, B, Y : real ;
    X       : integer ;

  procedure AXIS ;

    var
      TICK : integer ;
      TACK : string[ 1 ] ;

    begin
      VIEWPORT(  30, 250,  30, 170 ) ;
      FILLSCREEN( WHITE ) ;
      VIEWPORT(  40, 240,  40, 160 ) ;
      FILLSCREEN( BLUE ) ;
      PENCOLOR( NONE ) ;
      MOVETO(  40,  40 ) ;
      TURNTO( 0 ) ;
      PENCOLOR( BLACK2 ) ;
      for TICK := 1 to 9 do
        begin
          STR( TICK, TACK ) ;
          MOVE( 20 ) ;
          WSTRING( TACK ) ;
          TURNTO( 180 ) ;
          MOVE( 7 ) ;
          TURNTO( 0 ) ;
        end ;           (* for *)
      PENCOLOR( NONE ) ;
      MOVETO(  40,  40 ) ;
      TURNTO( 90 ) ;
      PENCOLOR( BLACK2 ) ;
      for TICK := 1 to 5 do
        begin
          STR( TICK, TACK ) ;
          MOVE( 20 ) ;
          WSTRING( TACK ) ;
          TURNTO( 180 ) ;
          MOVE( 7 ) ;
          TURNTO( 90 ) ;
        end ;           (* for *)
      PENCOLOR( NONE ) ;
      MOVETO(  40,  40 ) ;
    end ;     (* AXIS *)

  begin
    INITTURTLE ;
    TEXTMODE ;
    WRITE( 'ENTER SLOPE = ') ; READLN( M ) ;
    WRITE( 'ENTER INTERCEPT = ' ) ; READLN( B ) ;
    GRAFMODE ;
    AXIS ;
    PENCOLOR( NONE ) ;
    MOVETO(  40, TRUNC( 20 * B ) + 40 ) ;
    PENCOLOR( BLACK2 ) ;
    for X := 1 to 10 do
      begin
        Y := M * X + B ;
        MOVETO( TRUNC( 20 * X + 40 ), TRUNC( 20 * Y + 40 ) ) ;
      end ;     (* for X *)
  end.
```

Figure 8.8. PLOT

Figure 8.8 contains **procedure** AXIS that draws the BLUE coordinate system with a WHITE boundary and labels both axes with numbers. The WSTRING function outputs a string of characters to the picture screen. Notice how the integer value TICK is converted to a string of characters, TACK by intrinsic STR.

Each character of WSTRING takes 7 pixels in the X-axis direction. Thus after outputting the single-character numeral, we turn the turtle around to 180 degrees and walk back 7 pixels. Thus the sequence

```
WSTRING (TACK);
TURNTO (180)
MOVE (7)
```

performs the numerical labeling operation you see when PLOT is executed.

Clearly, the program in Figure 8.8 can be generalized. First, we could change the function plotted from a straight line to some other shape. For example, to plot a quadratic (parabola) function we write instead:

$$Y := M * SQR(X) + B;$$

Try substituting this in place of the straight-line formula of PLOT.

Another modification of PLOT would cause a bar-chart to be displayed in place of a line. For example, if BARCHART is a procedure, then we can replace the body of PLOT with:

```
for X := 1 to 10 do
   begin
      Y := M * X + B;
      BARCHART (Y,X);
   end;
```

where the VIEWPORT intrinsic is used to make bars.

```
procedure BARCHART (HEIGHT: real;
                           LOCATION : integer);
   var
      X, Y : integer;

   begin
      X := 20*LOCATION + 40;
      Y := TRUNC (20 * HEIGHT + 40);
      VIEWPORT ( X-10, X+10, 40, Y);
      FILLSCREEN (BLACK2);
   end;
```

This module draws a solid-color bar at location (X–10). The bar is 20 pixels wide and 20*HEIGHT pixels high.

The GRAFMODE routines can be summarized below.

INITTURTLE : initializes the GRAFMODE modules and places the turtle in the center of the screen.

TURN,TURNTO : turn the turtle through 0..360 degrees.

MOVE,MOVETO : moves the turtle a given distance in the direction given by TURN or TURNTO, moves to pixel coordinates given in the MOVETO intrinsic.

TEXTMODE, GRAFMODE : changes the mode from graphics to text or vice-versa.

PENCOLOR : selects the color of the turtle's pencil.

FILLSCREEN : color the viewport a given color.

VIEWPORT : selects a portion of the overall screen.

TURTLEX,TURTLEY : returns the (X,Y) location of the turtle.

TURTLEANG : returns the current direction of the turtle.

WCHAR, WSTRING: outputs a character or string of characters while in GRAFMODE.

SCREENBIT: returns FALSE if the pixel at location (X,Y) is BLACK.

DRAWBLOCK : draws an entire screen, a pixel at a time. See the next section.

CHARTYPE : sets the mode of output for all characters handled by WCHAR and WSTRING.

In the next section we study the last two intrinsics in more detail. We will also learn how to save a picture on disk, retrieve it, and display it once again. We will then be limited only by imagination!

8.3 ONCE IS NOT ENOUGH

One display of a picture may not be enough.[*] There are times when we may want to develop a picture, store it on disk, and then retrieve it from disk for re-display on the screen. Unfortunately, the Pascal intrinsics for reading a picture from the screen are very limited. In fact, we only have one intrinsic for doing this. The SCREENBIT (X,Y) function is TRUE if the pixel at location (X,Y) is *not* black. BLACK, BLACK1 or BLACK2 return FALSE through SCREENBIT.

Suppose we develop a program to save the straight-line plots of the previous section on disk. We will need an *image* of the screen as illustrated in Figure 8.9. The (XSCREEN, YSCREEN) coordinates designate the location of the picture relative to the pixels on the screen. This means we can place a picture anywhere in the range [0..191, 0..279]. If we choose to put the picture at location (30,30), then

---

*These programs were run using a separate display television. The reader may want to modify them to switch between TEXTMODE and GRAFMODE more often.

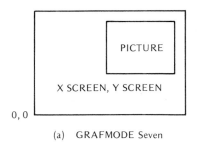

(a)   GRAFMODE Seven

Y STOP

. . .   PICTURE

Y START
        X START   . . .   X STOP
        _____/
                    WIDTH
(b)   Boolean Array [Y START . . . Y STOP, X START . . . X STOP]

Figure 8.9.   GRAFMODE Screen and Boolean Array

XSCREEN = 30
YSCREEN = 30

and we *map* the array of Figure 8.9(b) into the PICTURE region of Figure 8.9(a).

Suppose we define a region equal in size to the plots made by program PLOT, Figure 8.8.

type
    PICTURES = **packed array** [30..170, 30..250] **of boolean**;

Now, we can access every pixel inside this array by indexing the [Y,X] subscripts of a variable of type PICTURES. Suppose we create a disk file window variable of this type.

var
    PICFILE : **file of** PICTURES;

This allows us to store the pixels in a disk file, if only we can access the pixels on the screen. This is where function SCREENBIT comes in! The following section of Pascal copies the pixels from the screen into the file window variable and then stores the entire window on disk.

```
REWRITE (PICFILE, 'GRAF:PICTURES');

for Y := 30 to 170 do
  for X := 30 to 250 do
    PICFILE∧[Y,X] := SCREENBIT (X,Y);
PUT (PICFILE);
```

This method works, but unfortunately it has two drawbacks: (1) it is slower than an insurance claim, and (2) it does *not* copy the color of the pixels.

The two loops above repeat 140*220 = 30,800 times. This takes several minutes to complete! Each boolean value is packed into the file window, and this makes the section of iterative code even more delayed.

Curiously, the boolean values stored in the disk file PICFILE interact with the GRAFMODE modules so we can recreate colors using FILLSCREEN as shown in Figure 8.10. The **case** construct provides this, see the program.

We check the file by reading the first record back from disk:

```
RESET (PICFILE, 'GRAF:PICTURES');

DRAWBLOCK (PICFILE∧,
            28 ,        (*ROWSIZE *)
            0,0,        (* START *)
            220,140,    (* STOP *)
            30, 30,     (* X,Y-SCREEN *)
            10   );     (* MODE *)
```

The DRAWBLOCK procedure copies the array of pixels stored in PICFILE∧ onto the screen. The mapping is done just as shown in Figure 8.9. The ROWSIZE is computed from the definition of PICTURES. In general,

```
type
    PICTURES=packed array [XSTART..XSTOP, YSTART..YSTOP]
             of boolean;
```

Thus,

```
ROWSIZE:= 2*((XSTOP-XSTART + 15) div 16);
```

```
program PICFILES ;

  uses TURTLEGRAPHICS ;

  type
    PICTURES  =  packed array[ 30..170, 30..250 ] of boolean ;

  var
    PICFILE   :  file of PICTURES ;
    X, Y      :  integer ;
    COLOR     :  1 .. 5 ;
    CH        :  char ;

  procedure PLOT ;

    var
      M, B, Y : real ;
      X       : integer ;

    procedure AXIS ;

      var
        TICK : integer ;
        TACK : string[ 1 ] ;

      begin
        VIEWPORT(  40, 240,  40, 160 ) ;
        PENCOLOR( NONE ) ;
        MOVETO(  40,  40 ) ;
        TURNTO( 0 ) ;
        PENCOLOR( BLACK2 ) ;
        CHARTYPE( 6 ) ;
        for TICK := 1 to 9 do
          begin
            STR( TICK, TACK ) ;
            MOVE( 20 ) ;
            WSTRING( TACK ) ;
            TURNTO( 180 ) ;
            MOVE( 7 ) ;
            TURNTO( 0 ) ;
          end ;            (* for *)
        PENCOLOR( NONE ) ;
        MOVETO(  40,  40 ) ;
        TURNTO( 90 ) ;
        PENCOLOR( BLACK2 ) ;
        for TICK := 1 to 5 do
          begin
            STR( TICK, TACK ) ;
            MOVE( 20 ) ;
            WSTRING( TACK ) ;
            TURNTO( 180 ) ;
            MOVE( 7 ) ;
            TURNTO( 90 ) ;
          end ;          (* for *)
        PENCOLOR( NONE ) ;
        MOVETO(  40,  40 ) ;
      end ;    (* AXIS *)

    procedure PAINT ;

      begin

        WRITELN ( 'ENTER COLOR : ' ) ;
        WRITELN ;
        WRITELN ('[1]. WHITE.' ) ;
        WRITELN ('[2]. BLUE .' ) ;
        WRITELN ('[3]. GREEN.' ) ;
        WRITELN ('[4]. ORANGE' ) ;
        WRITELN ('[5]. VIOLET' ) ;
        WRITELN ;
```

Figure 8.10. PICFILES

```
            WRITE   ('[' ) ; READLN ( COLOR ) ;
            VIEWPORT( 30, 250, 30, 170 ) ;

            case COLOR of
              1 : FILLSCREEN( WHITE1 ) ;
              2 : FILLSCREEN( BLUE ) ;
              3 : FILLSCREEN( GREEN ) ;
              4 : FILLSCREEN( ORANGE ) ;
              5 : FILLSCREEN( VIOLET ) ;
            end ;

          end ;     (* PAINT *)

      begin              (* p l o t *)
          WRITE( 'ENTER SLOPE = ') ; READLN( M ) ;
          WRITE( 'ENTER INTERCEPT = ' ) ; READLN( B ) ;
          PAINT ;
          AXIS ;
          PENCOLOR( NONE ) ;
          MOVETO(  40, TRUNC( 20 * B ) + 40 ) ;
          PENCOLOR( BLACK2 ) ;
          for X := 1 to 10 do
            begin
            Y := M * X + B ;
            MOVETO( TRUNC( 20 * X + 40 ), TRUNC( 20 * Y + 40 )  ) ;
            end ;     (* for X *)
      end;            (* PLOT  *)

    begin              (* M A I N   P R O G R A M *)
      REWRITE( PICFILE, 'GRAF:PICTURES' ) ;

      INITTURTLE ;                            (* TEXTMODE? *)
      repeat
        PLOT ;

        for Y := 30 to 170 do
          for X := 30 to 250 do
            PICFILE^[ Y, X ] := SCREENBIT( X, Y ) ;

        PUT ( PICFILE ) ;
        WRITELN( ' DONE ? ' ) ; READLN ( CH ) ;
      until CH = 'Y' ;

      CLOSE( PICFILE, LOCK ) ;

      VIEWPORT( 30, 250, 30, 170 ) ;
      FILLSCREEN( BLUE ) ;

      RESET ( PICFILE, 'GRAF:PICTURES' ) ;
      DRAWBLOCK( PICFILE^, 28, 0, 0, 220, 140,30,30, 10 ) ;
      CLOSE ( PICFILE ) ;

    end.
```

Figure 8.10.   PICFILES

So we can state the DRAWBLOCK module as:

```
DRAWBLOCK   (ARRAY OF BOOLEANS,
             ROWSIZE,
             XSTART-XSCREEN,YSTART-YSCREEN
             XSTOP-XSTART,YSTOP-YSTART
             XSCREEN, YSCREEN,
               MODE  );
```

Actually, the XSTART, YSTART values can be set to skip over parts of the array; however, this practice is not recommended because it is error-prone. The values used in PICFILES were derived as follows:

XSCREEN=30
YSCREEN=30

XSTART =30
XSTOP =250

YSTART =30
YSTOP =170

Thus,

XSTART - XSCREEN =0
YSTART - YSCREEN =0

XSTOP-XSTART =250-30 =220
YSTOP-YSTART =170-30 = 140

ROWSIZE = 2*((250-30+15) div 16) =28

Hence, we can draw the array on the screen by issuing:

DRAWBLOCK (PICFILE∧, 28,0,0, 220, 140, 30, 30 MODE);

Everything is defined except the mode.

Figure 8.11 lists the actions taken by SCREENBLOCK when the MODE is given. The most useful modes are 10 and 6. Mode 10 copies the array onto the screen directly, while mode 6 *overlays* the new picture in array onto the current picture on the screen.

This idea is illustrated further by study of READPICS (Figure 8.12). This program reads the saved pictures from the disk file and displays them on the screen. Try the program with a variety of colors. For example, two plots stored on the screen (and disk file by program PICFILES) in BLUE and ORANGE are observed to take on new colors when displayed in MODE 10 or 6.

Under mode 10: A BLUE plot is colored BLUE when the BLUE or complement of BLUE is selected in READPICS.

Other results: BLUE becomes VIOLET when WHITE1, VIOLET, or GREEN is selected in READPICS.

If we select mode 6, many records can be overlaid onto the same screen area. The overlay is not always perfect, however, because *XOR* of an *XOR*ed

MODE	Action
0	FILLSCREEN (BLACK)
1	SCREEN = ARRAY *NOR* SCREEN
2	SCREEN = ARRAY *NOR* SCREEN
3	SCREEN = *COMPLEMENT* SCREEN
4	SCREEN = (*COMPLEMENT* ARRAY) *AND* SCREEN
5	SCREEN = *COMPLEMENT* ARRAY
6	SCREEN = ARRAY *XOR* SCREEN
7	SCREEN = ARRAY *NAND* SCREEN
8	SCREEN = ARRAY *AND* SCREEN
9	SCREEN = ARRAY *EQUALS* SCREEN
10	SCREEN = ARRAY
11	SCREEN = ARRAY *OR* (*COMPLEMENT* SCREEN)
12	SCREEN = SCREEN
13	SCREEN = (*COMPLEMENT* ARRAY) *or* SCREEN
14	SCREEN = ARRAY *OR* SCREEN
15	FILLSCREEN (WHITE)

Figure 8.11   The DRAWBLOCK Modes.

pixel erases it! Indeed, mode 6 is most commonly used to erase a figure after it has been displayed for awhile.

Be prepared to wait 4–5 minutes when executing program PICFILES, since the program is slow. Once the screen has been copied into a disk file, the display program is quite rapid.

A note: The CHARTYPE (6) function call in program PICFILES sets the mode (XOR) of character types. This mode forces the number to "show through" regardless of what may already be on the screen.

Let's review the approach taken to copy a picture from the screen onto disk. First, we must decide upon a screen region as defined by a *mapping* from the screen into a **packed boolean** array. Second, we copy the black-and-white pixels from SCREENBIT into the boolean array. This is a slow process, but once we have the copy, we can save it on disk. This disk file can be retrieved and displayed many ways by DRAWBLOCK. We must choose a MODE before employing DRAWBLOCK.

This brief introduction to computer graphics should stimulate many hours of experimentation. Color, shapes, and motion are all possible variations using TURTLEGRAPHICS.

We complete this introduction by reviewing the most important topics covered in this chapter.

A. Turtle graphics must be initialized using the INITTURTLE module.

```
program READPICS ;

  uses TURTLEGRAPHICS ;

  type
    PICTURES  =  packed array[ 30..170, 30..250 ] of boolean ;

  var
    PICFILE   :  file of PICTURES ;
    COLOR     :  1 .. 5 ;
    MO        :  integer ;

  begin
    RESET  ( PICFILE, 'GRAF:PICTURES' ) ;

    WRITE  ('ENTER MODE = ' ) ; READLN( MO ) ;
    INITTURTLE ;

  repeat

    WRITELN ( 'ENTER COLOR : ' ) ;
    WRITELN ;
    WRITELN ('[1]. WHITE.' ) ;
    WRITELN ('[2]. BLUE .' ) ;
    WRITELN ('[3]. GREEN.' ) ;
    WRITELN ('[4]. ORANGE' ) ;
    WRITELN ('[5]. VIOLET' ) ;
    WRITELN ;

    WRITE  ('[' ) ; READLN ( COLOR ) ;
    VIEWPORT( 30, 250, 30, 170 ) ;

    case COLOR of
      1 : FILLSCREEN( WHITE1 ) ;
      2 : FILLSCREEN( BLUE ) ;
      3 : FILLSCREEN( GREEN ) ;
      4 : FILLSCREEN( ORANGE ) ;
      5 : FILLSCREEN( VIOLET ) ;
    end ;

    DRAWBLOCK( PICFILE^, 28, 0, 0, 220, 140,30,30, MO ) ;
    GET ( PICFILE ) ;
  until EOF( PICFILE ) ;
  CLOSE ( PICFILE ) ;

  end .
```

Figure 8.12.   READPICS

B. TEXTMODE and GRAFMODE allow the user to switch screens.

C. The screen displays 0..23 lines of 0..79 characters in TEXTMODE and 191..0 pixels by 0..279 pixels in GRAFMODE.

D. TURTLE is an imaginary pencil that moves around the screen through MOVE, MOVETO, TURN and TURNTO modules.

E. Character output to the GRAFMODE screen is done via WCHAR and WSTRING modules.

F. The GRAFMODE screen is copied using SCREENBIT and recreated using the DRAWBLOCK module.

G. Only a portion of the screen can be viewed using the VIEWPORT module.

H. The TURTLE can be guided using PADDLE and BUTTON if we are careful to slow the computer to the speed of the paddle wheel.

8.4 A LITTLE GEOMETRY

We conclude this chapter with a brief review of geometry. A quick way to learn *analytical geometry* is by watching figures grow on the GRAFMODE screen.

Program GEOMETRY illustrated in Figure 8.13 can draw almost anything we give it. The heart of this program is the **repeat** loop in the middle of DRAW.

```
repeat
    ANGLE    := ANGLE + 5;
    RADIANS := (ANGLE / 180) *PI
    R  := EQUATION (ANGLE);
    X  := TRUNC (R * COS (RADIANS) + XORG);
    Y  := TRUNC (R * SIN(RADIANS) + YORG);
    MOVETO ( X, Y);
until TRUNC (ANGLE) >= 360;
```

The variable ANGLE *rotates* through 0..360 degrees defining a plane in 5 degree increments. However, the TRANSCEND functions, sine and cosine, operate on *radians* instead of degrees. Therefore, we must convert 360 degrees =2*PI radians into degrees.

$$RADIANS = \frac{2*PI}{360} * DEGREES$$

Next, we compute the distance from the origin to a point on the curve, as illustrated in Figure 8.14. This point is at location (R,ANGLE) in terms of *polar coordinates,* and at location (X,Y) in *Cartesian coordinates.* The transformation used by the DRAW routine is:

```
X := R * COS (RADIANS);
Y := R * SIN (RADIANS);
```

Since we must locate this point relative to the (XORIG, YORIG) center, we add these offsets to (X,Y) (see GEOMETRY). Now, turn to the **function** EQUATION. This formula can be changed to implement any geometric figure we want.

```
program  GEOMETRY ;

  uses TURTLEGRAPHICS, TRANSCEND ;

  const
    PI    = 3.141596 ;

  procedure AXIS ( XORG, YORG : integer ) ;

    begin
      FILLSCREEN( BLUE ) ;
      PENCOLOR ( NONE ) ;
      MOVETO ( 0, YORG ) ;
      PENCOLOR ( BLACK2 ) ;
      MOVETO ( 279, YORG ) :
      PENCOLOR ( NONE ) ;
      MOVETO ( XORG, 191 ) ;
      PENCOLOR ( BLACK2 ) ;
      MOVETO ( XORG, 0 ) ;
      MOVETO ( XORG, YORG ) ;
    end ;    (* AXIS *)

  procedure DRAW ( XORG, YORG : integer ) ;

    var
      X, Y   : integer ;
      R, ANGLE: real ;
      RADIANS : real ;

    function EQUATION ( ANGLE : real ) : real ;

      (*****  EQUATION OF GEOMETRIC FIGURE, IN POLAR FORM  *****)
      const
        C  = 30 ;
        A  = 90 ;

      var
        RAD : real ;

      begin
        RAD       := (( ANGLE - A ) / 180.0 ) * PI ;
        EQUATION  := 2 * C * COS( RAD ) ;
      end ;              (* EQUATION *)

    begin
      ANGLE    := 0 ;
      R        := EQUATION( ANGLE ) ;
      X        := TRUNC( R ) + XORG ;
      Y        := YORG ;
      PENCOLOR( NONE ) ;
      MOVETO ( X, Y ) ;
      PENCOLOR( BLACK2 ) ;

      repeat
        ANGLE  := ANGLE + 5 ;
        RADIANS:= ( ANGLE / 180.0 ) * PI ;
        R      := EQUATION( ANGLE ) ;
        X      := TRUNC( R * COS( RADIANS ) + XORG ) ;
        Y      := TRUNC( R * SIN( RADIANS ) + YORG ) ;
        MOVETO ( X, Y ) ;
      until TRUNC( ANGLE ) >= 360 ;

    end ;   (* DRAW *)

  begin      (*  G E O M E T R Y  *)
    INITTURTLE ;
    AXIS ( 139, 95 ) ;
    DRAW ( 139, 95 ) ;
  end.
```

Figure 8.13. GEOMETRY

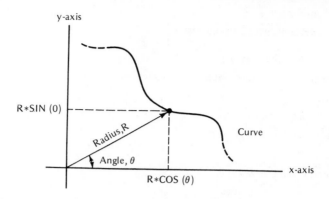

Figure 8.14.   Polar Coordinates and Cartesian, Too

The following formulas give various interesting shapes on the screen when used in place of the circle of EQUATION.

1. EQUATION := C * SIN(RAD) *SQR(COS(RAD))
   This draws a bifolium (butterfly).

2. EQUATION := C * SIN(N*RAD)
   This draws a circle when N=1, a 2*N-leafed rose when N-2,4,8,.., and an N-leafed rose when N is odd.

3. EQUATION := C / (1–COS(RADIANS));
   This draws a parabola.

4. EQUATION := SQRT(SQR(A*B) / (SQR(A*SIN(RADIANS)) + SQR(B*COS(RADIANS)))
   This draws an ellipse with major and minor semi-axes A and B.

5. A hyerbola is obtained using a minus in place of the + in 4. above.

6. EQUATION := SQRT(SQR(C) * COS(2*RADIANS))
   This gives the Lemniscate of Bernoulli (a fancy figure-eight).

7. EQUATION := C * RADIANS
   This simple equation gives the Spiral of Archimedes.

8. Motion. See the program ROTATE for rotation of a box through 2*PI (360 degrees) radians (Figure 8.15).

Notice that several of the formulas above are named after famous mathematicians. Archimedes, for example, was a brilliant ancient scholar who nearly succeeded in discovering calculus 1800 years before Newton! Perhaps after some experimentation, you can discover a graphical figure to bear your name!

```
program ROTATE ;

  uses TURTLEGRAPHICS, TRANSCEND ;

  const
    PI       = 3.14159 ;
    N        = 4 ;
    TOOSMALL = 1.0E-2 ;

  type
    LIST     = array[ 1..N ] of real :

  var
    DELTAX, DELTAY : real ;
    PIVOTX, PIVOTY : real ;
    X, NEWX        : LIST ;
    Y, NEWY        : LIST ;
    ANGLE0, RADIUS : LIST ;
    ANGLE          : real ;
    I              : 1 .. N ;

  procedure BOX ( var X,Y : LIST ; COL : SCREENCOLOR ) ;

    var
      POINT : integer ;

    begin
      PENCOLOR( NONE ) ;
      MOVETO  ( TRUNC( X[ 1 ] ), TRUNC( Y[ 1 ] ) ) ;
      PENCOLOR( COL ) ;
      for POINT := 2 to N do
        begin
          MOVETO( TRUNC( X[ POINT ] ),TRUNC( Y[ POINT ] ) ) ;
        end ;
      MOVETO( TRUNC( X[ 1 ] ), TRUNC( Y[ 1 ] ) ) :
    end ;                        (*    BOX    *)

  begin
    INITTURTLE ;                          (* TEXTMODE? *)
    WRITE  ( 'ENTER PIVOT POINT : ' ) ;
    READLN ( PIVOTX, PIVOTY ) ;
    WRITELN ( 'ENTER ', N:3, ' POINTS : ' ) ;
    for I := 1 to N do
      begin
        WRITE  ( 'POINT # ', I:3,' : ' ) ;
        READLN ( X[ I ], Y[ I ] ) ;
        DELTAX     := X[ I ] - PIVOTX ;
        DELTAY     := Y[ I ] - PIVOTY ;
        RADIUS[ I ] := SQRT( SQR( DELTAX ) + SQR( DELTAY ) ) ;
        if ABS( DELTAX ) < TOOSMALL
          then
            if ABS( DELTAY ) < TOOSMALL
              then ANGLE0[ I ] := 0
              else ANGLE0[ I ] := PI / 2.0
          else  ANGLE0[ I ] := ATAN( DELTAY / DELTAX ) ;
      end ;
    ANGLE    := 0 ;
    while ANGLE <= 2 * PI  do            (* SWEEP THRU 360 DEGREES  *)
      begin
        for I := 1 to N do              (* ROTATE BY ANGLE RADIANS *)
          begin
            NEWX[ I ] := PIVOTX + RADIUS[ I ] * COS( ANGLE+ANGLE0[ I ] ) ;
            NEWY[ I ] := PIVOTY + RADIUS[ I ] * SIN( ANGLE+ANGLE0[ I ] ) ;
          end ;
        BOX( X, Y, BLACK2 ) ;           (* ERASE THE PREVIOUS LINE *)
        BOX( NEWX, NEWY, BLUE ) ;       (* PAINT NEW LINES         *)
        for I := 1 to N do              (* COPY BACK INTO X,Y      *)
          begin
            X[ I ] := NEWX[ I ] ;
            Y[ I ] := NEWY[ I ] ;
          end ;
        ANGLE := ANGLE + 0.2 ;          (* SWEEP 0.2 RADIANS EACH PASS *)
      end ;   (*  while  *)
    end.
```

Figure 8.15.   ROTATE

TWENTY QUESTIONS

1. If both TV and RS232 terminals are used, do we need to switch between TEXTMODE and GRAFMODE?
2. How many pixels are on the screen?
3. Where is location (0,0)?
4. What color is the complement color of ORANGE?
5. What happens to drawings that go outside the VIEWPORT region?
6. What does PENCOLOR (NONE) do?
7. Can you draw a RED line on the screen?
8. Why do we need BLACK1, BLACK2, etc.?
9. What does INITURTLE do?
10. What is the difference between MOVE and MOVETO?
11. What are the range of values produced by PADDLE?
12. What does this statement do?

    while not BUTTON (1) **do;**

13. What does STR (35, TACK) **do?**
14. Can SCREENBIT (X,Y) copy a BLUE pixel from the screen?
15. How long does it take to get an insurance claim cheque?
16. What is the value of ROWSIZE in DRAWBLOCK for an array that copies all 280?
17. Which MODE (almost) does an overlay on the screen when using DRAW-BLOCK?
18. Which module is used to write text while in GRAFMODE?
19. Why?
20. Does DRAWBLOCK modify the array?

ANSWERS

1. No. Only if you want to display TEXT on the TV screen; otherwise the RS232 terminal.
2. 280 times 192.
3. Lower left-hand corner.
4. BLUE.
5. They are ignored.

6. Nothing. The pen does not draw.

7. No.

8. Some colors *run*; to get thin lines, we need special BLACK and WHITE colors.

9. Places the TURTLE in the middle of the screen in GRAFMODE, facing east (0 degrees).

10. MOVE causes TURTLE to move relative to its current location. MOVE-TO causes TURTLE to move in a specific location no matter where TURTLE is initially.

11. 0<=PADDLE <=2255.

12. Waits until the paddle button is pushed.

13. Converts 35 into a string equal to '35'.

14. Yes, but it copies it as a TRUE value, and is colorblind.

15. About as long as it takes to copy the screen.

16. ROWSIZE = 2*((280+15) div 16) = 36.

17. 6

18. WCHAR or WSTRING

19. Because.

20. No.

Chapter 9

Making Music

"I came from Al—a—bama, With my ban—jo on my knee; I'm goin' to Lou—si—ana, My true love for to see."

Stephen Foster

9.1 THEORY OF MUSIC

Musical scores are written much like computer programs. Both have a cryptic notation; both are for the purpose of directing the actions of a machine; both have to consider the human interface; and both have a history of jargon, technique, and style. Before we write a Pascal program to turn the Apple computer into an organ, suppose we review the theory of musical scoring.

Musical sounds are represented by symbols called notes. A WHOLE note is held for a whole beat; a HALF note is held for a half beat; a QTR note is held for a quarter of a beat, and so on. See Figure 9.1(a).

```
type
    LENGTH = (WHOLE,HALF,THIRD,QTR,EIGHT,DOT);
    NOTES  = (A,B,C,D,E,F,G);
```

Notes also are placed either on a *treble clef* or *base clef*, as shown in Figure 9.1(b) and (c). The treble and bass clefs are combined into a *Grand Staff* or eleven-line staff, as shown in Figure 9.1(d). The Apple Pascal system can play the notes from the treble clef only. The numbers written next to each note shown in Figure 9.1(d) are approximately equivalent to the sound produced by the NOTE intrinsic obtained from APPLESTUFF.

NOTE (DURATION,PITCH);

where;

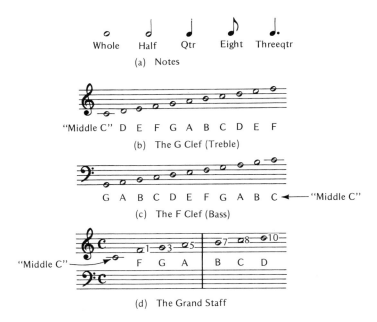

Figure 9.1.   Musical Notation

```
var
   DURATION  :  0..255;
   PITCH     :  0..50;
```

(Actually, PITCH>50 will cause sounds to be produced, but they are unreliable.)
To produce the six notes numbered in Figure 9.1(d), we might do the following:

```
program TESTNOTE;
uses APPLESTUFF;
var
   DURATION  :  0..255;
   PITCH     :  0..50;
begin
   NOTE (100, 1);
   NOTE (100, 3);
   NOTE (100, 5);
   NOTE (100, 7);
   NOTE (100, 8);
   NOTE (100,10);
end.
```

The treble clef has 5 lines, and so there are 5 notes that can be placed on each line. We remember them as "Every Good Boy Does Fine", e.g., E G B D F. Also, this clef has 4 spaces between the lines. We can remember the names of the notes in the spaces because they spell FACE!

All half-step notes (sharps and flats) as well as full-step notes are played by the Pascal NOTE intrinsic using the encoding scheme of Figure 9.2. The # sign means a half-step up, while the b sign means to take a half-step down in pitch. This encoding will be the first step taken to translate from sheet music to Pascal.

The Pascal encoding of Figure 9.2 shows how to obtain a numerical equivalent for each of the N = Natural notes and S = Sharp notes. If we use the ORD intrinsic, we get the appropriate value for PITCH in the NOTE (DURATION, PITCH) intrinsic.

```
var

    TONE : NOTES;

begin
    for   TONE := RST to SG2 do
          NOTE (100, ORD (TONE));
end.
```

Observe how zero is used as a rest space. The section of program above will play the scale from F to #G2 when executed (be sure to include **uses** APPLE-STUFF).

We need some more theory before we can conduct a symphony. The DURATION of each note is also important when reading music.

Every song is made of pieces. Each piece consists of *measures*, and each measure consists of notes and rests. This division is shown in Figure 9.3(a). The

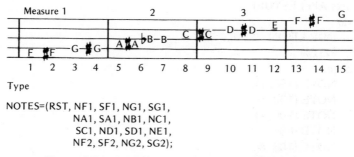

Type

NOTES=(RST, NF1, SF1, NG1, SG1,
       NA1, SA1, NB1, NC1,
       SC1, ND1, SD1, NE1,
       NF2, SF2, NG2, SG2);

Figure 9.2.   Correlation Between Music and Notes

chorus of Figure 9.3(a) is 8 measures long; each measure consists of 4 beats. Each measure contains one or more notes with duration of one, one-half, one-quarter, or one-eighth of a beat.

Figure 9.3(b) gives the equivalent encoding for Pascal score to be played in the next section. The notes are *natural* (N) or half-step sharps (S). Their duration is *not* illustrated in the example.

A musical *time signature* is indicated at the beginning of every piece. The 4/4 signature says every measure has 4 beats; the 3/4 signature is used to indicate 3 beats per measure and 2/4 signals, two beats per measure. The number of beats is used to determine the length of each note in the measure. Thus if the TEMPO is given, then 4/4-time means that each measure is played for TEMPO time units:

Note	Duration
WHOLE	TEMPO
HALF	TEMPO div 2
QTR	TEMPO div 4
EIGHT	TEMPO div 8
DOT	ADD 50% to previous note duration.

Now we can construct the data structure of a musical score consisting of a TEMPO, measures, notes, and their corresponding duration.

(a) The Musical Score

(b) The Pascal Score

SA1, SA1	ND1, ND1, ND1	NC1, NC1, NA1, NF1	NG1, NF1, NG1

NA1, NC1, NC1, ND1	NC1, NA1, NF1, NG1	NA1, NA1, NG1, NG1	NF1

Figure 9.3.   Chorus of "Oh! Susannah"

9.2 LISTEN TO THE MUSIC

The encoding of "Oh! Susanna" as given in Figure 9.3 is shown in Figure 9.4. The duration of each note is shown along with its pitch. Study this list carefully and notice how dotted notes are handled. To include a dot, the note must be encoded twice—once for its pitch and duration, and a second time to indicate that it is dotted. The note is played 50% longer when it is followed by a dot.

This tune is played at about the right speed when TEMPO=150; but it can be played faster by decreasing TEMPO to 50, or slower by increasing TEMPO to 250. The exact speed is up to the composer.

The structure of a score is given by the following data structures:

```
type
   NOTES =  (RST,NF1,SF1,NG1,SG1,NA1,SA1,NB1,
             NC1, SC1,ND1,SD1,NE1,NF2,
             SF2,NG2,SG2);
```

To play a note, we supply intrinsic NOTE with the order of a variable of scalar type NOTES:

```
SOUNDS := ORD (I);
```

Continuing:

```
BEATS = (ZERO,WHOLE,HALF,THIRD,QTR,EIGHT,DOT);
```

Since ORD (typeBEATSvariable) is 0,1,2,3,4,5,6, we can divide TEMPO by 1,2,3,4 to get whole, half, or quarter notes. The eighth note and dotted note are taken care of in the following **case** statement.

```
case  COUNT of
   1: COUNT := TEMPO; (* WHOLE NOTE :)
   2: COUNT := TEMPO div 2; (* HALF *)
   3: COUNT := TEMPO div 3; (* THIRD *)
   4: COUNT := TEMPO div 4; (* QTR *)
   5: COUNT := TEMPO div 8; (* EIGHT *)
   6: COUNT := (LEN [J–1] / div 2) * TEMPO;
end;
```

The last case clause above uses the duration of the previous note, LEN [J–1], to compute the duration of the J-th (current) note. This takes care of the DOT problem.

8 BARS
150 TEMPO

Measure	NO.	PITCH	KIND (DURATION)
1	2	SA1	HALF
		SA1	HALF
2	3	ND1	QTR
		ND1	HALF
		ND1	QTR
3	4	NC1	QTR
		NC1	QTR
		NA1	QTR
		NF1	QTR
4	4	NG1	HALF
		NG1	DOT
		NF1	EIGHT
		NG1	EIGHT
5	5	NA1	QTR
		NC1	QTR
		NC1	QTR
		NC1	DOT
		ND1	EIGHT
6	5	NC1	QTR
		NA1	QTR
		NF1	QTR
		NF1	DOT
		NG1	EIGHT
7	4	NA1	QTR
		NA1	QTR
		NG1	QTR
		NG1	QTR
8	2	NF1	HALF
		NF1	DOT

Figure 9.4. Encoding of "Oh! Susanna"

Next, we construct the components of a measure:

type
   MEASURES = **record**
                  N : 1..MAXN; (* number of notes here *)
                  BLASTS : **array** [1..MAXN] **of** 0..50;
                  LEN : **array** [1..MAXN] **of** 0..255;
                  end;

Therefore, each BLAST (note) is stored as a pitch number. Each measure has up to MAXN blasts (notes) in it. The note (blast) is of length LEN, so we must keep an array of durations also.

Finally, we will store the song on disk so it can be played over and over again. An entire song is a disk record:

```
SONGS = record
              TEMPO : 0..255;
              BARS : 1..MAXB;
              SCORE : array [1..MAXB] of MEASURES;
          end;
```

The number of measures is stored in BARS, and each measure is an entry in SCORE. To put this on disk we define DISK as a disk file.

```
var
    DISK : file of SONGS;
```

Figure 9.5 lists program SCORE, which inputs the encoded song. The score for "Oh! Susanna" in Figure 9.4 can be input to this program directly.

The string arrays NT and BT simply help to convert the English inputs into numeric values. Modules SOUNDS and KINDS do the conversion using NT and BT, respectively. These two modules employ a bit of treachery because they exit from the loop and the module as soon as the matching string is found.

Figure 9.6 shows how to retrieve the SCORE from disk and play it through the speaker. The core of this module is the two loops: one to recall each measure, another to recall each note of each measure.

```
for M := 1 to B do
    (* recall Measure M *)
    for J := 1 to N do
        (* recall each note *)
        NOTE (BLASTS [J], COUNT);
```

These programs store one song only, but they can be modified to add as many songs to the disk file as there is disk space. Composer and machine can then enjoy many hours of musical entertainment.

Remember the NOTE function works as follows:

A. It is in APPLESTUFF, so be sure to include uses APPLESTUFF in the program.

B. It works on integers only,
```
        NOTE ( PITCH, DURATION);
where,   PITCH       : 0..50;
         DURATION  : 0..255;
```

```
program  SCORE ;

  uses APPLESTUFF ;

  const
    MAXN  = 16 ;
    MAXB  = 20 ;

  type
    NOTES        = ( RST, NF1, SF1, NG1, SG1, NA1, SA1,
                     NB1, NC1, SC1, ND1, SD1, NE1, NF2,
                     SF2, NG2, SG2  ) ;

    BEATS        = ( ZERO, WHOLE, HALF, THIRD, QTR, EIGHT, DOT ) ;

    MEASURES     = record
                     N      : 1 .. MAXN ;
                     BLASTS : array[ 1..MAXN ] of 0..50 ;
                     LEN    : array[ 1..MAXN ] of 0..255 ;
                   end ;

    SONGS        = record
                     TEMPO  : 0 .. 255 ;
                     BARS   : 1 .. MAXB ;
                     SCORE  : array[ 1..MAXB ] of MEASURES ;
                   end ;

  var
    B, M        : 1 .. MAXB ;
    T           : 0 .. 255 ;
    J           : 1 .. MAXN ;
    DISK        : file of SONGS ;
    NT          : array[ NOTES ] of string[ 3 ] ;
    BT          : array[ BEATS ] of string[ 5 ] ;

  function  HOWMANY : integer ;

    var
      N  :  1 .. MAXN ;
    begin
      WRITE  ( 'enter number of notes in this measure = ' ) ;
      READLN ( N ) ;
      HOWMANY := N ;
    end ;      (*  HOWMANY  *)

  function  SOUNDS : integer ;

    var
      S  :  string[ 3 ] ;
      I  :  NOTES ;

    begin
      repeat
        WRITE  ( 'ENTER NOTE : ' ) ;
        READLN ( S ) ;
        for I := RST to SG2 do
          begin
            SOUNDS := ORD( I ) ;
            if S = NT[ I ] then exit( SOUNDS ) ;
          end ;
```

Figure 9.5. SCORE   191

```
            WRITELN ( 'ERROR IN INPUT !!' ) ;
         until FALSE ;
      end ;                 (*  SOUNDS  *)

   function  KINDS : integer ;

      var
         S  : string[ 5 ] ;
         I  : BEATS ;
      begin
         repeat
            WRITE  ( 'ENTER KIND OF NOTE : ' ) ;
            READLN ( S ) ;
            for I := ZERO to DOT do
               begin
                  KINDS := ORD( I ) ;
                  if S = BT[ I ] then exit( KINDS ) ;
               end ;
            WRITELN( 'ERROR IN INPUT !!' ) ;
         until FALSE ;
      end ;            (* KINDS *)

begin
   NT [ RST ] := 'RST' ;        BT [ ZERO ]  := 'ZERO' ;
   NT [ NF1 ] := 'NF1' ;
   NT [ SF1 ] := 'SF1' ;        BT [ WHOLE ] := 'WHOLE' ;
   NT [ NG1 ] := 'NG1' ;
   NT [ SG1 ] := 'SG1' ;        BT [ HALF ]  := 'HALF' ;
   NT [ NA1 ] := 'NA1' ;
   NT [ SA1 ] := 'SA1' ;        BT [ THIRD ] := 'THIRD' ;
   NT [ NB1 ] := 'NB1' ;
   NT [ NC1 ] := 'NC1' ;        BT [ QTR ]   := 'QTR' ;
   NT [ SC1 ] := 'SC1' ;
   NT [ ND1 ] := 'ND1' ;        BT [ EIGHT ] := 'EIGHT' ;
   NT [ SD1 ] := 'SD1' ;
   NT [ NE1 ] := 'NE1' ;        BT [ DOT ]   := 'DOT' ;
   NT [ NF2 ] := 'NF2' ;
   NT [ SF2 ] := 'SF2' ;
   NT [ NG2 ] := 'NG2' ;
   NT [ SG2 ] := 'SG2' ;

   WRITELN( 'ENTER A SONG :' ) ;
   WRITE  ( 'ENTER NUMBER OF BARS = ' ) ; READLN( B ) ;
   WRITE  ( 'ENTER TEMPO ( 1..255 )=' ) ; READLN( T ) ;

   REWRITE( DISK, 'SONGS.DATA' ) ;
   DISK^.TEMPO  := T ;
   DISK^.BARS   := B ;

   for M := 1 to B do
      with DISK^.SCORE[ M ] do
         begin
            N   := HOWMANY ;
            for J := 1 to N do
               begin
                  BLASTS[ J ] := SOUNDS ;
                  LEN[ J ]    := KINDS ;
               end ;
         end ;      (*  with  *)

   PUT( DISK ) ;
   CLOSE( DISK, LOCK ) ;
end .
```

Figure 9.5. (Continued)

```
program  PLAY  ;

  uses APPLESTUFF ;

  const
    MAXN  = 16 ;
    MAXB  = 20 ;

  type
    MEASURES    = record
                    N       : 1 .. MAXN ;
                    BLASTS  : array[ 1..MAXN ] of 0..50 ;
                    LEN     : array[ 1..MAXN ] of 0..255 ;
                  end ;

    SONGS       = record
                    TEMPO  : 0 .. 255 ;
                    BARS   : 1 .. MAXB ;
                    SCORE  : array[ 1..MAXB ] of MEASURES ;
                  end ;

  var
    B, M        : 1 .. MAXB ;
    T           : 0 .. 255 ;
    J           : 1 .. MAXN ;

    DISK        : file of SONGS ;
    COUNT       : integer ;

  begin
    RESET ( DISK, 'SONGS.DATA' ) ;
    T := DISK^.TEMPO ;
    B := DISK^.BARS ;

    for M := 1 to B do
      with DISK^.SCORE[ M ] do
        for J := 1 to N do
          begin
            COUNT := LEN[ J ] ;
            case COUNT of
            1 : COUNT := T ;
            2 : COUNT := T div 2 ;
            3 : COUNT := T div 3 ;
            4 : COUNT := T div 4 ;
            5 : COUNT := T div 8 ;
            6 : COUNT := ( LEN[ J-1 ] div 2 ) * T ;
            end ;
            NOTE( BLASTS[ J ], COUNT ) ;
          end ;

    CLOSE( DISK ) ;
  end.
```

Figure 9.6. PLAY

C. The musical scale can be shifted up or down, but we "calibrated" it with an organ to give the scale shown in Figure 9.2. Adding 12 to the pitch will shift the notes one *octave* higher.

D. The duration of a note is relative to the arbitrary members 0..255. To speed the PLAY program, decrease the TEMPO; to slow it down, increase the TEMPO.

E. A measure is a unit of music which "uses up" TEMPO beats. A note is a unit of music which "uses up" a fraction of a measure.

F. A bar and a Measure are the same thing.

TWENTY QUESTIONS

1. What type of parameters are required by NOTE?
2. Can we play Middle C with NOTE?
3. What gives a click?
4. Where is NOTE kept?
5. What does NF2 mean?
6. What does SA1, and B1 flat do?
7. What instrument did Nero play?
8. How many "voices" can NOTE play simultaneously?
9. Could we draw notes on the GRAFMODE screen while playing them at the same time?
10. How many octaves can NOTE play?
11. When does **repeat . . . until** FALSE; stop?
12. Can music be stored on a disk?
13. When did Johann Sebastian Bach become famous?
14. Which of the following are false: Beethoven (1) never married, (2) became deaf, (3) died as an unknown musician.
15. How do we program a pause instead of a note?
16. How do we cause a sixteenth note to be played?
17. What does this do?

```
repeat
    NOTE (20,100);
until KEYPRESS;
```

18. Who is Eric Clapton?

THE STOCKTON HILTON

2323 Grand Canal Boulevard
Stockton, California 95207
209/957-9090

19. Who is Donnie Osmond?

20. What is the score to "Shave-and-a-hair-cut, six bits"?

ANSWERS

1. Integers only.

2. Yes, by scaling the notes just right, but we did not do this (Changing the "key").

3. NOTE (1,1).

4. In APPLESTUFF.

5. Natural F in the second octave.

6. The same thing.

7. The fiddle.

8. One, unfortunately.

9. Yes, but the screen might not keep up.

10. Each octave as 12 notes, so 50 **div** 12 is 4.

11. Never. The **exit** is used instead.

12. Indirectly, by storing an encoded pitch and duration.

13. Not until 50 years after he died.

14. Obviously, number 3.

15. NOTE (0,100);

16. TEMPO **div** 16.

17. Screams until any keyboard key is pressed.

18. If you know, you are over 30.

19. If you know, you are under 21.

20. Try 3 measures of:
    3, NE1, HALF
    NC1, QTR
    NC1, QTR
    2, ND1, HALF
    NC1, HALF
    3, RST, HALF
    NE1, QTR
    NF2, QTR

Chapter 10

File Structures Supreme

He appeared on the beach surrounded by admiring disciples. A soft glimmer danced on his skin as he spoke to the group.

He appeared under the glare of the stadium lights, his body slightly leaning forward in anticipation as the crowd filtered into the stadium.

He appeared in the living room of millions as his long-awaited soliloquy began, and the words branded their minds:

"We are but swirling molecules to the carefree butterfly . . . giants among the insects . . . and insignificant beneath the sun and stars." The crush of humanity fell silent everwhere.

"Yet which is more intricate, the system of flesh we know as a human, or the system of stars and planets we call the Universe?" He stepped forward, and for a slight moment it was as if his image blurred.

"Is it our size that matters or the dreams we dream? What force can divert a determined people? What greater power hath humanity than achievement of the impossible, conception of an original idea, pursuit of the elusive goal?"

But before he was done, the soft glimmer faded, his image wrinkled, and finally the hologram of his "presence" vanished from 200 million "locations".

The people stirred and began a low rumble of conversation as they picked up their beach blankets or moved slowly to an exit. It would be another week before the experiment was continued. The mass consciousness of 200 of the world's greatest thinkers had been pooled tonight into a collective thought captured by telecommunications and broadcast to anyone with a hologram receiver. Next week's program would feature the collective thought of 300 musicians.

10.1 MEANWHILE, BACK TO FILES

Every data processing problem requiring large amounts of data requires a *file* to store the data, a *file structure* to organize the data, and a *file access method* in order to retrieve information from a file structure. We have used the elementary Pascal file system many times throughout this book. It is now possible to introduce some new ideas for advanced processing of file structures. Be-

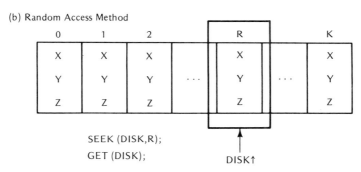

Figure 10.1. Pascal File Organization

fore doing so, however, we briefly review the capabilities of Pascal file structures and access methods.

Figure 10.1 illustrates the logical view of the following Pascal file:

```
type
   INFO   =  record
                 X :  integer;
                 Y :  real;
                 Z :  char;
              end;
var
   DISK : file of INFO;
```

We can read or write an INFO record by: (1) sequentially accessing each record in order from record item zero up to the last record item K, or (2) "randomly" accessing each record item by a *direct access,* SEEK followed by a GET or PUT.

In Figure 10.1(a) we simply opened the file and retrieved the first (zero-th) record item by

RESET (DISK, 'FILETITLE');

The FILETITLE is any valid file name, and the RESET intrinsic opens the file, sets the file pointer to the first (zero-th) record item, and reads the first record into the *window* variable DISK∧. The up-arrow indicates that DISK *points to* the record item containing X, Y, and Z.

Subsequent accesses to DISK∧ will cause the subsequent record items to be retrieved. If we wish to move record item #2 into the window variable, we must perform two additional accesses:

GET (DISK);
GET (DISK);

DISK∧ now contains record item #2.

In Figure 10.1(b) we illustrate how to *directly* access a given record item without sequentially moving the file pointer through other items. The SEEK intrinsic allows a direct or random access. We can skip around from one item to another as follows.

SEEK   (DISK, 3);
GET   (DISK);
SEEK   (DISK, 0);
GET   (DISK);
SEEK   (DISK, 5);
GET   (DISK);

Be warned that every SEEK must be followed by an access before subsequent SEEKs are performed. The following is *not accepted.*

SEEK (DISK, 3);
SEEK (DISK, 0);
SEEK (DISK, 5);
GET (DISK);

The typical pattern employed in an application program is a blend of sequential and random access. We can create and build a file sequentially and then process it using random access. For example,

REWRITE (DISK, 'MY.DATA');
    for I := 1 to N do
        begin
            READLN (X, Y, Z);
            PUT (DISK);
        end;

will create a new file titled MY.DATA, and then fill it with N values of INFO, numbered zero through (N–1). Each PUT moves the window pointer forward through the file.

We can process the sequential file in any order we wish as follows:

```
RESET (DISK, 'MY.DATA');
    repeat
      WRITE ('ENTER RECORD ITEM NUMBER :');
      READLN (M);
        if M >= 0
          then
          begin
            SEEK    (DISK,M);
            GET     (DISK)
            WRITELN (DISK∧.X,
                     DISK∧.Y,
                     DISK∧.Z);
          end;
      until M < 0;
```

This section of Pascal code continues to provide random access to any record item we desire simply by retrieving the M-th item. If M>=0, the record is retrieved; otherwise the loop terminates.

Notice the use of GET and PUT when dealing with files. We use READ and WRITE whenever we perform input and output to the pseudo-files INPUT and OUTPUT; so why not use READ and WRITE for access to disk files?

The READ and WRITE intrinsics may be used to perform I/O on a special kind of file called TEXT. Thus, if we define DISK to contain only characters, we can use READ and WRITE as before.

```
var
    DISKT : TEXT;
```

or also,

```
var
    DISKT : file of char;
```

We must include the file window in the intrinsic READ or WRITE procedure.

```
WRITE (DISKT, 'ANY TEXT');
READ (DISKT, STRING);
```

Also,

```
WRITELN (DISK, 'ANY TEXT');
READLN (DISKT, STRING);
```

Be careful to match WRITE and READ when using this form as well as WRITELN and READLN. The LN form places a carriage return delimiter in the TEXT file and conversely expects it to be there when a READLN is done.

UCSD Pascal also allows a special file type called INTERACTIVE. The definition of INTERACTIVE (as well as TEXT) files means that *no pre-fetch is assumed when the file is RESET or REWRITE opened.*

```
var
    DSK : INTERACTIVE;

begin
    RESET (DSK, 'MY.DATA');
    . . .
    READ (DSK, CHARACTERS);
    :
end.
```

The first record of file DSK is *not* retrieved automatically when the file is opened with RESET. This affects the way end-of-line, EOLN, is used, because the file must be read before EOLN is set.

The main use of TEXT and INTERACTIVE is in implementing the Pascal System itself, and this will not be pursued here. There are three predeclared TEXT files always open in Pascal: INPUT, OUTPUT, and KEYBOARD. INPUT accepts input characters from the console and echoes them back to the CRT screen. OUTPUT displays characters on the CRT screen only, and KEYBOARD accepts input characters from the keyboard but does not display them on the CRT screen. We can use KEYBOARD to enter a "secret" password into a secure application program.

Table 10.1 summarizes the differences among INTERACTIVE, TEXT, and any other Pascal file.

Unfortunately, many applications require even more powerful and flexible file structures in order to process large amounts of data. For example, we may want to store PAYROLL records sequentially and then retrieve a select subset of PAYROLL records by a unique key rather than by number.

```
type
    PAYROLLS  = record
                LAST        :     string [16] ;
                FIRST       :     string [12] ;
                MIDDLE      :     char;
                RATE        :     real;
                HRS         :     integer;
                DEPENDS     :     0..8;
                PAY         :     MONEY;
                end;
```

Table 10.1

Intrinsic	File Type	Comment
REWRITE	**file of**	Opens a new file. Pre-fetches record zero.
	TEXT INTERACTIVE	Opens a new file, but no pre-fetch of record zero.
RESET	**file of**	Opens an old file. Pre-fetches record zero.
	TEXT INTERACTIVE	Opens an old file, but no pre-fetch of record zero.
CLOSE	all files	Closes the file.
SEEK	**file of**	Random access of a record item.
GET,PUT	**file of**	Access and copy a record into the file window.
WRITE,WRITELN READ,READLN	TEXT INTERACTIVE	Access and copy a character(s) into a variable.

var
    PERSONS : **file of** PAYROLLS;

We can thus store a file of PAYROLLS in order, but turn around and access each record one at a time directly. The problem, however, is that we cannot use SEEK to solve this problem because the search key is not an integer.

Suppose we use PERSONS∧.LAST as a key (a unique identifier) to retrieve a record. How do we find the record containing the unique value stored in PERSONS∧.LAST?

One method is called *hashing* (discussed in Chapter 6). A hashing function is a function that converts a key into a number. The key may be any string or numeric value, but the hashed key must be an integer between zero and the record number of the last item in the file. We also require that the file be of fixed length, N, and that *some* of the entries be vacant. When a file is *hashed*, we use the hashing function H to tell us where to write the record with key K, and also where to locate the record with key K when it is retrieved.

$$\text{location} = H\,(K)$$

We studied an example of hashing in Chapter 6, so we will not investigate the method further here. For a detailed explanation, refer to the French-to-English Dictionary program.

A second (more general) method of retrieval using unique keys is called *indexing*. An *index file* is a file containing keys and their associated record item numbers.

```
type
    INDEXES  =  record
                    KEYS          :      string [16] ;
                    LOCATION   ;      integer;
                end;


var
    INDEX : file of INDEXES;
```

We can *index* the PAYROLLS of the PERSONS file by stripping the unique key from each record and inserting it into the INDEX file along with the corresponding record item number. See Figure 10.2.

Notice how the INDEX file contains redundant information that is also contained within the master file, PERSONS. This is the penalty we must pay for the convenience of an index file.

The advantages of an INDEX file are:

1. The index is shorter and contains just enough information to access the master file.

2. The hashing function or some other method can be used to convert a key into an item number (location) quickly.

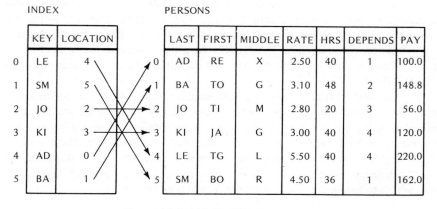

Figure 10.2. Index File Structure

3. Many index files can be used on a single data file in order to access each record of data in more than one way. See Figure 10.3.

The disadvantages of an index file are:

1. The index file contains redundant information which takes valuable disk space.
2. The access is slower because we must make at least two SEEKs to get a single master-file record.
3. The index *may* be difficult to maintain and update.
4. The index operation may be slow and time consuming.

In spite of the disadvantages, most business, professional, and scientific applications use index files to solve the problem of unique key access. In fact, we can overcome many of the objections to the index file structure by a clever index file structure discussed in the next section. We develop a complete, working file system called *Index Sequential Access Method* (ISAM), using the extremely versatile B-tree structure.

10.2   THE VERSATILE B-TREE

Suppose we want to index a master file containing telephone directory information as shown in Figure 10.4. In Figure 10.4(a) we show how the data records *might* be entered into the system. They are randomly selected and inserted into the directory according to *lexicographical order*, i.e., in alphabetical order by last name. Figure 10.4(b) shows the directory after it has been con-

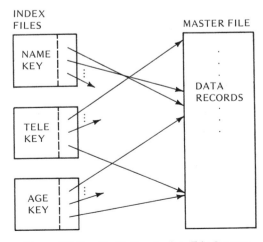

Figure 10.3.   Multi-Key Index File System

(a) Unordered List of Entries

Lewis	57 Isabella	451-2968
Jones	125 Oak	258-5991
Smith	82 Park	451-3688
Adams	109 Eddy	452-8080
Wilson	95 Williams	259-6613
Barton	118 Walnuto	258-6119

(b) Ordered List of Entries

Adams	109 Eddy	452-8080
Barton	118 Walnuto	258-6119
Jones	125 Oak	258-5991
Lewis	57 Isabella	451-2968
Smith	82 Park	451-3688
Wilson	95 Williams	259-6613

Figure 10.4   A Section Of A Telephone Directory

structed as an ascending-order list; therefore, one of the requirements we typically demand of an index file is that it place the keys of a data file in some order.

A quick and easy way to build a list of names in alphabetical order is shown in Figure 10.5. This illustrates a *binary search tree* as it is constructed one name at a time. The tree is binary because each path from the root of the tree to a leaf takes one of two possible turns. If the search key is less than the key stored at a "node", then the next node searched is to the left (left-side link); otherwise, the next node searched is to the right.

The binary search tree is ordered from left-to-right as indicated by the numbering of the final tree of Figure 10.5 (f). We can not only use the binary tree as an indexing structure, but we could also use it to sort the master file items shown by the index of Figure 10.6.

Beginning at the ROOT of the index file tree, we can list all data items in alphabetical order by following the left-side link through LEWIS, JONES, and finally ADAMS. We print ADAMS from the master file at record item 3 (following the DATA LINK field of Figure 10.6). Since there is a right-side link at index file ADAMS, we move to the index file item 5 and locate the record with key = BARTON. This is printed; thus we have printed the records in alphabetical order:

ADAMS
BARTON

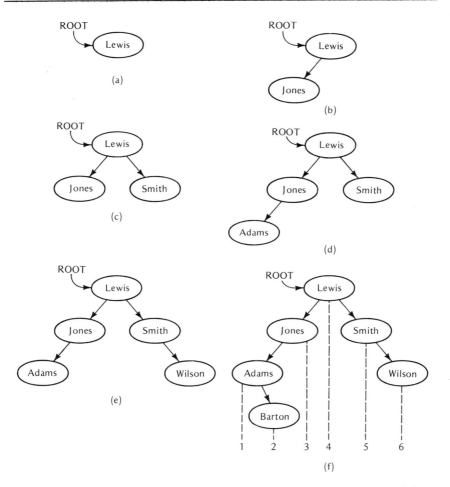

Figure 10.5.   Binary Search Tree Grown With Names of Figure 10.4(a)

Next, we must *backup* from BARTON because both left-side and right-side links are empty. Hence, backup the same way we came; so ADAMS is checked to see if there are any more links to follow. We have followed all of the links in ADAMS, so we backup to JONES. This node is also exhausted; so we backup again to LEWIS. We have not traced the path from LEWIS to the right-side item located at item 2 of the index file. Therefore, we begin by locating SMITH, printing SMITH's data record in item 2 of the master file, and then following the right-side pointer to WILSON, etc.

If we use a *pushdown stack* to "remember" where we came from, then searching a binary search tree is simple. Here is how it is done.

Index File

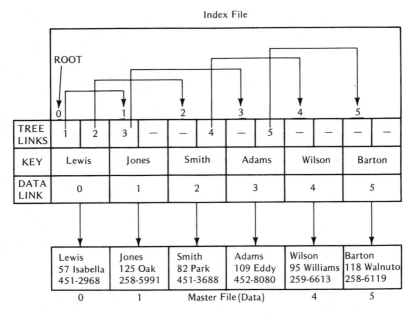

Figure 10.6.   Binary Search Tree Index File Structure

1. Initialize a pushdown stack to NULL (nothing) entree.
2. Read the root item of the index.
3. Repeat this until the stack is NULL again.

    3.1.   Read an item from the master file.

    3.2.   If a tree link exists that has not been searched, push the location of the current index item onto the stack and follow the tree link.

    3.3   If no tree link remains unexamined, then pop a backup location from the stack and backup to a previously visited item in the index.

4. Done. All master items have been searched in order.

This algorithm uses a pushdown stack, which we can implement very simply as an *array*. To *push* an item on the stack we update the array subscript and copy:

STOP := STOP +1;
STACK [STOP] := ITEM

Similarly, we can *pop* a previously pushed item by the converse —

ITEM := STACK [STOP];
STOP := STOP - 1;

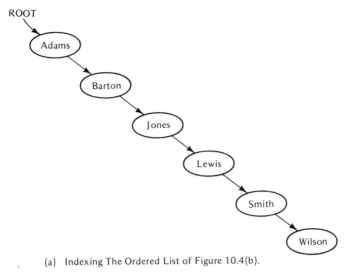

(a)   Indexing The Ordered List of Figure 10.4(b).

Figure 10.7.   Unbalanced Binary Search Tree

where STOP is the "stack-top" subscript.

The binary search tree is a big advance over earlier designs for index file structure, but it has definite limitations. First, it is difficult to keep the tree "balanced" or tuned so it is fast. Figure 10.7 shows what happens to the index tree when an ordered file is indexed. The tree is lopsided, leading to long search times.

Second, a binary search tree is not a very good model of the physical characteristics of a disk device. The major delay in retrieving information from a disk device is in the SEEK time. If we must perform one seek for every access to the index file item plus one additional seek to retrieve the master file item, then the search tree is itself a bottleneck.

The number of SEEKs performed to search an index tree is equal to the number of *levels* plus one; thus the number of seeks for locating BARTON in Figure 10.5 (f) is 5. The number of seeks to locate any item in Figure 10.5 (f) is no larger than 5, but bounded by 7 in the unbalanced tree of Figure 10.7. How can we reduce the number of seeks?

The index items are typically short entries containing the key and a few pointers. Suppose we group them into clusters, each group occupying no more than a single disk track, sector, or whatever. This idea means we can retrieve *many* keys from the index tree in a *single* SEEK. This is called a *B-tree*.

A B-tree can be constructed so that it is *always* balanced, no matter what order of inputs. In addition, all leaves of a B-tree are always at the same level, so we have a worst-case and best-case retrieval time that is the same for all records. Finally, a B-tree keeps the items in order just like a binary tree. Figure 10.8 shows the growth of a B-tree of *order* 3 for the master file in Figure 10.4(a).

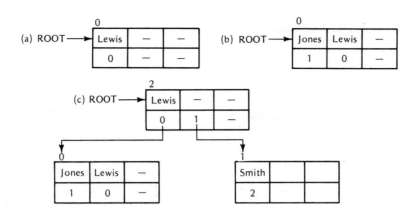

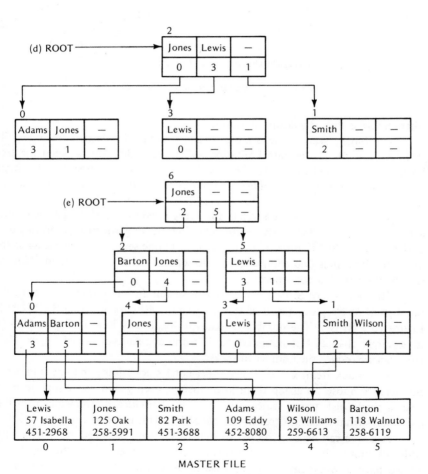

Figure 10.8. Growing a B-Tree: (a) Lewis, (b) Jones, (c) Smith, (d) Adams, (e) Complete Tree

Let's study the B-tree of Figure 10.4(c). The tree is updated by inserting SMITH into the tree of Figure 10.4(b). Since the tree is of order 3 (this means 3 links will be stored in each "node" of the tree), the ROOT item can hold two keys and three links. If we were to insert SMITH into the existing item at zero, the item would "overflow". Notice how the two keys already in item zero are in order—JONES followed by LEWIS. We must *split* this item into two items #0 and #1. Thus, SMITH is placed in item #1, and a new root item, item two, is created. The new root contains a key less than or equal to all keys at its left-side link, and a link to all keys at its middle link (all keys are greater than LEWIS). Hence, the B-tree in Figure 10.8(c) is in order, all leaves are at the same level, and keys are grouped together where possible.

In Figure 10.8(d) we see that adding to the tree causes another split to take place. We search down the tree of Figure 10.8(c): at root, ADAMS is less than LEWIS, so we locate the group of keys at item zero; continuing, ADAMS is less than JONES, so we *insert* ADAMS into item zero causing it to split (overflow).

In Figure 10.8(d) the result of splitting item zero into item zero and 3 causes additional expansion of the *parent* item above item zero in the tree. Thus JONES is inserted into item 2, causing LEWIS and the link to item 1 to be moved to the adjacent right-side links.

We see the completed index tree and the master file in Figure 10.8(e). After several more splits the root "node" has become item 6, and all leaf nodes contain keys in order, from left-to-right. It is important to notice how a B-tree grows from the top up! The binary tree grew from the leaves down, but a B-tree grows by creating new root nodes whenever more space is needed.

A B-tree index is ordered, balanced, and flexible enough to be searched rapidly because it conserves the number of disk seeks required. The *order* of a B-tree may be any N>2, but it is usually designed around the capacity of a disk sector or track. Each sector stores one item (a node) containing keys and links.

Suppose we set the order of the B-tree to a constant, N, and create nodes with a record format as shown in Figure 10.9. The FLAG component is TRUE if the POINTER [I] component links to a master data record and FALSE if the POINTER [I] links to another index (B-tree node) item. The keys are stored in SUBKEY and are up to 10 characters in length each.

We will need a pushdown stack to search down the B-tree and then backup as we split nodes, etc. We will also need a "list of available disk space" to manage the creation of new root nodes. Here is a pseudocode description of the B-tree algorithm.

B-Tree Insert Design

1. Given a record at location #ITEM and identified by a string in variable KEY, insert into the B-tree. Assume **no** duplicate KEY values, and the order of the tree is constant, N.

(a) *type*

    KEYS   = *string* [10] ;

    POINTERS = *integer;*

    NODES   = *record*

              FLAG   : *boolean;*

              POINTER: *array* [1 . . . N] *of* POINTERS;

              SUBKEY : *array* [1 . . . N] *of* KEYS;

              end;

(b)

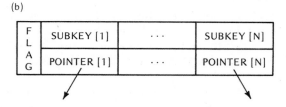

Figure 10.9.   Format of B-Tree Nodes

2. Find the last node (a leaf) in the index tree that should contain the new ITEM and KEY. This is done by searching from the root of the B-tree index down to the leaf, using a pushdown stack to "remember" the path back to the node.

3. When the appropriate leaf is found, the value of subscript I should be such that:

    KEY <= SUBKEY [I]

    POINTER [I] points to the location for KEY.

The SUBKEY and POINTER arrays are as shown previously.

4. Add the new item, ITEM and KEY, by pretending that the located node can hold (N+1) pointers (by appending a temporary pointer call TEMPTR), and insert the new item into the located node (in proper order).

5. If there is room in the located node, then update the index record in the B-tree on disk and EXIT (INSERT). We are done.

6. If, however, the insertion in step 4 was responsible for an "overflow" in the node, we must subdivide the node into two nodes of TRUNC ((N+1)/2) and N-TRUNC ((N+1)/2) entries, respectively. The remaining "middle" entry is moved up to the parent node of these two nodes. Thus, we must create a "brother" node consisting the N-TRUNC ((N+1)/2) high-order entries. The

original (sister) node is updated to show null entries where we have removed the high-order entries.

7. Request storage space for the newly created brother node and write it to disk. "Null-out" the removed entries and update the located (sister) node.

8. Now, we must find a place to insert the middle entry which resulted from the split in steps 6-7. This means the parent of the brother and sister node must be located and the middle entry inserted into it, etc.

9. Pop the location of the parent node from the stack that was used (in step 2) to "remember" the path from root node to leaf node. If the stack has the location of a node in the tree, then go to step 4.

10. If the stack (in step 9) was "empty", then we must have split the root node. In this case, the root node is no longer a root, so we must create a new root node and insert the locations of brother and sister into it. Be sure to update the pointer to this new root node so that subsequent searches can find it.

11. Exit the insert routine, EXIT (INSERT);

This algorithm and the B-tree structure are widely used to maintain ISAM files for numerous applications. The technique is a valuable one, but the user should be aware of its limitations as well. There are three disadvantages to the B-tree file organization as compared to simpler (sequential) organization.

Actung #1. There may be a considerable waste of storage in a B-tree index file because every item is a fixed-sized item, possibly containing many "empty" entries.

Actung #2. Entries may be deleted (removed) by removing them from both master and index file, but the resulting deletion may leave "holes" in the index file (aggravating problem #1) and require a "coelescing" algorithm for merging adjacent empty items. This can be done, but it may slow the file system.

Actung #3. The Pascal programs for implementing this algorithm are "type-dependent," that is, we must modify the program in order to change the key type, size, etc. This can be done also, but it will require some understanding of the (complex) code.

It is not unusual to run the B-tree file system with $50 <= N <= 99$. The "best" size depends on the size of the keys and the capacity of the disk device.

To make sure you understand the method, examine the result obtained in Figure 10.10 for inserting ALAIN into the B-tree of Figure 10.8(e). Notice how the nodes are split, leading to a parent node split, leading to an insertion in the root node! Figure 10.10 shows only the left half of the B-tree after the insertion is completed.

The program of Figure 10.11 is actually a system including the following menu selections:

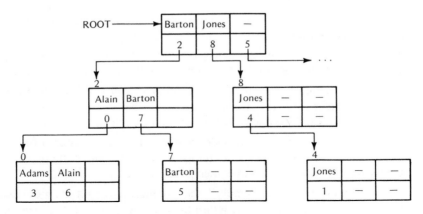

Figure 10.10.   Recursive Split Example: Insert ALAIN

1. SEQUENTIAL FILE DATA ENTRY.

2. INDEX A SEQUENTIAL FILE.

3. RETRIEVE AN INDEXED RECORD.

4. READ INDEXED SEQUENTIAL FILE IN ORDER.

5. STOP.

The first selection allows a user to create and enter data into a master file. The second selection allows a user to build the B-tree index from the master file using a portion of the master file as a key (the program must be modified to alter the format shown in Figure 10.9).

Once the file is entered and indexed, selections 3 and 4 allow retrieval. Selection 3 allows a user to retrieve any record, one at a time. Selection 4 dumps the entire file in order, one after the other. What modifications would be needed to dump all records from a key value of KEYSTART to KEYSTOP?

Obviously, selection 5 terminates the FILESYS program. Notice how the program of Figure 10.11 is segmented to overlay a piece at a time into main memory. Each segment is a subsystem corresponding to the menu selections.

The FILESYS program uses a **goto** statement to backup through the B-tree and insert new keys into the appropriate parent nodes. We must do two things in Pascal before a **goto** is allowed.

First, the G+ option must be turned on so the compiler will recognize and accept a **goto**. Second, the label must be declared in the scope (procedure) of the **goto**. This must be the *first* data definition statement in the procedure.

label
   4;

```
program  FILESYS ;
(*$G+ *)
  const
    SIZE  =  20 ;              (* NUMBER OF NODES IN B TREE, MAX. *)
    N     =   3 ;              (* ORDER OF B TREE                 *)
    NULL  =  -1 ;              (* NULL OR EMPTY POINTER           *)

  type
    KEYS     = string[ 10 ] ;  (* 10 CHARACTER KEYS               *)
    POINTERS = integer ;       (* FILE POINTERS IN B TREE         *)
    NODES    = record
                 FLAG : boolean ;(* TRUE=NODE CONTAINS DATA POINTERS*)
                                 (* FALSE=NODE HAS INDEX POINTERS   *)
                 POINTER : array[ 1..N ] of POINTERS ;
                 SUBKEY  : array[ 1..N ] of KEYS ;
                 end ;
    EMPTIES  = record
                 TREESIZE : 0 .. SIZE ;
                 AVAIL    : array[ 0..SIZE ] of boolean ;
                 ROOT     : POINTERS ;
                 end ;
    INPUTS   = record
                 SNAME : KEYS ;
                 SADDR : string[ 20 ] ;
                 STELE : string[  8 ] ;
                 end ;

  var
    I, K, LAST : integer ;     (* WORKING COUNTERS, ETC           *)
    NEW, TEMP  : NODES ;       (* WORKING NODES                   *)
    NEWNODE,
    NODE,
    TEMPPTR    : POINTERS ;    (* WORKING POINTERS                *)
    STOP       : -1 .. 20 ;    (* STACK POINTER                   *)
    STACK      : array[ 0..20 ] of POINTERS ;
    SFILE      : file of INPUTS;(* SEQUENTIAL FILE, INPUT RECORDS *)
    BTREE      : file of NODES ;(* THE B TREE                     *)
    AVAILIST   : file of EMPTIES;(*THE LIST OF AVAILABLE RECORDS  *)
    KEY        : KEYS ;        (* THE SEARCH KEY                  *)
    ITEM       : POINTERS ;    (* THE DATA RECORD POINTER TO SFILE*)
    FILENAME   : string[ 16 ] ; (* TITLE TO SEQUETIAL FILE, INPUT *)
    INDEXNAME  : string[ 16 ] ; (* TITLE TO BTREE INDEX, OUTPUT   *)
    MENU       : 1 .. 5 ;      (* 5 SELECTIONS FROM SCREEN        *)
    NUMBER     : POINTERS ;    (* RECORD NUMBER IN SFILE          *)

procedure CLSCREEN ; forward ;
procedure WRITENODE ( ITEM : POINTERS ) ; forward ;

segment procedure ENTRY ;

  const
    BLANK  = '                        ' ;
```

Figure 10-11.   FILESYS. (Continued next page.)

```
begin
  CLSCREEN ;
  GOTOXY(15, 7 ); WRITELN( 'SEQUENTIAL FILE DATA ENTRY.' );
  GOTOXY(11, 9 ); WRITE  ( 'ENTER FILE NAME : ' ); READLN( FILENAME ) ;
  REWRITE ( SFILE, FILENAME ) ;
  with SFILE^ do
    begin
      repeat
        GOTOXY( 20,14 ); WRITE( BLANK ) ;
        GOTOXY(  8,14 ); WRITE( 'ENTER NAME : ' ); READLN( SNAME ) ;
        if SNAME <>''
          then
            begin
              GOTOXY( 23,16 );WRITE( BLANK ) ;
              GOTOXY(  8,16 );WRITE( 'ENTER ADDRESS : ' );READLN( SADDR );
              GOTOXY( 32,18 );WRITE( BLANK ) ;
              GOTOXY(  8,18 );WRITE( 'ENTER TELEPHONE NUMBER : ' );
              READLN( STELE ) ;
              PUT( SFILE ) ;
            end ;
      until SNAME = '' ;
    end ;      (* with *)
  CLOSE( SFILE, LOCK ) ;
end ;                              (* ENTRY *)

segment procedure INDEX ;

  procedure CREATE ;
  begin      (*  C R E A T E  *)
    (*     OPEN LIST OF AVAILABLE RECORDS      *)
    REWRITE( AVAILIST, 'AVAILIST.DATA' ) ;
    AVAILIST^.AVAIL[ 0 ] := FALSE ;
    for I := 1 to SIZE do
      with AVAILIST^ do
        AVAIL[ I ] := TRUE ;
    AVAILIST^.TREESIZE := SIZE ;
    AVAILIST^.ROOT     := 0 ;
    PUT( AVAILIST ) ;
    CLOSE( AVAILIST, LOCK ) ;
    (*     OPEN INDEX FILE     *)
    GOTOXY( 11, 9 ); WRITE( 'ENTER INDEX NAME : ' );
    READLN( INDEXNAME ) ;
    REWRITE( BTREE, INDEXNAME ) ;
    with BTREE^ do
      for I := 1 to N do
        begin
          POINTER[ I ] := NULL ;
          SUBKEY [ I ] := '' ;
        end ;
    BTREE^.FLAG   := TRUE ;
    PUT( BTREE ) ;
    CLOSE( BTREE, LOCK ) ;
end ;                              (* CREATE *)
```

Figure 10-11.   (Continued)

```
procedure FINISH ;
  begin
    SEEK ( AVAILIST, 0 ) ;
    PUT ( AVAILIST ) ;
    CLOSE( AVAILIST, LOCK ) ;
    CLOSE( BTREE, LOCK ) ;
    CLOSE( SFILE ) ;
  end ;                          (* FINISH *)

function ALOCATE : integer ;
  var
    I  :  integer ;
  begin
    with AVAILIST^ do
      begin
        for I := 0 to TREESIZE do
          if AVAIL[ I ]
            then
              begin
                AVAIL[ I ] := FALSE ;
                ALOCATE    := I ;
                EXIT ( ALOCATE ) ;
              end ;             (* IF-THEN-FOR *)
      end ;                     (*    WITH      *)
  end;                          (*   ALOCATE    *)

  procedure LOOKUP ;

  begin
    STOP := 0 ; STACK[ STOP ] := NULL ;
    STOP := 1 ; STACK[ STOP ] := NULL ;
    NODE := AVAILIST^.ROOT ;        (* START AT ROOT NODE      *)
    repeat
      I := 1 ;
      SEEK( BTREE, NODE ) ;
      GET ( BTREE ) ;
      with BTREE^ do
        begin
          while ( SUBKEY[ I ] <> '' )
                    and
                ( SUBKEY[ I ] < KEY )
              do I := SUCC( I ) ;       (* FIND INSERT PLACE        *)
          STOP := STOP + 1 ; STACK[ STOP ] := NODE ;
          STOP := STOP + 1 ; STACK[ STOP ] := I ;
          NODE := POINTER[ I ] ;
        end ;                         (* with *)
    until ( NODE = NULL ) or ( BTREE^.FLAG );
  end ;                               (*  LOOKUP  *)
```

Figure 10-11.   (Continued)

```
procedure SPLIT ;
  begin
    with  BTREE^ do
      begin
        NEW.FLAG := FLAG ;
        LAST    := (N + 1) div 2 ;
        K       := 1 ;
        while LAST+K <= N do
          begin
            NEW.POINTER[ K ] := POINTER[ LAST + K ] ;
            NEW.SUBKEY [ K ] := SUBKEY [ LAST + K ] ;
            K := SUCC ( K )` ;
          end ;                (* while *)
        NEW.POINTER[ K ] := TEMPPTR ;
        NEW.SUBKEY [ K ] := '' ;
        for K := K+1 to N do
          begin
            NEW.POINTER[ K ] := NULL ;
            NEW.SUBKEY [ K ] := '' ;
          end ;               (* while *)
      end ;               (* with  *)

  (*   STEP   7   *)

  TEMP    := BTREE^ ;
  BTREE^  := NEW ;
  NEWNODE := ALOCATE ;
  SEEK( BTREE, NEWNODE ) ;
  PUT ( BTREE ) ;
  BTREE^  := TEMP ;
  with BTREE^ do
    begin
      KEY  := SUBKEY[ LAST ] ;
      for K := LAST+1  to N do
        begin
          SUBKEY [ K ] := '' ;
          POINTER[ K ] := NULL ;
        end ;                     (* for  *)
    end ;              (* with *)
  SEEK( BTREE, NODE ) ;
  PUT ( BTREE ) ;
end ;              (* SPLIT *)

procedure INDEXKEY ;

  label
    4 ;                    (*  WARNING : GOTO MAY BE HARMFULL  *)

  begin

    (*   STEP   2   *)

    LOOKUP ;

    (*     STEP    3    *)

    I       := STACK[ STOP ] ; STOP := STOP - 1 ;
    NODE    := STACK[ STOP ] ; STOP := STOP - 1 ;
    NEW.FLAG := TRUE ;
```

Figure 10-11. (Continued)

```
(*     STEP   4       *)

4:
with BTREE^ do
  begin
    TEMPPTR := POINTER[ N ] ;
    for K := N downto I + 1 do
      begin
        POINTER[ K ] := POINTER[ K - 1 ] ;
        SUBKEY [ K ] := SUBKEY [ K - 1 ] ;
      end ;
    POINTER[ I ] := ITEM ;
    SUBKEY [ I ] := KEY ;
    FLAG          := NEW.FLAG ;
  end ;                (*  with  *)

  (*   STEP   5     *)

  if BTREE^.SUBKEY[ N ] = ''
    then
      begin
        SEEK( BTREE, NODE ) ;
        PUT ( BTREE ) ;
        EXIT( INDEXKEY ) ;
      end ;
  (*   STEP  6       *)

  SPLIT ;

  (*  STEP  8 & 9   *)

  ITEM   := NODE ;
  I      := STACK[ STOP ] ; STOP := STOP - 1 ;
  NODE   := STACK[ STOP ] ; STOP := STOP - 1 ;
  if NODE = NULL
    then
      begin

          (*   step    10    *)

          with  BTREE^ do
            begin
              FLAG := FALSE ;
              POINTER[ 1 ] := ITEM ;
              SUBKEY [ 1 ] := KEY ;
              POINTER[ 2 ] := NEWNODE ;
              SUBKEY [ 2 ] := '';
              for K := 3 to N do
                begin
                  POINTER[ K ] := NULL ;
                  SUBKEY [ K ] := '' ;
                end ;
              NEWNODE := ALOCATE ;
            end ;            (* with *)
          SEEK( BTREE, NEWNODE ) ;
          PUT ( BTREE ) ;
          AVAILIST^.ROOT := NEWNODE ;
          EXIT( INDEXKEY ) ;
      end ;      (* IF-THEN  *)
```

Figure 10-11. (Continued)

217

```
              SEEK( BTREE, NODE ) ;
              GET ( BTREE ) ;
              BTREE^.POINTER[ I ] := NEWNODE ;
              NEW.FLAG := FALSE ;
              goto 4 ;

      end;                      (* INDEXKEY  *)


  begin      (*   I N D E X   *)
    CLSCREEN ;
    CREATE ;
    GOTOXY( 11, 9 ); WRITE( 'ENTER SEQUENTIAL FILE NAME : ' );
    READLN( FILENAME ) ;
    GOTOXY( 11, 9 ); WRITELN('INDEXING IS IN PROCESS......' );
    RESET ( SFILE, FILENAME ) ;
    RESET ( BTREE, INDEXNAME ) ;
    RESET ( AVAILIST, 'AVAILIST.DATA' ) ;
    NUMBER := 0 ;                    (* RECORD NUMBER OF INPUT        *)
    repeat
      if not EOF( SFILE )
        then
          begin
            KEY       := SFILE^.SNAME ;
            ITEM      := NUMBER ;
            INDEXKEY ;              (* INSERT KEY & ITEM INTO TREE*)
            GET ( SFILE ) ;        (* GET NEXT SEQUENTIAL RECORD *)
            NUMBER    := NUMBER + 1 ;
          end ;
      until EOF( SFILE ) ;
    FINISH ;
  end ;                        (* INDEX *)


segment procedure LOOKUP ;

  procedure SEARCH ( NODE : POINTERS ) ;
    var
      I          : integer ;
    begin
      SEEK ( BTREE, NODE ) ;
      GET  ( BTREE ) ;
      while TRUE do
        begin
          if BTREE^.FLAG                     (* IS IT A LEAF ??  *)
            then
              begin
                I := 1 ;                      (* YES. OUTPUT EACH *)
                while BTREE^.POINTER[ I ] <> NULL do
                  begin
                    if BTREE^.SUBKEY[ I ] = KEY
                      then
                        begin
                          WRITENODE ( BTREE^.POINTER[ I ] );
                          EXIT( SEARCH ) ;
                        end;    (*  if    *)
```

Figure 10-11. (Continued)

```
                I := I + 1 ;
              end ;          (*  while  *)
            WRITELN( 'NOT FOUND' ) ;
            EXIT ( SEARCH ) ;
          end          (* IF-THEN *)
        else
          begin                        (* NOT A LEAF, SO GO DOWN A SUBTREE *)
            I := 1 ;
            while ( BTREE^.SUBKEY [ I ] < KEY )
                        and
                  ( BTREE^.SUBKEY [ I ] <> '' )
              do  I := I + 1 ;
          end ;          (*  if-then-else  *)
      SEEK ( BTREE, BTREE^.POINTER[ I ] ) ;
      GET  ( BTREE ) ;
    end ;      (* LOOP FOREVER *)

  end ;          (*  SEARCH  *)


begin
  RESET ( AVAILIST, 'AVAILIST.DATA' ) ;
  NODE := AVAILIST^.ROOT ;
  CLOSE ( AVAILIST ) ;
  CLSCREEN ;
  GOTOXY( 11, 9 ) ; WRITE( 'ENTER INDEX NAME : ' ); READLN( INDEXNAME );
  GOTOXY( 11,11 ) ; WRITE( 'ENTER FILE NAME  : ' ); READLN( FILENAME ) ;
  RESET ( BTREE, INDEXNAME ) ;
  RESET ( SFILE, FILENAME  ) ;
  GOTOXY( 11,14 ) ; WRITE( 'ENTER KEY FOR SEARCH : ' ); READLN( KEY ) ;
  while KEY <> '' do
    begin
      SEARCH ( NODE ) ;                (*  RECURSIVE DESCENT THRU BTREE  *)
      GOTOXY( 11,14 ) ; WRITE( 'ENTER KEY FOR SEARCH : ' );
      READLN( KEY ) ;
    end ;
  CLOSE  ( BTREE );
  CLOSE  ( SFILE ) ;

end ;                          (* LOOKUP *)


segment procedure DUMP ;

procedure SEARCH ( NODE : POINTERS ) ;
  var
    I        : integer ;

  begin
    SEEK ( BTREE, NODE ) ;
    GET  ( BTREE ) ;
    if BTREE^.FLAG                      (* IS IT A LEAF ??  *)
      then
        begin
          I := 1 ;                      (* YES. OUTPUT EACH *)
          while BTREE^.POINTER[ I ] <> NULL do
            begin
              WRITENODE ( BTREE^.POINTER[ I ] );
              I := I + 1 ;
            end ;
```

Figure 10-11. (Continued)

```
      end       (* if-then *)
    else
      begin                    (* NOT A LEAF, SO RECURIVELY SEARCH *)
        I := 1 ;
        while BTREE^.POINTER[ I ] <> NULL do
          begin
            SEARCH ( BTREE^.POINTER[ I ]  ) ;
            SEEK ( BTREE, NODE ) ;
            GET  ( BTREE ) ;
            I := I + 1 ;
          end ;
      end ;          (*  if-then-else  *)

      end ;          (*  SEARCH  *)

  begin                    (*   D U M P   *)

    RESET ( AVAILIST, 'AVAILIST.DATA' ) ;
    NODE := AVAILIST^.ROOT ;
    CLOSE ( AVAILIST ) ;
    CLSCREEN ;
    GOTOXY( 11, 9 ) ; WRITE( 'ENTER INDEX NAME : ' ); READLN( INDEXNAME );
    GOTOXY( 11,11 ) ; WRITE( 'ENTER FILE NAME  : ' ); READLN( FILENAME ) ;
    GOTOXY( 11,14 ) ; WRITE( 'PROCESSING FILE IN ORDER .......' ) ;
    RESET ( BTREE, INDEXNAME ) ;
    RESET ( SFILE, FILENAME  ) ;

    SEARCH ( NODE ) ;              (*  RECURSIVE DESCENT THRU BTREE  *)
    CLOSE  ( BTREE );
    CLOSE  ( SFILE ) ;

  end ;                      (* DUMP  *)

  procedure CLSCREEN ;
    var
      LINE    : 1 .. 25 ;
    begin
      for LINE := 1 to 25 do
        WRITELN ;
    end ;                      (* CLSCREEN *)

  procedure WRITENODE ;
    var
      PAUSE : char ;
    begin
      SEEK ( SFILE, ITEM ) ;
      GET  ( SFILE ) ;
      CLSCREEN ;
      GOTOXY ( 11, 9 ) ; WRITE( 'NAME    : ', SFILE^.SNAME ) ;
      GOTOXY ( 11,10 ) ; WRITE( 'ADDRESS: ', SFILE^.SADDR ) ;
      GOTOXY ( 11,11 ) ; WRITE( 'TELE # : ', SFILE^.STELE ) ;
      GOTOXY ( 11,13 ) ; WRITE( 'STRIKE <RET> TO CONTINUE : ' ) ;
      READLN ( PAUSE ) ;
    end ;            (*  WRITENODE  *)
```

Figure 10-11.   (Continued)

```
begin                        (*  F  I  L  E  S  Y  S  *)
  repeat
    CLSCREEN ;
    GOTOXY( 15, 7 ); WRITE ( 'BTREE FILE SYSTEM' ) ;
    GOTOXY( 11, 9 ); WRITE ( '[1]. SEQUENTIAL FILE DATA ENTRY.' );
    GOTOXY( 11,10 ); WRITE ( '[2]. INDEX A SEQUENTIAL FILE.' );
    GOTOXY( 11,11 ); WRITE ( '[3]. RETRIEVE AN INDEXED RECORD' );
    GOTOXY( 11,12 ); WRITE ( '[4]. READ INDEXED SEQUENTIAL FILE IN ORDER');
    GOTOXY( 11,13 ); WRITE ( '[5]. STOP.' );
    GOTOXY( 11,16 ); WRITE ( '[ ]. ENTER CHOICE.' ); GOTOXY( 12,16 );
    READLN( MENU ) ;
    case MENU of
        1 : ENTRY ;
        2 : INDEX ;
        3 : LOOKUP ;
        4 : DUMP ;
        5 : EXIT ( FILESYS ) ;
      end ;                       (* CASE *)
    until FALSE ;                 (* REPEAT  FOREVER *)
  end.
```

While **gotos** are a poor programming practice, they may be useful in rare circumstances. We could have avoided the **goto** 4; but the program would have been obscured; so we used one, anyway.

Several EXIT statements can also be found in the FILESYS program. They are controlled forms of **goto**, which also should be avoided unless readability is impaired.

FILESYS manages three files: (1) the master file containing data items, (2) the B-tree index file containing B-tree links and keys, and (3) the AVAILIST/DATA file containing a list of available disk items for use by the expanding B-tree. This file also contains the item number of the root node.

If AVAILIST.AVAIL [K] is true, the corresponding item is free and may be allocated for use in the B-tree.

In the next section we explore possible applications of the B-tree index structure and suggest some ideas for a general index structure. Remember these important features of an ISAM file structure:

A. ISAMs may have as many index files as needed, and each index file can use a different key to access the master file.

B. B-trees are a compromise between speed, flexibility, and memory utilization—thus they are a good index file structure.

C. The expected number of SEEKs in searching a B-tree of order N containing K keys:

$$\# \text{seeks} \le LOG_{N/_2} \left\{ \frac{K+1}{2} \right\}$$

If we store 2,000,000 keys in a B-tree, it takes no more than 6 seeks to retrieve any record when N=20.

D. B-tree indexes can be easily updated, searched, and constructed, but they may be wasteful of disk space.

10.3 NEVER SORT A FILE

One of the advantages of low-cost microcomputers is the widespread availability of "in-house" computers. This means that businesses no longer need the services of a time-shared central computer or a service bureau. Instead, small businesses can afford to install a small computer and run it themselves.

Furthermore, the "in-house" computer can give "immediate" answers if it is properly programmed and used. Unfortunately, the traditional methods of implementing business applications on large central computers are not always applicable to the small in-house computer system. This is because centralized computers are more efficiently run in *batch mode*, while small in-house computers are better suited to *interactive mode* of operation. Indeed, they must be programmed much more carefully to deal with human interaction because they deal with humans *directly*. This causes severe problems unless we rethink the old ways and devise new ways of implementing systems.

As an example, suppose we rethink the old way of implementing a billing system (accounts receivable). In an A/R (accounts/receivable) system, we must keep a master file which contains at least a name, address, and current balance for every account to be billed at the end of the month, year, etc. In addition, each master-file record must contain a unique identifier called its key, which allows us to match this account to its *transaction*. A transaction is either a payment (the bill is paid), a charge (a new purchase), or other (adjustments due to interest, errors, etc.). A *transaction file* must be established for recalling all transactions carried out during the day, week, month, etc.

We can imagine a transaction file containing many transactions with identical keys, because one client may generate many charges or make several payments in a month. We cannot index a transaction file like we could a master file. Figure 10.12(a) illustrates the "traditional view" of this situation, and Figure 10.12(b) shows a typical modification of the system used in many in-house systems.

Both the organizations in Figure 10.12 fail to provide timely, up-to-date information for the in-house A/R system. Here is why.

1. The transaction file must be sorted into order and posted against the balance stored in the master file before the current balance is updated. This all takes time, and so it is postponed until the end of the month.

2. The master file in Figure 10.12(a) cannot be rapidly accessed at random because the index is slow to be created. Without the index, processing is sequential.

(a)   Traditional Organization of A/R Files

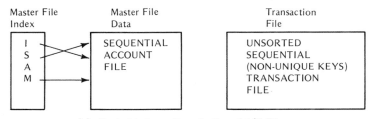

(b)   Typical In-house Organization of A/R Files

Figure 10.12.   Organization of A/R Files

3. The current transactions cannot even be retrieved without reading the entire transaction file, because the transactions for a single account are scattered (randomly) throughout the file. They are appended to the file in the order they arrive.

One of the reasons for an in-house computer is to get instantaneous results; yet this view of the system seems to prevent the user's access to information except once a month, etc.

Let's rethink the problem. One obstacle is the disorder of the transaction file, while another obstacle is the lack of an up-to-date access method. If we could index the transaction file, we could rapidly access any entries in it; but it contains non-unique keys, so this is not possible.

Every transaction must have a corresponding master file account or else we have violated an accounting principle. Furthermore, we can index the master account file because it contains unique keys. This suggests a B-tree ISAM structure with linked lists as shown in Figure 10.13.

Every item in the master file is indexed via a B-tree index file. This means we never sort the master file, and we never go for a period of time without immediate access to every account in the master account file.

Every item in the transaction file is also indexed through the same B-tree index. In the case of a transaction entry, the master file record contains a link to the transaction file as well as containing the data for the account.

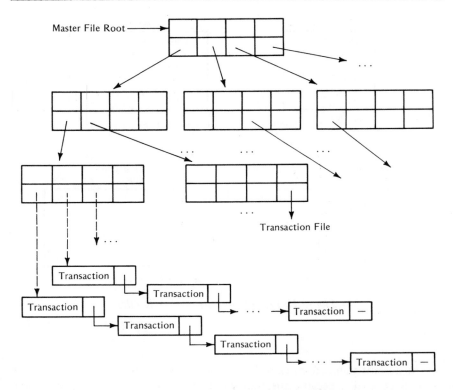

Figure 10.13.   Interactive A/R File System

Since the transaction file contains non-unique entries, we simply link to-gether all transactions with the same key value as shown in Figure 10.13. When-ever we want to look at them, process them, or whatever, we can do so without reading the entire transaction file. We use SEEK to access directly the subset of transaction records pertaining to the master file account.

The advantages of this structure are not limited to A/R. Most business systems operate on a "master" and "transaction" file. For example, a payroll system consists of a master file containing employee information, e.g., name, mailing address, social security number, pay rate, number of dependents, and miscellaneous (insurance) information. The transaction file contains a list of hours worked, what shift, what pay rate adjustment (time-and-one-half), etc.

An accounts payable (A/P) system works the same way. Every master account corresponds with a debtor, and every transaction means another charge against the company to be paid to the debtor.

The pervasive general-ledger system is a collection of journals (transaction files) and balance sheets (master files). The inventory system runs in conjunction with A/R, but it contains a list of inventory (master file) and a list of "sold" items or "bought" items (the transactions). Again, the model of Figure 10.13 fits the situation.

This section suggests some ideas for using Pascal to implement useful and flexible systems. We hope you will be able to put these ideas to work.

TWENTY QUESTIONS

1. What is the difference between a random access and a sequential access in UCSD Pascal?
2. What is the difference between a TEXT file and an ordinary Pascal file?
3. What happens if we SEEK beyond the end of a file?
4. Is this legal in Pascal?

   DISK∧ := NEW;

5. What is the question? The answer is Boeing, Bayer, or?
6. Which of these is incorrect?

   GET (DISK); or SEEK (DISK,R);
   GET (DISK);   SEEK (DISK,R+1);

7. What is the item number of the first item of a file?
8. What is file OUTPUT?
9. How can we access a file by key instead of by item number?
10. What is the main drawback of an index file?
11. What is the main advantage of an index file?
12. Draw a binary search tree for these items (use them in this order): D, DA, E, B, F, G, A, I.
13. Is the tree in 12 balanced?
14. A binary tree grows from its _____ to its _____.
15. A B-tree grows from its _____ to its _____.
16. A pushdown stack can be implemented as an _____.
17. In a B-tree of order N=20 containing 1999 keys, how many disk SEEKs can be expected?
18. What is the main disadvantage of B-tree index?
19. What do we have to do to use a **goto** in a Pascal program?
20. What is the difference between *batch* and *interactive* systems?
21. Bonus question: How was the book?

ANSWERS

1. A random access must be preceded by a SEEK.
2. TEXT and INTERACTIVE files hold text only, allow the READ, WRITE intrinsics, and do not prefetch the first item.
3. Nothing—literally.
4. Yes, if DISK is a file window and NEW is of the same type as the base type of DISK.
5. Who was B?
6. The pair of SEEKs.
7. Zero.
8. CONSOLE:
9. Use a hashing function, an index file, or some means of converting the key into a number.
10. It is redundant, takes more space, and is slower.
11. It converts a key into an item number which directly locates the data item. This can be done on any number of keys.
12.

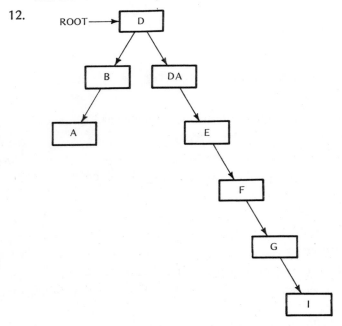

13. No!
14. From its root to its leaves.
15. From its leaf to its roots.

16. Array structure.
17. Less than 3.
18. Wasted storage due to unused nodes.
19. We must direct the compiler to accept **gotos**, G+, and we must declare the labels in a label statement.
20. A world. An interactive system must respond, quickly, and it must interface with naive users.
21. Keep the cards and letters coming.

Chapter 11

BASIC Versus Pascal

"Step right up, gentlemen, and listen well," the barker shouted to the crowd. "Here is a pound of gravel and a pound of gold, my friends. Now tell me, which weighs the most?"

"Well, any fool knows the difference between rock and gold," an old man shouted from the dusty road.

"But tell me sir, which is the heavier burden to carry?" the huckster retorted.

The old man's eyes brightened against his red face as he found the answer. "Gold tis no burden at all — the pound of gravel is the heavier of the two!" The others that had gathered nearby nodded their approval.

11.1 INTERPRETATION VERSUS COMPILATION

The most immediate difference between Pascal and BASIC is the manner in which each is typically implemented. Pascal is usually compiled in a separate step from its execution. Therefore, Pascal is inherently more tedious to code initially.

BASIC is usually implemented as an interpreter. This means that each statement of BASIC is immediately ready to be executed without a separate translation step. The benefits of this immediate feedback are tremendous, especially when debugging a new program. In some cases, program coding and testing are accelerated by 5 to 10 times over the effort needed to program and test a corresponding Pascal program.

Why then is Pascal used when BASIC lowers the effort needed to code and test a similar program? The answer lies in two phenomena observed by computer scientists over the past decade.

1. Most of the effort in designing, developing, testing, maintaining and enhancing computer software is in maintaining and enhancing, *not* coding and debugging.

2. As the size of a program grows, the effort needed to implement and maintain

it grows even faster. Indeed, doubling the number of lines of code more than doubles the effort needed to implement it.

The first observed law puts BASIC at a disadvantage unless the program is used only once and then thrown away. The second law says that Pascal is better for large programs because it uses modules (procedures, functions, units) to reduce the size of each program unit. We can summarize as follows:

Achtung #1.   BASIC is best for small programs that are run once or twice and then thrown away.

Achtung #2.   Pascal is best for large-scale programs that have a long lifecycle and therefore must be maintained and enhanced.

In the age of million-dollar programs running on ten-dollar computers, the advantages of Pascal are obvious. Until an even greater "mechanical advantage" comes along, Pascal will continue to be the best software tool available.

The details of each language may differ, but does Pascal really offer a "more powerful" software development tool than BASIC? Let's compare the two languages at the programmer level and see what happens.

11.2 SYNTACTIC COMPARISONS

The data-chunking features of Pascal are far superior to the data-chunking capabilities of BASIC. The following excerpts show how to define data types, write assignment statements, and perform the fundamental operations of programming in both BASIC and Pascal.

The . . . notation means "some other statements," and the statement numbers used in the BASIC illustrations are of no special significance.

Pascal	*BASIC*
var	
X : **array**[1..10] **of real** ;	10 DIM X(10)
Y : **array**[1..10,1..20] **of real**;	15 DIM Y(10,20)
S : **string**[10] ;	20 DIM S$(10)
I,J : **integer** ;	
X[I] := Y[I,J] + 5 ;	110 X(I) = Y(I,J) + 5
if X[I] = 0	350 IF X(I) <> 0 THEN 390
then begin	360 REM THEN
. . .	. . .
end	380 GOTO 400
else begin	390 REM ELSE
. . .	. . .
end ;	400 REM ENDIF

```
for I := 1 to 10 do                          500 FOR I = 1 TO 10
   begin                                     510 REM BEGIN
   . . .                                         . . .
   end ;                                     590 NEXT I

while X[ I ] > 0 do                          700 IF X(I) <= 0 THEN 780
   begin                                     710 REM BEGIN
   . . .                                         . . .
   end ;                                     770 GOTO 700
                                             780 REM END

repeat                                       800 REM REPEAT
. . .                                            . . .
until X[ I ] <= 0 ;                          880 IF X(I) > 0 THEN 800

case I of                                    900 ON I GOTO 910, 920, 930
1 : . . .                                    910 . . .
                                             919 GOTO 990
2 : . . .                                    920 . . .
                                             929 GOTO 990
3 : . . .                                    930 . . .
end ;                                        990 REM END

procedure RUB ;                              1000 REM RUB
   begin                                     1010 . . .
   . . .                                         . . . . . . .
   end ;                                     1100 RETURN
   . . .
   RUB ;                                     1210 GOSUB 1000
```

It is true that many dialects of BASIC have structures borrowed from Pascal-like languages. For example, some dialects allow an IF-THEN-ELSE statement similar to the Pascal choice structure. In general, however, Pascal offers many features not found in BASIC. Here are a few of these "new" structures.

Data types   :   **char, boolean, set, record, file**
Control types :   **nested procedures, segments, EXIT, and more versatile case-selection.**

Some people claim that Pascal is more "expressive" than previous computer languages. However, the "expressiveness" of a computer language is only vaguely understood. Instead, we might say that Pascal is "higher-level" than some other language; but again we must define what we mean by "high-level "

Fitzsimmons and Love discuss Halstead's measure of language level in the March 1978 *Computing Surveys* article, "A Review and Evaluation of Software Science." We suggest that Pascal is somewhere between ALGOL — 58 and PL/I in expressiveness (as defined by Fitzsimmons and Love using Halstead's measure), while BASIC is somewhere between Pilot and FORTRAN. The levels of these languages are shown below, relative to English prose.

Langauge	*Level*
English Prose	1.00
PL/I	0.50
ALGOL-58	0.31
FORTRAN	0.28
PILOT	0.18
CDC Assembler	0.17

According to this table Pascal is roughly twice as high-level as BASIC, using Halstead's measure of language level. This means we can understand a program in Pascal twice as easily as in BASIC, and for large programs requiring maintenance and enhancements, this is a big advantage.

The value of a programming language is a controversial subject, and each language has its following, all of whom claim their language as the best one. In the final analysis the reader will have to decide which language is the best for each purpose.

Index